OECD Economic Surveys: Netherlands 2012

This document and any map included herein are without prejudice to the status of or sovereignty over any territory, to the delimitation of international frontiers and boundaries and to the name of any territory, city or area.

Please cite this publication as:
OECD (2012), *OECD Economic Surveys: Netherlands 2012*, OECD Publishing.
http://dx.doi.org/10.1787/eco_surveys-nld-2012-en

ISBN 978-92-64-12790-6 (print)
ISBN 978-92-64-12791-3 (PDF)

Series: OECD Economic Surveys
ISSN 0376-6438 (print)
ISSN 1609-7513 (online)

OECD Economic Surveys: Netherlands
ISSN 1995-3305 (print)
ISSN 1999-0367 (online)

The statistical data for Israel are supplied by and under the responsibility of the relevant Israeli authorities. The use of such data by the OECD is without prejudice to the status of the Golan Heights, East Jerusalem and Israeli settlements in the West Bank under the terms of international law.

Photo credits: Cover © Andrew Ward/Life File.

Corrigenda to OECD publications may be found on line at: *www.oecd.org/publishing/corrigenda*.
© OECD 2012

You can copy, download or print OECD content for your own use, and you can include excerpts from OECD publications, databases and multimedia products in your own documents, presentations, blogs, websites and teaching materials, provided that suitable acknowledgment of OECD as source and copyright owner is given. All requests for public or commercial use and translation rights should be submitted to *rights@oecd.org*. Requests for permission to photocopy portions of this material for public or commercial use shall be addressed directly to the Copyright Clearance Center (CCC) at *info@copyright.com* or the Centre français d'exploitation du droit de copie (CFC) at *contact@cfcopies.com*.

Table of contents

Executive summary 8

Assessment and recommendations 9

    The government is facing both short- and long-term challenges 9
    Sizeable fiscal consolidation is under way 18
    Globalisation and policies for the business sector 25
    Preparing the labour market for further globalisation and population ageing 28
    Promoting competition and cost control in the health care sector 31
    Bibliography 36
    Annex A1. Progress in structural reform 38

Chapter 1. **Reforming policies for the business sector to harvest the benefits of globalisation** 41

    The benefits and challenges of globalisation 42
    Benefiting from globalisation by strengthening the business environment 50
    Notes 65
    Bibliography 66

Chapter 2. **The Dutch labour market: Preparing for the future** 71

    The effect of globalisation on labour demand 72
    Policies to foster labour mobility 77
    Notes 92
    Bibliography 92

Chapter 3. **Health care reform and long-term care in the Netherlands** 97

    Performance of the health care system 98
    The health care sector was substantially reformed in the second half of the 2000s 103
    The next wave of reform 114
    Population ageing will put pressure on a costly long-term care system 117
    Conclusion 122
    Notes 124
    Bibliography 124

Boxes

    1. Correcting external imbalances via structural reform 12
    2. Mortgage indebtedness of households 15
    3. The Spring 2012 fiscal consolidation package 18

TABLE OF CONTENTS

4. Global warming and flood protection	22
5. The ambitiousness of the Dutch social model induces high ageing costs	24
6. Main fiscal policy recommendations	25
7. Main business sector policy recommendations	28
8. Main labour market recommendations	31
9. Main health policy recommendations	36
1.1. The port of Rotterdam and the surge in re-exports	44
1.2. New policies for the business sector	50
1.3. Top Consortia for Knowledge and Innovation (TKIs)	54
1.4. The design of R&D tax credits	58
1.5. Reducing red tape	62
1.6. Recommendations to strengthen the business environment	65
2.1. Wage bargaining and a shift to decentralisation	81
2.2. Life-long learning incentives	83
2.3. Polices to attract high-skilled workers	85
2.4. Integrating the disabled in the labour market	90
2.5. Recommendations to support labour reallocation and activation of underutilised labour resources	91
3.1. Mental health care reform – a step too far?	108
3.2. Will the organisation of GPs into primary care groups improve cost-efficiency?	112
3.3. Main reform measures in the hospital sector 2012-15	115
3.4. A comprehensive public long-term care system	117
3.5. The decentralisation of home help has improved cost-efficiency	119
3.6. The government's reform agenda for long-term care	120
3.7. Recommendations to promote a more efficient and competitive health sector	123

Tables

1. Demand, output and prices	11
2. Households' mortgage debt	15
3. Public and private age-related spending	24
1.1. Foreign controlled enterprise activity	48
1.2. The main dates in the formulation of the new policies of the business sector	50
1.3. Tax measures to foster innovative activities (main features per scheme)	58
1.4. Top 10 problematic factors for doing business in the Netherlands	64
2.1. Workers covered by collective agreements	83
2.2. Lowest collective agreement wage per age category	90
3.1. Mortality rates of infants and mortality by leading causes	100
3.2. Private spending as a share of total health expenditure	102
3.3. Public expenditures for health care and long-term care	103
3.4. Public health care expenditure (ZVW) by category	103
3.5. Profitability of health insurance	106
3.6. Concentration of the health insurance market	106
3.7. Expenditures on curative mental care covered by ZVW	108
3.8. Changes in negotiated average prices in the hospital segment B	109
3.9. Remuneration, as ratio to average wage in each country	110
3.10. General practitioners and specialists per 1 000 population	111

Figures

1. Short-term economic indicators	10
2. Labour market developments	11
3. The average funding ratio and share of pension funds with a funding ratio below the legal minimum	13
4. Interest rate and housing prices developments	14
5. Competitiveness indicators	16
6. Dutch export performance in selected commodities	17
7. Labour productivity growth	17
8. The fiscal stance is pro-cyclical in 2012	20
9. Imbalances in the euro area countries	21
10. Sustainability gaps in European countries	22
11. Public debt path before and after the crisis	23
12. Population ageing	23
13. Average total pension	25
14. Modest exports to emerging markets	26
15. Job mobility is low	29
16. Health care cost now and in 2060	35
1.1. Openness has increased	43
1.2. Competitiveness indicators	44
1.3. Re-exports have surged	45
1.4. Export performance to the emerging economies	46
1.5. Modest exports to emerging markets	47
1.6. Relatively high in- and outward FDI	48
1.7. Private R&D spending is low	49
1.8. Services exports specialised in professional business, communication as well as royalties	53
1.9. The share of graduates with a science or engineering degree is low	56
1.10. High explicit barriers to trade and investment in emerging markets	56
1.11. Dutch R&D tax incentives have strong SME focus	59
1.12. Business R&D by size class of firms	59
1.13. Excellent research system but mediocre business linkages	60
1.14. Venture capital market is relatively small	62
1.15. Administrative burdens on start-up	63
1.16. Entry regulation for a selection of sectors	63
1.17. Fast growing (innovative SME) enterprises	64
2.1. Labour market indicators	73
2.2. Beveridge curve	73
2.3. Employment shifts to knowledge intensive services	74
2.4. Employment of high-skilled workers increased	75
2.5. Wage dispersion is relatively small	75
2.6. Labour productivity growth	76
2.7. Population ageing	77
2.8. Job mobility is low	78
2.9. Employment Protection Legislation (EPL) for workers with permanent contracts remains high	79
2.10. High tenure premia for men	80

2.11.	Unit labour costs have increased relatively fast	82
2.12.	Immigrants in high-skill jobs	84
2.13.	High incidence of female part-time employment	87
2.14.	Low average annual hours actually worked per worker	87
2.15.	The average retirement age is increasing	88
2.16.	The number of disability recipients remains high	89
3.1.	Life expectancy indicators	99
3.2.	Health risks	101
3.3.	The Netherlands has high health expenditures	102
3.4.	Health care consultations and hospital resource use	104
3.5.	Health care resources	105
3.6.	Expenditure on outpatient prescription drugs	113
3.7.	Main features of the envisaged reorganisation of the long-term care system	120

This Survey is published on the responsibility of the Economic and Development Review Committee of the OECD, which is charged with the examination of the economic situation of member countries.

The economic situation and policies of the Netherlands were reviewed by the Committee on 26 April 2012. The draft report was then revised in the light of the discussions and given final approval as the agreed report of the whole Committee on 14 May 2012.

The Secretariat's draft report was prepared for the Committee by Jens Høj, Mathijs Gerritsen and Stéphane Sorbe under the supervision of Pierre Beynet. Statistical assistance was provided by Sylvie Foucher-Hantala. The Survey also benefited from external consultancy work.

The previous Survey of the Netherlands was issued in June 2010.

This book has...

StatLinks
A service that delivers Excel® files from the printed page!

Look for the *StatLinks* at the bottom right-hand corner of the tables or graphs in this book. To download the matching Excel® spreadsheet, just type the link into your Internet browser, starting with the *http://dx.doi.org* prefix.
If you're reading the PDF e-book edition, and your PC is connected to the Internet, simply click on the link. You'll find *StatLinks* appearing in more OECD books.

BASIC STATISTICS OF THE NETHERLANDS, 2011

THE LAND

Area (1 000 km^2):		Major cities (thousand inhabitants, 31 December 2010):	
Total	41.5		
Agricultural area (1 000 km^2)	19.1	Amsterdam	779
Woodland	3.7	Rotterdam	610
		The Hague	495

THE PEOPLE

Population (thousands)	16 574	Total employment (thousands)	8 533
Natural increase (thousands)	48	Employment (% of total):	
Number of inhabitants per km^2	494	Agriculture	2.5
		Industry	15.3
		Other	82.2

PRODUCTION (2010)

Gross domestic product (in billion EUR)	588.4	Gross fixed capital investment:	
Gross domestic product per head (thousand EUR)	35.4	In % of GDP	18.6
		Per head (EUR, 2010)	6 452.0

THE GOVERNMENT

Public consumption (% of GDP)	28.1	Composition of Parliament (seats):	150
General government (% of GDP):		People's Party for Freedom and Democracy	31
Current disbursements	48.7	Dutch Labour Party	30
Current receipts	45	Party for Freedom	23
		Christian Democratic Appeal	21
		Socialist Party	15
		Others	30
		Last election: June 2010	
		Next election: September 2012	

FOREIGN TRADE

Exports of goods and services (% of GDP)	82.6	Imports of goods and services (% of GDP)	74.5

THE CURRENCY

Monetary unit: Euro	Currency unit per USD, average of daily figures:	
	Year 2011	0.72
	April 2012	0.76

Executive summary

The Netherlands is expected to see growth resume only slowly, implying further increases in unemployment in the short term. Current fiscal targets imply a pro-cyclical stance for the next couple of years. In the medium term, economic performance will be affected by continued globalisation and ageing of the labour force. In this perspective, structural fiscal consolidation measures are necessary to secure fiscal sustainability, but the government should also prepare the business sector for the ongoing challenges of globalisation, and adapt labour market institutions for an older and shrinking labour force.

- **Government finances should be brought under control to support confidence, comply with the rules of the Stability and Growth Pact, and secure fiscal sustainability.** In the case of a severe economic downturn, fiscal consolidation should avoid excessive pro-cyclicality as this could endanger the economic recovery and potentially aggravate current account imbalances within the euro area. Improving fiscal sustainability should be pursued once the recovery has become self-sustained, focusing on structural spending measures combined with reforms to boost employment and participation rates.

- **Globalisation is presenting new market opportunities.** The economy has benefited from globalisation via stronger international trade and higher foreign direct investments. Looking ahead, continued globalisation would push companies to become more innovative and search for new activities and markets. To further this process, the government is reforming policies for the business sector. Part of the reform agenda is a targeted approach to strengthen key sectors. However, attention should be paid to avoid that the new approach becomes a vehicle for favouring particular firms or industries. The other part of the agenda is to improve framework conditions, which is commendable and should be combined with other framework policies, notably in the area of labour and product markets.

- **Preparing the labour market for the future.** Globalisation has benefited workers via higher real wages (with a larger positive effect for high-skilled workers) and long periods of high employment and low unemployment. However, if the economy is to benefit more from globalisation, there is a need to reform employment protection for workers with permanent contracts and wage formation to increase the ability of the labour market to allocate increasingly scarce labour resources to their most productive use. Also, underutilised labour resources should be mobilised.

- **Controlling health expenses is the key to securing fiscal sustainability.** Health spending, particularly in the area of long-term care, is set to increase with population ageing, which is also going to change health service demands. To meet both objectives, the government is introducing more competition. To fully reap the benefits of competition, this should be combined with measures to strengthen the hand of health insurers by addressing asymmetric information problems. This notably requires enabling performance-based contracting and addressing information asymmetries. In the area of long-term care, controlling costs would require giving care purchasers adequate financial incentives and improving targeting.

Assessment and recommendations

The government is facing both short- and long-term challenges

The economy is expected to emerge from the recent weakness in the course of 2012. As the recovery gathers pace, a major task for the government will be to maintain its fiscal consolidation efforts, which are necessary to restore fiscal sustainability. In the longer term, the government is faced with the challenge of ensuring that the economy continues to benefit from globalisation, which requires efforts in adjusting business sector and labour market policies (the subjects of Chapters 1 and 2, respectively). The government also needs to prepare the economy for population ageing by expanding the revenue base by extending working lives, mobilising underutilised labour resources and containing pension and health care costs. The last requires a cost-efficient health sector, which the government is promoting via more competition (Chapter 3).

The international confidence crisis slowed the economy

The economy contracted in the last two quarters of 2011, reflecting both a weakening of the domestic economy and an abrupt deceleration of world trade under the influence of renewed global financial turmoil. Domestic demand slowed as business investments were scaled back and private consumption declined. Despite the weakening economy, consumer price inflation edged up under the influence of higher energy prices, reaching 2½ per cent in early 2012. Forward-looking indicators suggest that economic weakness is likely to continue in most of the first half of 2012 (Figure 1).

Unemployment rose to 5.0% in early 2012 – the highest since 2005 – reflecting less labour hoarding than in 2009. Part of the explanation comes from the sluggishness of the employment recovery in 2010-11, as firms have struggled to restore productivity losses arising from the extensive labour hoarding in 2009. As this process was not completed, firms probably still have relatively high employment levels compared with their level of production. Moreover, firms are probably left with a relatively thin buffer of workers that can easily be dismissed (of mainly younger workers with temporary contracts) suggesting that further reductions of the labour force may increasingly affect workers with permanent contracts (Figure 2). Moreover, unemployment has probably been kept down by self-employed reacting to the slowdown in activity by reducing their hours worked rather than registering as unemployed.

A slow recovery is expected

Looking ahead, the recovery is likely to resume in the second half of 2012 (Table 1). Its strength will depend mostly on the vigour of the expected pick-up in world trade. The associated acceleration in exports will feed into the domestic economy largely via business investment, which, however, will be restrained by the low capacity utilisation rate. Private

Figure 1. **Short-term economic indicators**

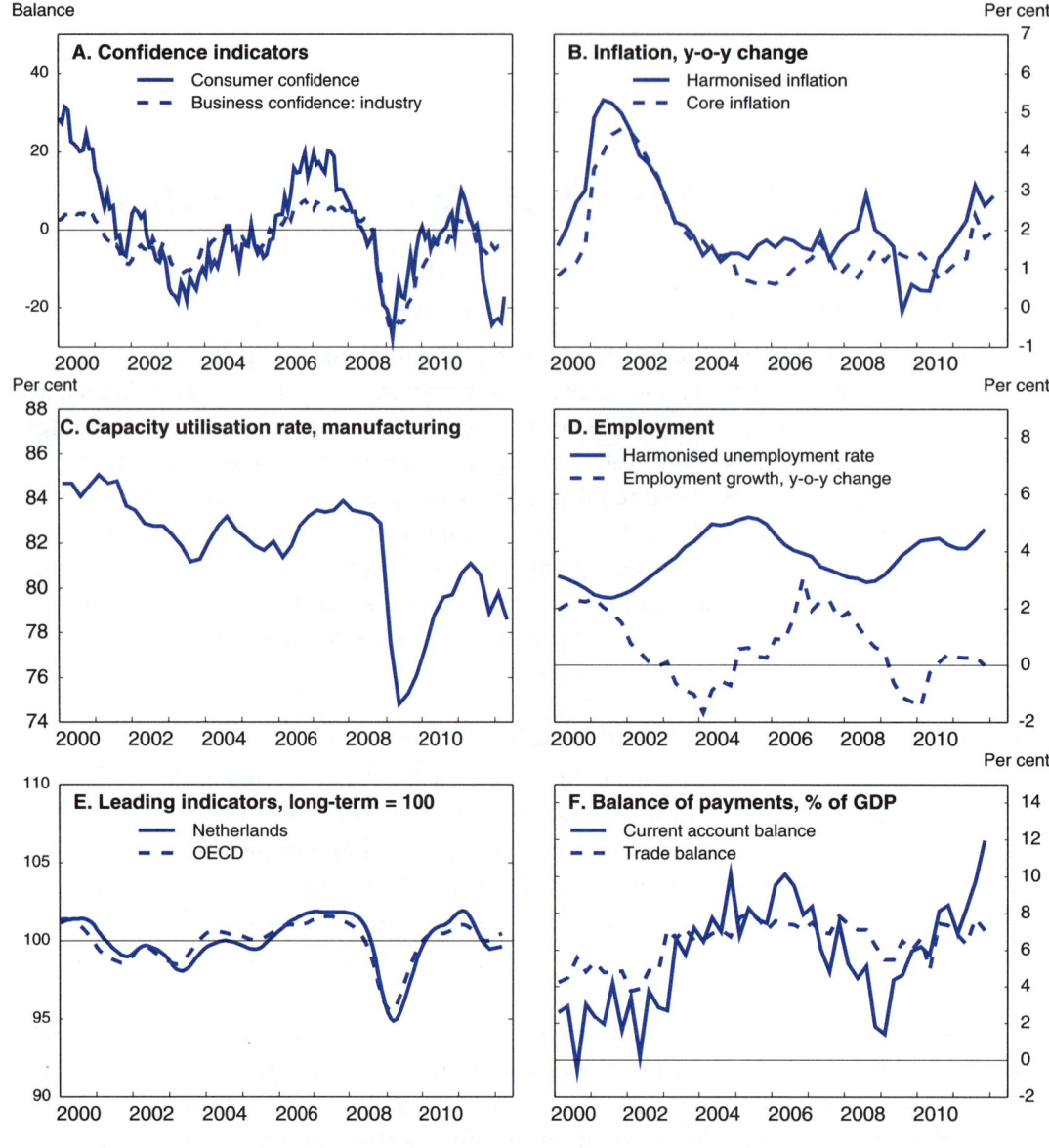

Source: OECD (2012), OECD Economic Outlook and Main Economic Indicators Databases.
StatLink http://dx.doi.org/10.1787/888932613940

consumption, on the other hand, is likely to remain subdued until the uncertainties surrounding pensions, house prices and financial wealth begin to dissipate. Thus, domestic demand is likely to be relatively weak over the next years. The slow expansion of domestic demand also means that unemployment is set to increase further, possibly until end-2013. The weak labour market should reduce inflation pressures to well within the ECB target range. The export-driven recovery will leave the current account surplus at its elevated level. Within the context of correcting the European imbalances, there is a role for structural reform to help reducing the large Dutch current account surplus, although the effects on reducing the surplus will probably only materialise beyond the current projection horizon (Box 1).

Figure 2. **Labour market developments**

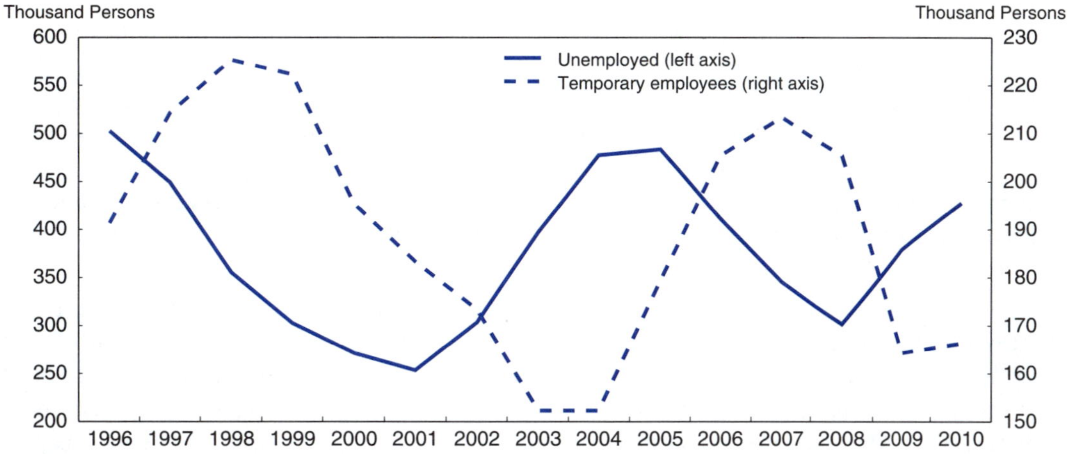

Source: Statistics Netherlands (2012), CBS Statline.

StatLink ⟶ http://dx.doi.org/10.1787/888932613959

Table 1. **Demand, output and prices**
Percentage changes, volume (2005 prices)

	2008 Current prices EUR billion	2009	2010	2011	2012	2013
Gross domestic product	594.7	−3.5	1.6	1.3	−0.6	0.7
Private consumption	270.4	−2.6	0.4	−1.1	−0.7	−0.2
Government consumption	152.8	4.8	1.0	0.2	−0.7	−1.3
Gross fixed capital formation	121.8	−10.2	−4.4	5.8	−1.9	2.5
Public sector	20.5	4.5	−2.6	−2.3	−6.6	−3.5
Residential	37.5	−14.6	−11.5	6.3	−3.8	−0.3
Business	63.8	−12.2	−0.9	8.7	0.6	5.6
Final domestic demand	545.1	−2.2	−0.4	0.7	−0.9	0.0
Stockbuilding[1]	0.2	−0.8	1.2	0.1	−0.5	0.0
Total domestic demand	545.3	−3.1	0.9	0.8	−1.5	0.0
Exports of goods and services	453.4	−8.1	10.8	3.8	5.4	5.4
Imports of goods and services	404.0	−8.0	10.6	3.5	4.7	5.0
Net exports[1]	49.4	−0.7	0.9	0.5	0.9	0.8
Memorandum items:						
Harmonised index of consumer prices		1.0	0.9	2.5	2.4	1.5
Unemployment rate[2]		3.7	4.4	4.4	5.3	5.7
Households saving ratio[3]		6.4	3.9	5.5	6.4	7.0
Government financial balance[4]		−5.5	−5.0	−4.6	−4.3	−3.0
General government gross debt (Maastricht definition)[4]		60.7	62.9	65.1	70.9	73.5

1. Contributions to real GDP growth.
2. As a percentage of labour force.
3. As a percentage of disposable income.
4. As a percentage of GDP.

Source: OECD Economic Outlook, No. 91.

ASSESSMENT AND RECOMMENDATIONS

> **Box 1. Correcting external imbalances via structural reform**
>
> The current account surplus has increased to reach nearly 10% of GDP in 2011, reflecting a larger surplus on the trade balance. As analysed in the previous Survey, the trade balance is the main factor behind the large and sustained current account surplus and reflects large trade surpluses vis-à-vis the European Union that are partly offset by a trade deficit with Asia – a pattern that is largely the result of the large volume of re-exports that typically channel (Chinese) products through to Germany. The capital flow side of the current account balance shows that the surplus is mainly related to Dutch non-financial firms' foreign direct investments as they – *inter alia* – benefit from globalisation opportunities.
>
> Recent OECD work suggests that structural reform can help to address imbalances in the euro area. In surplus countries – Germany and the Netherlands – reforms should aim at stimulating investment and support domestic demand, while deficit countries should focus on product and labour market reform (OECD, 2012; Kerdrain et al., 2010). Structural reform discussed in this *Survey* may reduce the current account surplus. The government's new policy for the business sector aims at improving broad framework conditions, which is likely to stimulate business investment. Domestic demand is best strengthened through competition policies as well as via measures to secure the solvency of the labour market pension funds and to remove uncertainties in the housing market, which would lower precautionary savings. In addition, the Dutch approach of preserving external competitiveness through wage moderation rather than through productivity gains is likely to have dampened consumption.
>
> The concerns within Europe about excessive imbalances have increased, as witnessed by the introduction of the Excessive Imbalances Procedures, which includes preventive recommendations and fines. An early warning system with a scoreboard of ten indicators is covering the major sources of macroeconomic imbalances. The Netherlands is currently above the indicative thresholds for public debt, private debt and export market share losses (EC, 2012).

Wealth losses have been substantial and pose, together with high household indebtedness, risks to the recovery

Private consumption is being held back by slow income growth and wealth losses. Real disposable income fell in 2009 and has since expanded only slowly. However, falling values of households' second-pillar pension savings, houses and financial wealth have contributed to a sharp fall in consumer confidence. In 2011, most pension funds again became insolvent for regulatory purposes (solvency ratio below the legal minimum of 105%) as financial market turbulence depressed share prices and lowered interest rates (Figure 3). This induced around 100 funds (representing about 40% of all pensioners) to announce average reductions of 2¼ per cent in nominal pensions from 2013 – a move that for many pensioners follows a period of partial, if any, indexation of pensions. In view of the ongoing financial market turbulence, the regulator decided in 2011 to use a three-month average of the yield curve rather than the year-end observation as the discount rate to assess the solvency ratio. This was a step towards the last *Survey*'s recommendations of using a more stable long-term interest rate. More substantively, the solvency of pension funds should benefit from the legislated increase in the retirement age (see below).

Real house prices have fallen by more than 15% since 2008 (Figure 4). At the same time, households' (gross) mortgage debt continued to increase to an internationally high level (Table 2). The combined effect has been to leave at least 10% of (mostly younger) house owners

Figure 3. **The average funding ratio and share of pension funds with a funding ratio below the legal minimum**

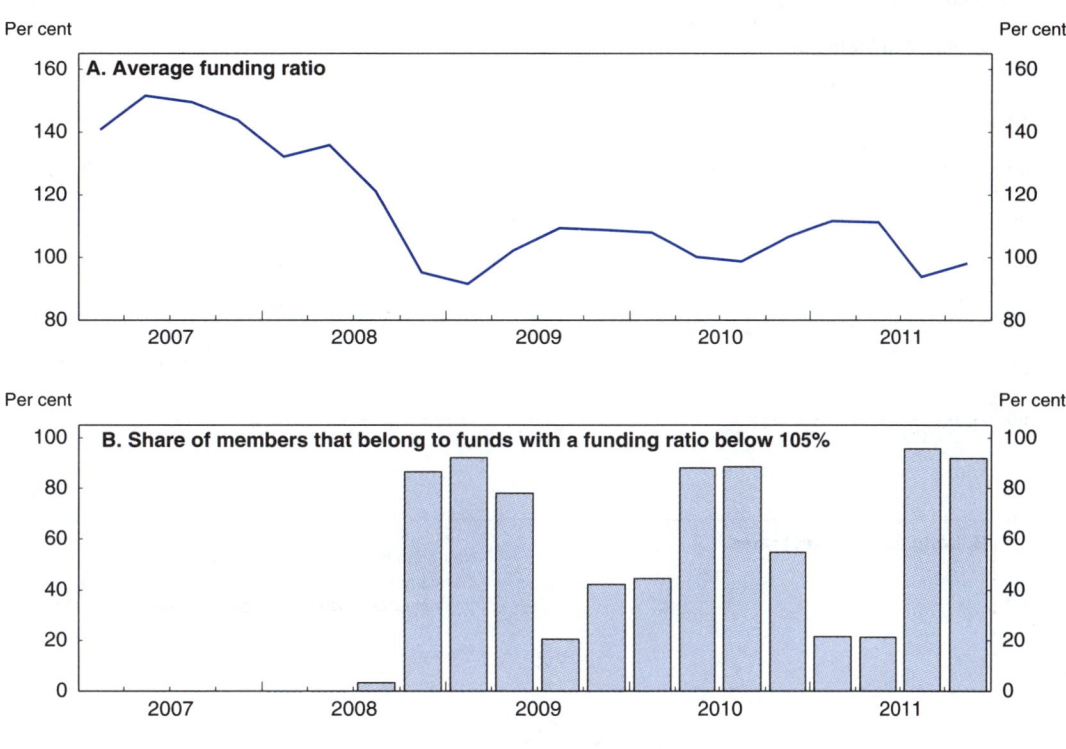

Source: Dutch National Bank.

StatLink ⟶ http://dx.doi.org/10.1787/888932613978

with negative equity. A contributing factor to the depressed prices is that the mortgage rate has remained relatively high; unlike the rate on government bonds that has followed similar German rates down. The high mortgage rate reflects that banks have become more reluctant to issue housing credit (Box 2). In addition, the withdrawal of some foreign banks from the Dutch market has reduced competitive pressures in mortgage lending. More generally, a main issue in the current conjuncture is that the high indebtedness of private households combined with sustained housing market weakness may depress private consumption and hamper labour mobility (Box 2). In addition, the government's backstop function via the National Mortgage Guarantee Fund constitutes a risk to public finances. Other downside risks include a sharper and more prolonged contraction of international trade and continued euro crisis. Indeed, if these two risks materialised simultaneously, economic growth could turn out much weaker than projected. On the upside, improved solvency of the pension funds could boost consumer confidence.

In 2011, the housing transaction tax was temporarily lowered from 6% to 2% to stimulate the market. However, the temporary nature of the measure together with ongoing discussions about housing taxation (particularly about removing the tax deductibility of mortgage interest) creates expectations of future changes in tax treatment of housing. Thus, to create more stable expectations, the reduction in the transaction tax should be made permanent and financed by higher taxation of real estate, which could take the form of a reduction in the value of the tax deductibility of mortgage interest

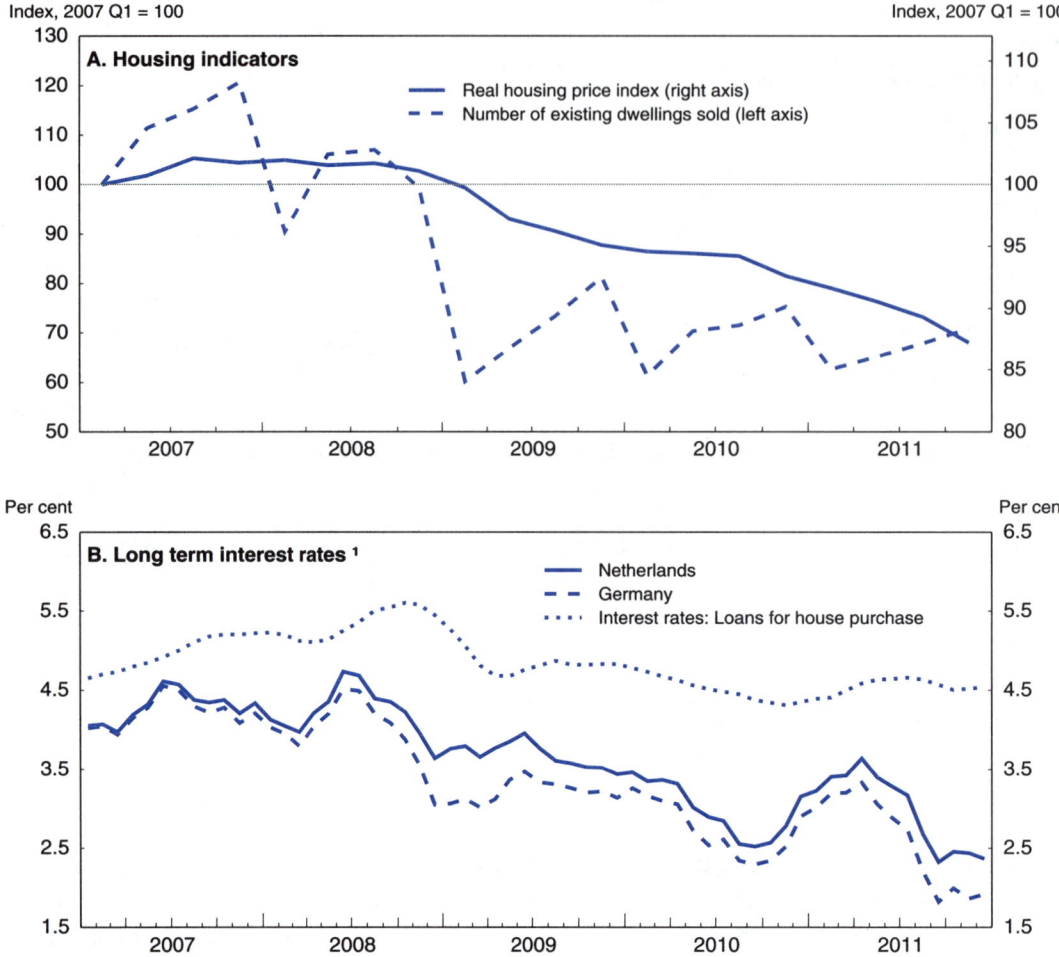

Figure 4. **Interest rate and housing prices developments**

1. 10-year central government bonds for the Netherlands, 10-year government bonds for Germany. Loans for house purchase cover all type of house purchase loans.
Source: OECD, *Analytical Database*, Central Bureau of Statistics and Dutch National Bank.
StatLink http://dx.doi.org/10.1787/888932613997

payments or higher taxation of imputed rent as recommended in the previous *Survey* (OECD, 2010). Higher taxes on real estate should be phased in gradually to avoid abrupt effects on the housing market and to provide certainty.

The economy has enjoyed relatively good trade performance

The Netherlands is likely to benefit more than other countries from a recovery in world trade. The Dutch export market performance has been relatively good with an overall gain in export market shares over the past decades, in contrast to the falling export market shares experienced in many other OECD countries – as a consequence of emerging economies becoming important exporters (Figure 5). However, the good performance is due in large parts to the growing volume of re-exports of goods (with little Dutch value-added), reflecting Rotterdam's position as a main gateway for European trade (see Chapter 1). When subtracting this effect, domestically produced goods have lost about a fifth of their export market shares – similar to the losses (without subtracting those countries' re-exports) of many other European countries, such as France and the United Kingdom. Indeed,

Table 2. **Households' mortgage debt**
As a percentage of GDP

	1995	2000	2005	2010
Austria	36.9	41.2	47.5	50.9
Belgium	33.8	36.4	41.0	51.4
Denmark	..	..	108.9	133.9
Euro area[1]	..	43.9	54.4	62.0
Finland	..	..	45.7	59.8
France	32.5	33.3	40.8	53.1
Germany	55.9	67.8	66.0	58.5
Ireland	..	..	80.2	113.6
Italy	13.1	18.9	30.6	41.4
Netherlands	**56.7**	**83.6**	**109.1**	**123.0**
Norway	58.8	54.2	70.6	83.8
Spain	28.4	43.0	68.2	82.5
Sweden	45.9	50.2	64.3	82.2
United Kingdom	54.7	56.4	76.9	85.4

1. Euro area for 17 countries.
Source: Eurostat (2012), *Annual National Accounts*, Financial balance sheets.

Box 2. **Mortgage indebtedness of households**

The high mortgage debt of households reflects the effects of housing tax policy and especially the tax deductibility of mortgage interest. Mortgage interest for the primary residence can be fully deducted from taxable income during 30 years, leading many households to maintain a high gross mortgage debt, which is often coupled with a long-term tax-friendly savings account.

Falling house prices combined with this high indebtedness have already put 10% of households in a situation of negative equity, meaning that their total net assets (including non housing related assets but not pension funds' reserves) are negative (DNB, 2011a and 2011b). However, mortgage defaults are still rare, at less than 0.1% of mortgages (Rabobank, 2012). Thus, the main issues with negative equity may be depressive effects on households' consumption and labour mobility, as households that intend to move to a new house have to refinance or repay their negative equity. It should be noted that labour mobility is already being undermined by housing market rigidities, as described in the 2010 *Survey*.

Households are somewhat cushioned against their mortgage indebtedness by their large net financial assets (166% of GDP) which have been affected only to a relatively small extent by the 40% decline in share prices since the 2007 peak as only a quarter of assets are invested in shares. This leaves Dutch households in a better position than those in other European countries to face such shocks that, together with the relatively low number of layoffs, may explain the low mortgage default rate. An additional cushion for many households is that the government-owned National Mortgage Guarantee Fund settles any residual debt with lenders in cases of forced sales of (eligible) property.

Households' large mortgage debt is mirrored in banks' balance sheets by funding needs that are larger than deposits. The resulting funding gap – close to EUR 500 billion – used to be financed through short-term capital markets. However, the euro crisis has made these markets less accessible because of the increase in risk-aversion (DNB, 2011a). This has led banks to strengthen their lending criteria, contributing to the higher-than-usual spread between mortgage interest rates and government bonds' rates. As an additional and alternative source of financing, banks have begun to emit more covered bonds – using mortgage assets as collateral – which make banks more vulnerable to large falls in house prices. Nevertheless, the larger banks' solvency ratios are among the highest in Europe and their profitability is still positive, albeit declining because of worsening economic conditions. In addition, last year's stress tests of the banking sector concluded that they needed no additional recapitalisation.

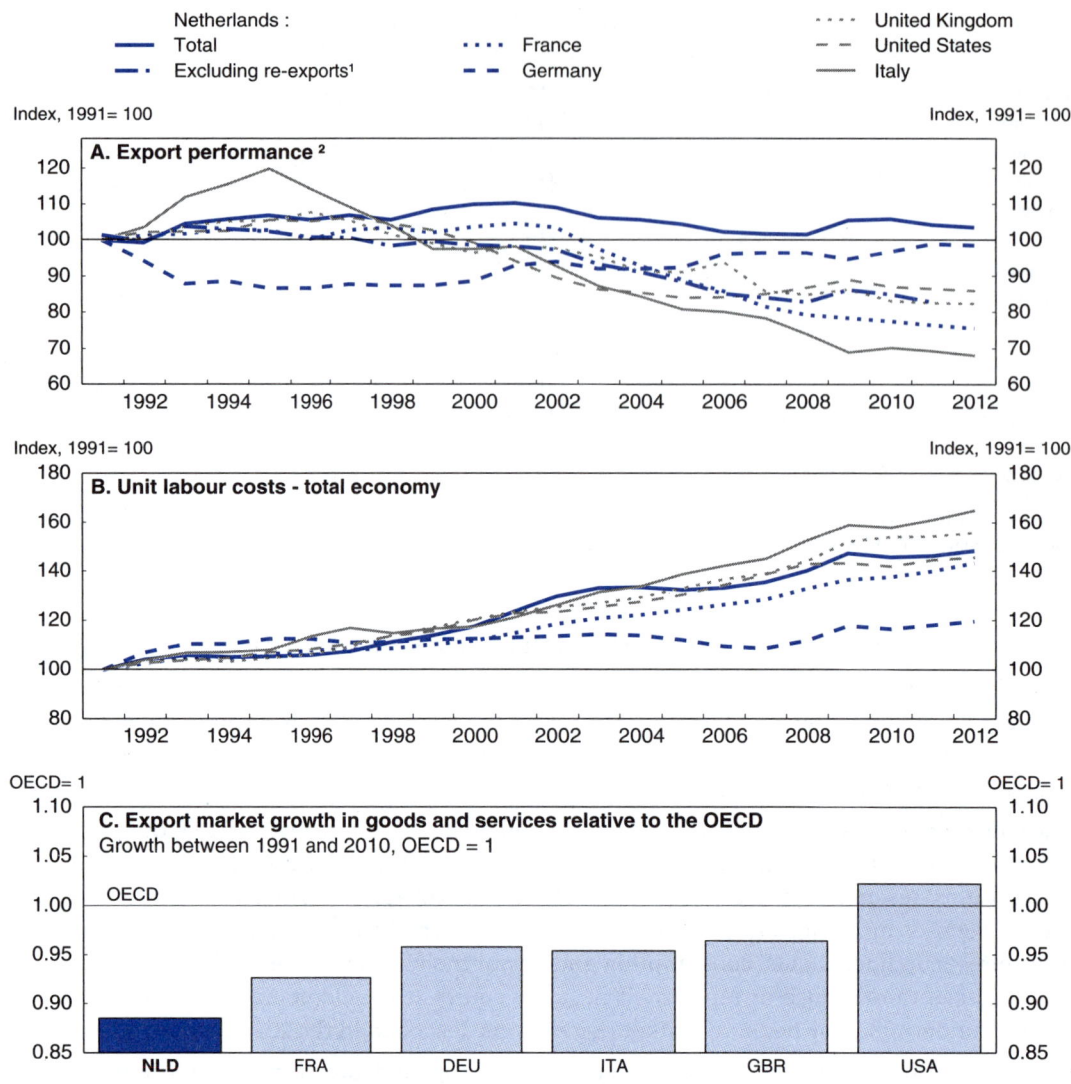

Figure 5. **Competitiveness indicators**

1. Re-exports according to Dutch classification.
2. Export performance is measured as actual growth in exports relative to the growth of the country's export market.
Source: OECD (2012), *OECD Economic Outlook Database*.

StatLink ☞ http://dx.doi.org/10.1787/888932614016

high-technology goods have not gained markets shares in fast growing markets (Figure 6) (Groot *et al.*, 2011). Moreover, the weighted Dutch export market growth has been less vigorous than for other countries, as the main geographical orientation of Dutch exports is still the traditional and relatively slow growing export markets in Europe and North America. Emerging markets are becoming more important export destinations (with the BRIC countries, *i.e.* Brazil, Russian Federation, India and China, accounting for 4% of total exports) but less than observed for other EU countries, leading to – as discussed in Chapter 1 – concerns that Dutch firms could benefit more from globalisation (Groot *et al.*, 2011).

A factor preventing better export performance is eroding competitiveness due to increasing unit labour costs (Figure 5, Panel B). Over the past 1½ decades hourly labour (and multifactor) productivity growth has tended to be below those in many other countries

Figure 6. **Dutch export performance in selected commodities**[1]

Annual world sectoral trade growth, 2000-2010

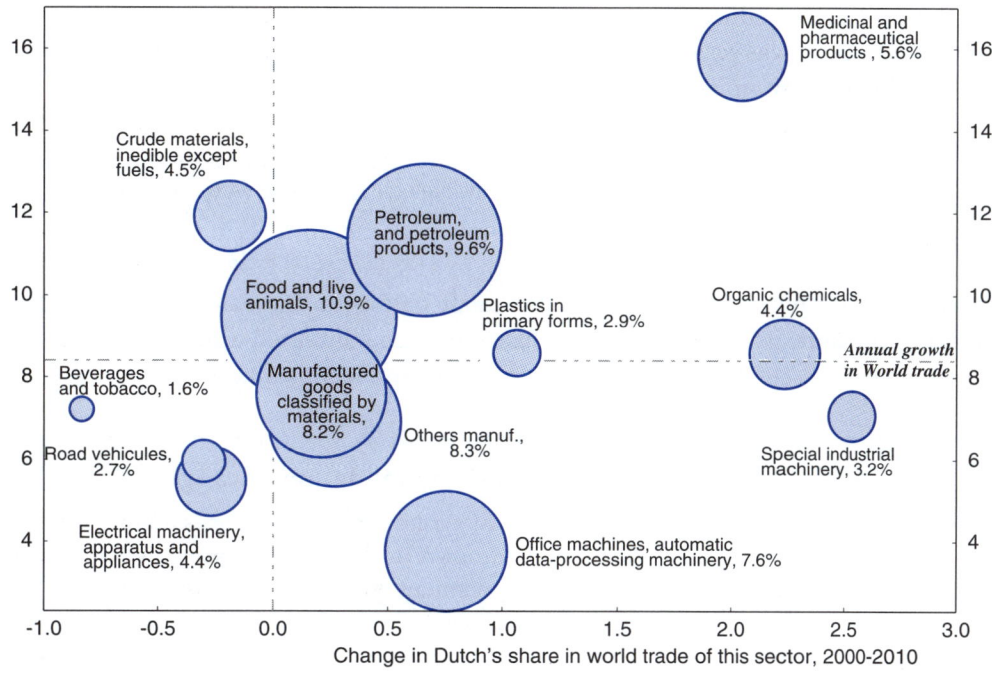

1. Selected commodities based on SITC Rev.3 classification, represent 74% of total nominal exports. The size of the bubble indicates the share of the sector in total Dutch's exports in 2010, which is indicated next to the category.
Source: OECD/UN (2012), *International Trade by Commodity Statistics, Joint Database*.

StatLink http://dx.doi.org/10.1787/888932614035

Figure 7. **Labour productivity growth**
5-year moving average of GDP per hour worked

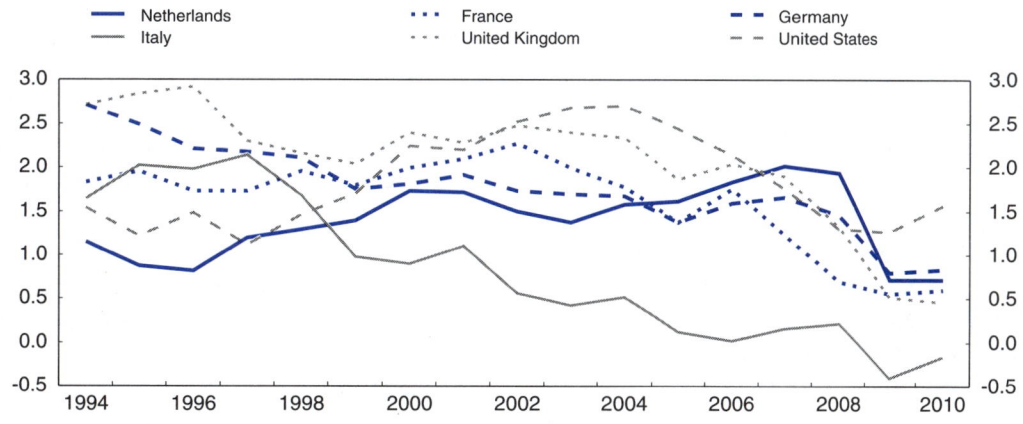

Source: OECD (2012), *Labour Productivity Database*.

StatLink http://dx.doi.org/10.1787/888932614054

(Figure 7). Part of this reflects the extensive labour hoarding that has characterised the labour market during recessions, but it is also an indication that the labour market may not be sufficiently effective in transferring labour resources to new and faster growing sectors and adapting to new productivity-enhancing technologies.

ASSESSMENT AND RECOMMENDATIONS

Sizeable fiscal consolidation is under way

The government's 2012 budget is an important step in the implementation of its consolidation plan to reduce the deficit by a cumulated 3% of GDP by 2015, which in the Coalition Agreement was expected to almost close the sustainability gap (The Government, 2011). The 2012 Budget projects an improvement of the structural deficit of over 1% of GDP, while letting the automatic stabilisers support the weak economy. The additional consolidation package in Spring 2012 and already planned measures should roughly double the consolidation efforts in 2013, before the effort falls back to ½ per cent of GDP the following two years (Box 3) (CPB, 2010a). The cumulative medium-term consolidation effort is significant and should bring the deficit down to at least 3% of GDP in 2013, but will only reduce the public spending-to-GDP ratio by about half of its increase since 2007. On the other hand, the Spring 2012 consolidation package also contained a number of structural reforms, particularly in the area of housing, pension and labour markets.

Box 3. The Spring 2012 fiscal consolidation package

In early 2012, it became clear that the weakening of economic activity necessitated additional fiscal consolidation to achieve the 3% of GDP objective laid down in the EU's excessive deficit procedure. The minority government tried to reach a consolidation agreement with its usual support party in Parliament, but ended with calling for general elections in September 2012. Subsequently, the caretaker government and three opposition parties agreed on a package, which contained fiscal consolidation and structural reforms in a number of key areas such as the labour market, pensions and the housing market. Savings from the package are expected to reach 12 billion (2% of GDP) in 2013.

The package consists of the following main measures:

- The standard VAT-rate will be increased by 2 percentage points to 21% in October 2012 (yielding additional revenues of EUR 4.1 billion in 2013) and there will be higher duties on tobacco and alcohol (extra revenues of EUR 625 million in 2013). The rise in indirect taxes will be increasingly compensated for by lower income taxes as of 2013, particularly for low-income employees.

- All wages in the public sector (excluding health care) will be frozen for two years, generating savings of EUR 900 million in 2012 and EUR 1.7 billion in 2013 and onwards.

- Health care expenditures will be limited by higher co-payments (lower income households will be compensated via higher health care subsidies) and a reduction in the scope of the basis insurance package. Stringent arrangements will be made with health care institutions to secure overall health care savings of EUR 1.6 billion in 2013.

- The statutory retirement age of 65 will be gradually increased, starting in 2013, to 66 in 2019 and 67 in 2024. Thereafter it will be linked to changes in life expectancy. In addition, the tax advantages for building up private pensions (Witteveenkader) will be reduced as the eligibility age for private pensions will be increased from 65 to 67 in 2014 and the maximum annual fiscal accrual rate for pension savings will be reduced, implying a lower tax-exempt pension contribution.

- Employers will pay unemployment benefits for the first six months of a worker's spell of unemployment. In addition, employers have to invest in training programmes and job-to-job assistance. In return, steps are taken for a more flexible labour market, by simplifying dismissal procedures and lowering costs of dismissal.

> **Box 3. The Spring 2012 fiscal consolidation package** *(cont.)*
>
> - As of January 2013, new mortgages need to be paid off in full (and at least as annuity) over the course of the loan agreement of 30 years in order to continue to obtain access to the mortgage interest deduction facility (leading to structural savings of EUR 5.4 billion). In addition, the maximum Loan-to-Value ratio will be gradually lowered to 100%. Moreover, the temporary lowering of the transaction tax from 6% to 2% will become permanent.
> - In social housing, rents for tenants with an annual income between EUR 33 000 and EUR 43 000 can be increased yearly by inflation +1% (the additional revenue for property owners will be subject to a rental tax as of 2013).
> - New environmental measures will include additional measures to support insulation of houses and durable construction, among others. The use of fossil fuels will be discouraged by increasing taxes on coal and gas and road use charges for heavy goods vehicles ("Eurovignette"), and by abolishing tax advantages for using diesel for specific industrial and commercial use ("red diesel").

As outlined in the Coalition Agreement, the 2012 consolidation focuses on the expenditure side, amounting to 0.9% of GDP, with cuts concentrated on social benefits, the public wage bill and subsidies (The Government, 2010). The focus on spending restraint is growth enhancing in the long term. The reduction in child care spending may negatively affect female labour market participation. To avoid breaking the overall expenditure ceiling in the Coalition Agreement, additional measures were added, mainly to contain health care expenditures (CPB, 2011c). Further fiscal consolidation comes from higher revenues of ½ per cent of GDP, including increased household and corporate taxes (via the phasing of the 2009 crisis related measure of accelerated depreciation of investment) employers' social security contributions, and health care premiums.

Determining a suitable fiscal stance is particularly complex in the current economic situation. Sticking to the planned nominal fiscal targets would allow the Netherlands to meet its European obligations and ensure a rapid improvement of fiscal sustainability, which could potentially contribute to calm financial markets' sovereign debt concerns and support the AAA rating of Dutch government bonds. On the other hand, attention should be paid that an overly rapid fiscal consolidation does not have an excessive negative impact on activity, especially at a time when the economy is particularly fragile owing to the weak housing market and the solvency issues surrounding the pension funds. In addition, hysteresis effects may reduce potential growth, aggravating fiscal sustainability problems. Moreover, since several euro area members are under fiscal stress and have no other choice but to implement drastic fiscal consolidation, a less vigorous pace of fiscal consolidation in the Netherlands could help support activity and correct imbalances in the euro area (Figure 9). On balance and based on the OECD's central projection of a gradual recovery, the overall fiscal stance seems appropriate in terms of moving public finances onto a sustainable path over the next few years despite fiscal policy being somewhat pro-cyclical (Figure 8).

A fiscal rule adopted in the Coalition Agreement stipulated that if the budget deficit deviated by more than 1 percentage point of GDP from the government's medium-term baseline, the government needed to take action to ensure that the projected deficit was back on track by the end of its term. Since the presentation of the 2012 Budget, the economic outlook worsened and the Spring 2012 CPB projection showed a sufficient deviation to trigger

Figure 8. **The fiscal stance is pro-cyclical in 2012**

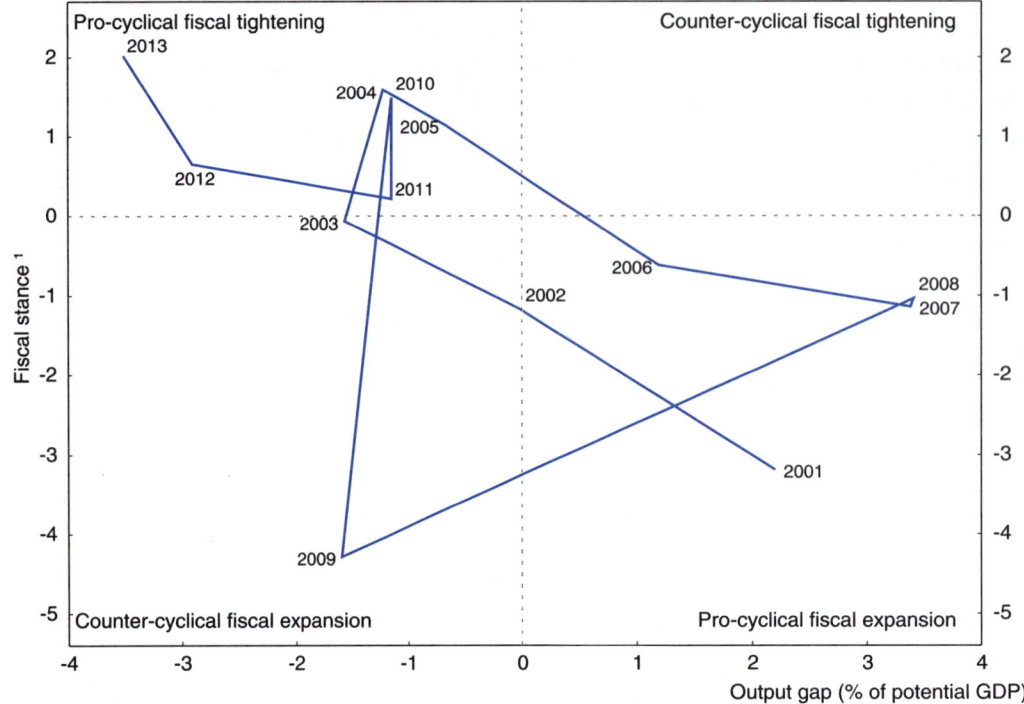

1. Fiscal stance is measured by the changes in cyclically-adjusted primary balance, excluding natural gas revenues.
Source: OECD Economic Outlook Database, No. 90 and CPB Central Plan Bureau.

StatLink ⟶ http://dx.doi.org/10.1787/888932614073

the rule. The rule was a strong instrument to secure fiscal consolidation, but in this instance was pro-cyclical. Notwithstanding such rules, in case of a drastic worsening of the economic outlook, for example like the risk scenario in the OECD Economic Outlook, No. 90 (roughly equal to the 2009 recession), the government should use fiscal policy to support the economy as in the 2009 recession. The resulting delay in fiscal consolidation would need to be offset by credible medium-term consolidation via structural measures.

The main long-term fiscal challenge is to close the large sustainability gap

The fiscal sustainability gap was estimated by the European Commission to be 9¼ per cent of GDP in 2010, which is high in a EU context (Figure 10). The CPB estimate is 4½ per cent of GDP in 2015 (before implementation of the 2010 Coalition agreement) – the lower estimate reflects lower expected costs of ageing, expected structural improvements arising from pre-2010 measures, and a recovery of the corporate tax elasticity (CPB, 2010b; European Commission, 2011). Moreover, these estimates do not take into account higher future flood protection costs associated with global warming, pointing to a need for a more cost-efficient water management system (Box 4).

The 2010 Coalition Agreement aims at reducing the sustainability gap by 4 percentage points by 2015 via fiscal consolidation and structural reform mainly in the area of pension, health and long-term care (see Chapter 3). The retirement age in the state (first pillar) pension system was to increase from 65 to 66 in 2020 and thereafter be linked to life expectancy – a measure that will be emulated in the labour market (second pillar) pension system. The measure will be combined with more generous indexation to actual rather than

Figure 9. **Imbalances in the euro area countries**
As a percentage of GDP, 2011

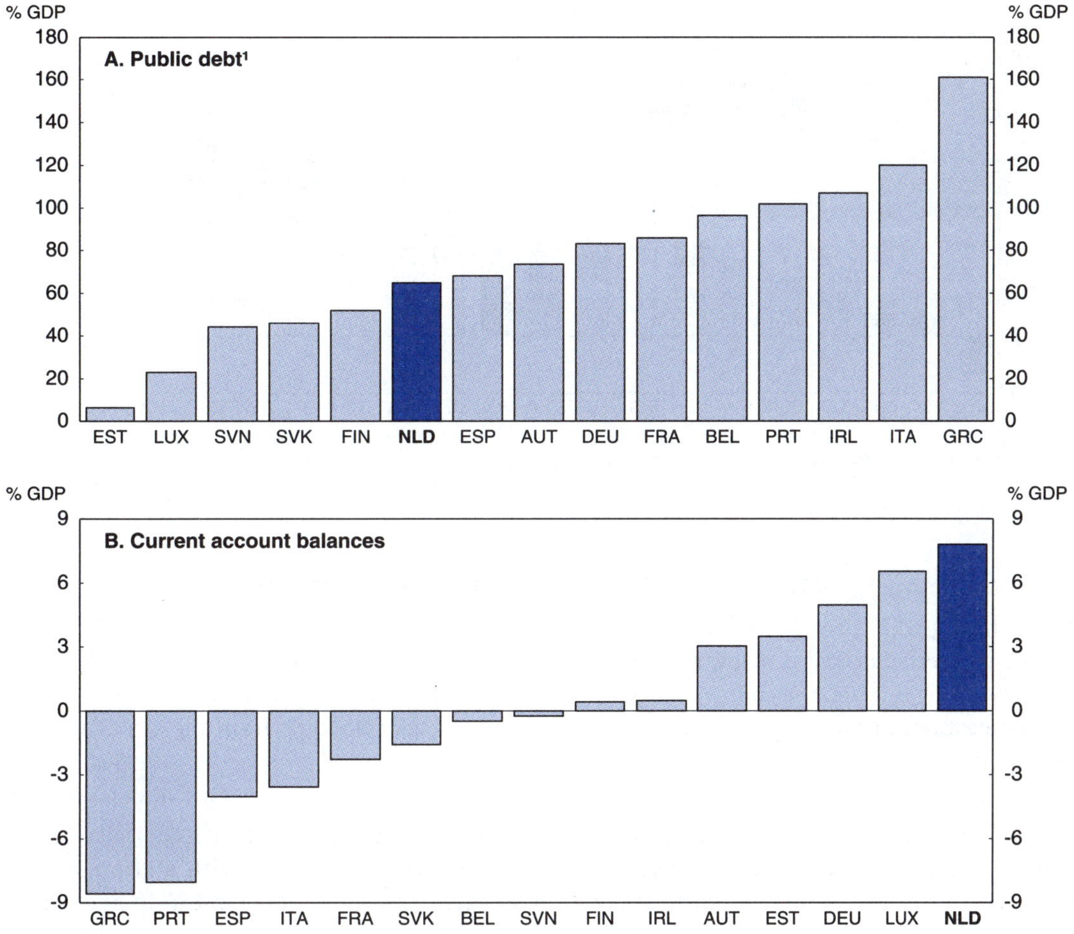

A. Public debt[1]

B. Current account balances

1. The debt data is estimated on the basis of *OECD Economic Outlook*, No. 90.
Source: OECD (2011), *OECD Economic Outlook Database*, No. 90.

StatLink http://dx.doi.org/10.1787/888932614092

negotiated wages. Later retirement will also be promoted via a *bonus-malus* system where early retirement leads to a 6½ per cent reduction in state pension per year and late retirement to a 6½ per cent increase. In addition, a "Vitality" scheme will promote longer working lives by enhancing training, continuation, mobility, and career incentives for older workers through tax credits and bonuses (CPB, 2011c). In all, these measures should improve fiscal sustainability by ¾ per cent of GDP (CPB, 2011). From a political economy perspective, the current crisis is an opportune moment to implement substantial structural reform, which could partly contribute to the closing of the fiscal sustainability gap. The economic crisis has sharply increased the public debt-GDP ratio relative to the pre-crisis level, narrowing the room to cope with population ageing (Figure 11).

The government expects that with the current consolidation plans, the public debt-GDP ratio will stabilise in 2015 at a level that is 40 percentage points higher than previously projected. Higher debt and an expected normalisation of interest rates imply higher cost of debt servicing just as population ageing commences in earnest (Figure 12). Nevertheless, the Netherlands is better prepared than many European countries with a public debt ratio that is

Figure 10. **Sustainability gaps in European countries**
2010

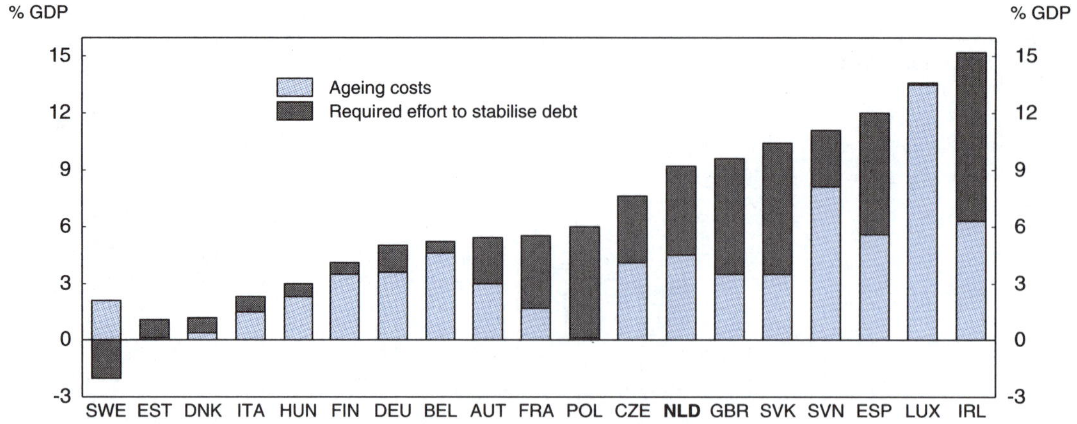

Source: European Commission (2011), *Commission Staff Working Paper*.
StatLink http://dx.doi.org/10.1787/888932614111

Box 4. Global warming and flood protection

Global warming will raise the sea level and increase precipitation. The sea level rise will increase the share of the Netherlands that is below sea level and the increased precipitation means that the volume of river water flooding through the country will swell and have more peak periods. As a result, substantial and prolonged investment programmes in dikes are required to prevent flooding from the sea as well as from the rivers.

Various scenarios indicate that global warming of 2-6 degrees Celsius will cause the sea level to rise between 15-35 cm by 2050 and by another 50-85 cm in the following 50 years (KNMI, 2006; Delta Commissie, 2008). In addition, there will be an increase in river discharges into the sea with a stronger seasonal variation, even possible creating dry summers with insufficient water for transport in inland waterways. Moreover, there is likely to be an increase in extreme weather events, which not only will challenge the capacity of drainage infrastructures and sewage systems, but also create more situations where storms are creating extraordinarily high tides, preventing the emptying of rivers into the sea.

About a quarter of the country is below the sea level and more than half of the population and two-thirds of economic activity is found in flood prone areas. The protection of these areas requires substantial flood defences, including about 3 800 km of dikes and dunes in the primary defences and another 17 000 km in secondary defences. The current maintenance and updating of these defences demands annual water infrastructure investments of about ¾ per cent of GDP. The necessary additional flood protection required by global warming could required almost another ¼ percentage of GDP per year over the longer term.

Water management is in the hands of five different levels of government (the central government, the provinces, the water boards, the municipalities, and the water companies) where the most important in terms of flood protection is the 25 water boards (the oldest democratic institution in the Netherlands, dating back from the middle ages). This multi-level structure has also led to numerous water charges (to cover water supply, dike maintenance, sewage systems, etc.) which are mostly set on a cost-plus basis and show a high regional variation. Part of these large regional differences reflect differences in efficiencies related to a lack of economies of scale, political boards not focusing on cost efficiency, or lack of financial incentives for efficient operation.

Figure 11. **Public debt path before and after the crisis**
As a percentage of GDP

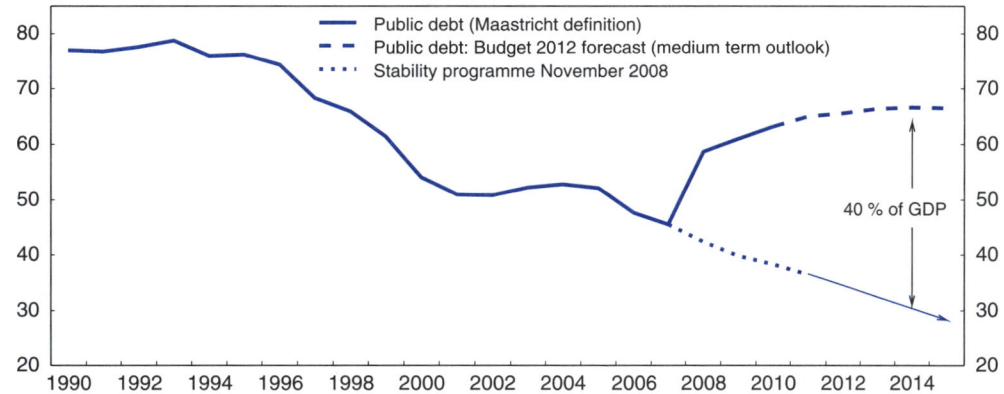

Source: OECD Economic Outlook Database, Dutch 2012 budget and 2008 Stability Programme.
StatLink ⇒ http://dx.doi.org/10.1787/888932614130

Figure 12. **Population ageing**

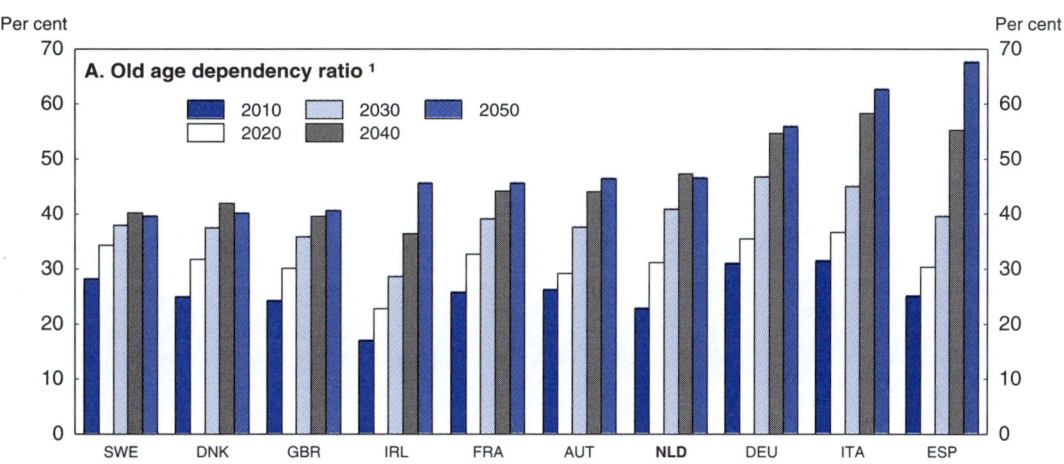

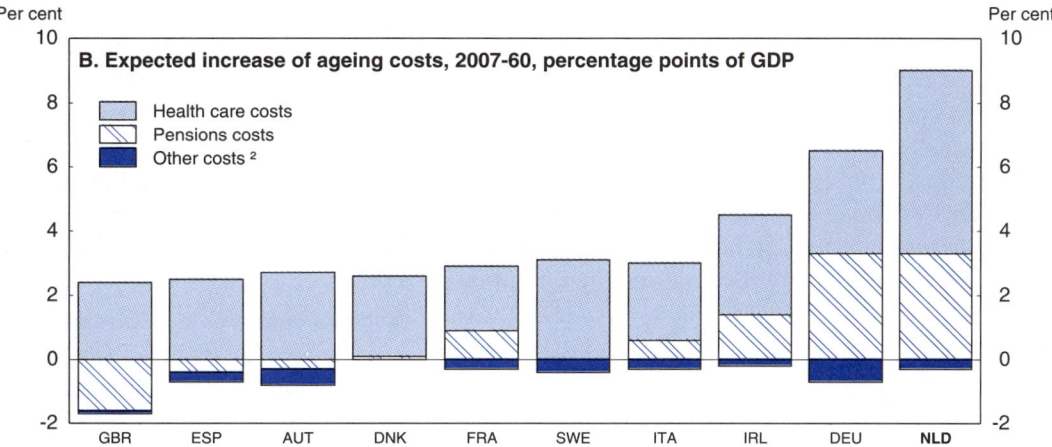

1. Population 65 years and over divided by 15-64 years population.
2. Unemployment benefits and education costs.

Source: OECD (2011), *Historical Population Data and Projections Database (1950-2050)* and European Commission (2009), "2009 Ageing Report: Economic and budgetary projections for the EU-27 Members States (2008-2060)".
StatLink ⇒ http://dx.doi.org/10.1787/888932614149

more than 30 percentage points lower than the euro area average and with accumulated private labour-market pension assets of 135% of GDP in 2010. The relatively high future ageing costs reflect the ambitiousness of the Dutch social model, rather than especially unfavourable demographics (Box 5). To secure fiscal sustainability, the government should focus its attention on curbing ageing related increases in pension and health spending. In this context, the planned increase in the retirement age is an important step and the 2012 health care reform (see below) could contribute in this direction. If necessary, the government should be ready to implement additional measures in both areas.

> Box 5. **The ambitiousness of the Dutch social model induces high ageing costs**
>
> The Netherlands faces one of the highest ageing costs in Europe according to the latest estimates (European Commission, 2009). Based on pre-2009 policy, public spending is set to increase by almost 10% of GDP over 2007-60, against an increase of 5½ per cent of GDP for the euro area (Table 3). This high cost mainly reflects the ambitiousness of the Dutch social model, especially in terms of pensions and long-term care.
>
> Table 3. **Public and private age-related spending**
> As a percentage of GDP
>
> | | Netherlands | | | Euro area | | |
> |---|---|---|---|---|---|---|
> | | 2007 | 2060 | Change 2007-60 | 2007 | 2060 | Change 2007-60 |
> | Public pensions | 6.6 | 10.5 | 3.9 | 11.0 | 13.8 | 2.8 |
> | Health care | 4.8 | 5.8 | 1.0 | 6.7 | 8.1 | 1.4 |
> | Long term care | 3.4 | 8.1 | 4.7 | 1.3 | 2.7 | 1.4 |
> | **Total public spending** | **14.8** | **24.4** | **9.6** | **19.0** | **24.6** | **5.6** |
> | Private pensions | 5.2 | 12.1 | 6.9 | n.a. | n.a. | n.a. |
> | **Total spending** | **20.0** | **36.5** | **16.5** | **n.a.** | **n.a.** | **n.a.** |
>
> Source: European Commission (2009), "2009 Ageing Report: Economic and budgetary projections for the EU-27 Members States (2008-2060)".
>
> In 2007, Dutch pensioners enjoyed the highest purchasing power in Europe, with the average pension (public plus private) representing 74% of the average wage in the economy (Figure 13). While the average pension is projected to rise to 81% of the average wage by 2060, most other countries expect a decline as past pension reforms will lower initial pensions and reduce their subsequent indexation. For example, French pensions are now indexed on prices and German indexation directly takes into account sustainability considerations. In contrast, the Dutch pension reform implies longer working life, but more generous pensions, in total leading to a lowering of pension outlays in 2060 by more than ¾ per cent of GDP. However, whether these favourable pensions will fully materialise depend on the second-pillar occupational pensions system's ability to fulfil its pension promises – a somewhat doubtful proposition given that many funds are currently lowering their nominal pensions.
>
> Regarding long-term care, the Dutch system is more than twice as costly as the European average (Table 3), primarily reflecting the comprehensiveness of the Dutch system, which includes accommodation costs in nursing homes and home help for domestic activities. At the same time co-payments for home care are internationally low (see Chapter 3).

> Box 5. **The ambitiousness of the Dutch social model induces high ageing costs** (cont.)
>
> Figure 13. **Average total pension**
> As a percentage of the economy-wide average wage
>
>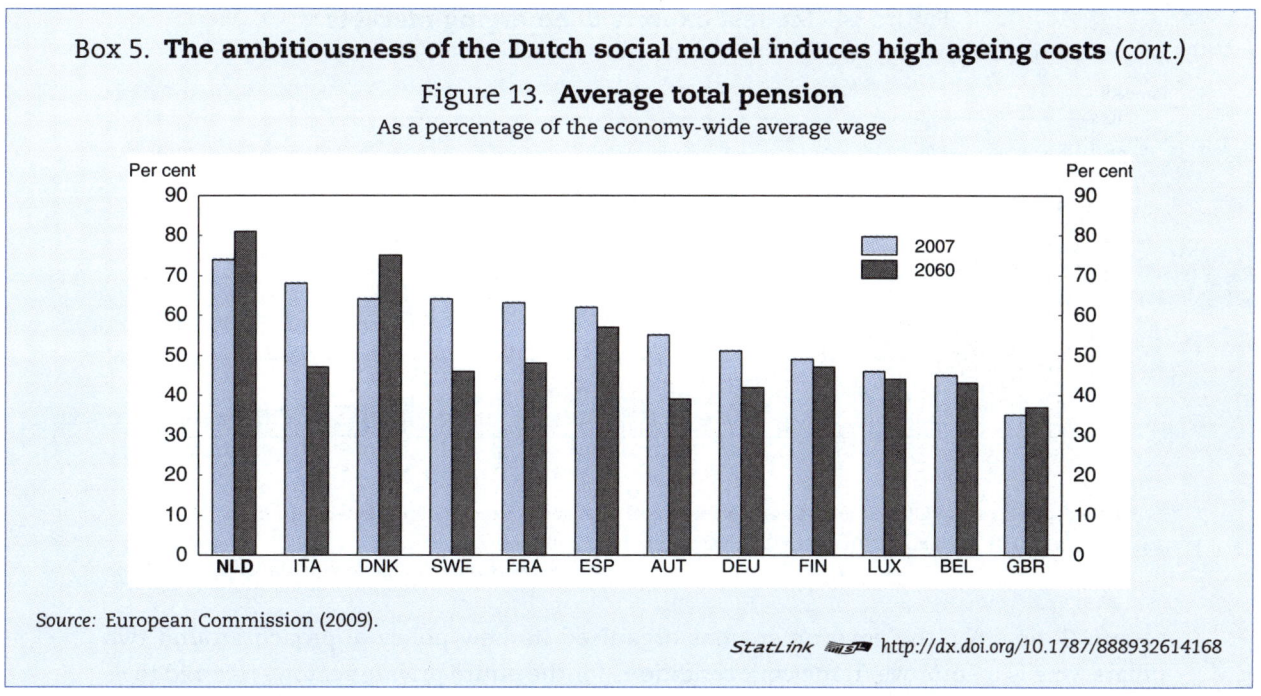
>
> Source: European Commission (2009).
>
> StatLink http://dx.doi.org/10.1787/888932614168

> Box 6. **Main fiscal policy recommendations**
>
> Government finances should be brought under control, but fiscal consolidation should avoid excessive pro-cyclicality in the event that downside risks materialise.
>
> Secure long-term fiscal sustainability by implementing planned measures, such as increasing the retirement age in the state pension system and introducing more competition in the health sector, to curb ageing-related spending growth in the area of pensions and health spending as well as being ready to adopt additional measures if necessary.

Globalisation and policies for the business sector

Globalisation has had a significant positive impact on the Dutch economy. The increase in world trade has allowed the Netherlands to reap huge benefits via Rotterdam's position as the main trade gateway to the rest of Europe, leading particularly to a surge in re-exports. Globalisation and better communication allow for faster adoption of new technologies, helping productivity growth. Consumers have benefited from downwards pressure on prices via cheaper imports from emerging economies and greater choice. Both inward and outward foreign investments have increased, allowing for the transfer of new technologies and efficiency enhancing separation of production. However, a concern is that exports of domestically produced goods remain focused on slow-growing traditional European markets and not sufficiently on emerging countries (Figure 14). In addition, globalisation is pushing companies to become more innovative and to search for new activities.

The government is reforming policies for the business sector

To face the opportunities and challenges arising from globalisation, such as establishing trade and investment linkages with emerging countries and boosting innovative activities, the Dutch government is reforming the policies for the business

Figure 14. **Modest exports to emerging markets**
Exports of goods to BRIC countries,[1] as percentage of total, 2010 or latest year available

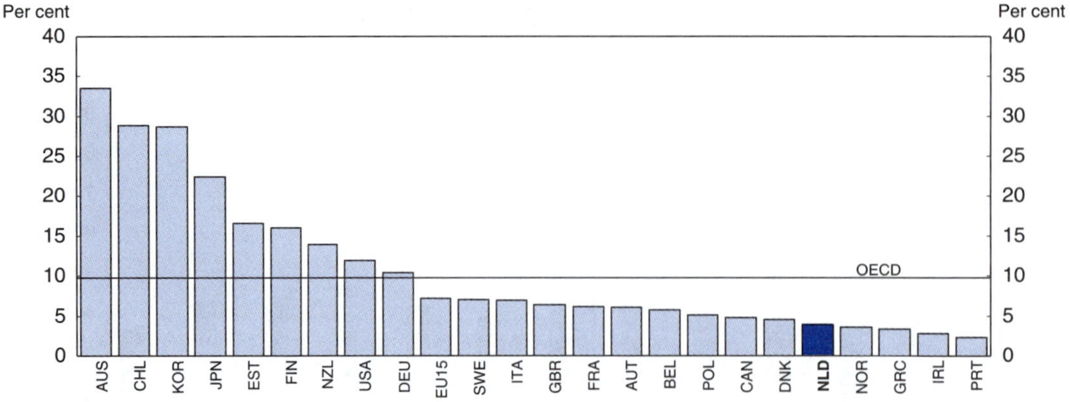

1. Total goods exports to BRIC countries as a percentage of total goods exports of presented countries.
Source: OECD (2012), International Trade and Commodities Statistics Database.

StatLink ⟶ http://dx.doi.org/10.1787/888932614187

sector. Concretely, the government has organised its new policy approach around two pillars. One is to improve framework conditions for the entire private sector – referred to as the "economic agenda" – and the other is to focus on nine areas of excellence in the form of a "top sector approach". Such a reform has to strike a balance between targeted policies to address market failures policies and to improve broad framework conditions to foster a market-based promotion of comparative advantages.

Regarding top sector support, the objective is to identify and address market and government failures at the sector level and prioritise research and development activities. These failures are particularly a limited knowledge transfer from universities, a co-ordination failure among different branches of the government, overly detailed sector regulation, and an insufficient supply of skilled workers. The aim is to develop sector specific policies across the full breadth of the government, including education, innovation, and foreign policies as well as reducing regulatory burdens. To facilitate the new demand-driven bottom-up process, so-called top teams for each sector have been formed, comprising sector experts, high ranking civil servants, SME entrepreneurs and representatives from research institutions. The top teams are to identify opportunities and challenges for each sector and formulate sector specific policy proposals to the government as well as to themselves. Based on the recommendations from the top teams, the government is currently working out detailed policy measures with implementation starting in the first half of 2012. Top teams can exploit a broad range of experiences and insights to improve the formulation of framework policies, particularly within industries. Indeed, this represents a possibility for ensuring that sector regulation is as uniform as possible to promote general framework conditions. Drawing on the experience with the current top teams, the government should consider establishing similar teams for more sectors to provide information and suggestions about how to make sector regulation more growth friendly. In terms of globalisation, such regulation is particularly important to secure for service sectors as they provide important inputs to the export sectors and account for an increasing share of the economy and exports.

The definition of the selected sectors may also be too broad, as not all industries need specific attention to promote exports and R&D and some would be better served by the application of general framework conditions (such as competition policy) to ensure favourable framework conditions. For example, the selected logistic sector could include industries as different as international and domestic road haulage and taxis. Thus, to secure an efficient use of available public funds, the scope of the top sectors should become more clearly defined in terms of only including industries where there is an objective need for public support. This would also contribute to enabling the planned move towards evidence based policy making.

Using top sectors to identify regulatory burdens may address asymmetric information problems, insofar as they exist. However, the approach also raises issues of regulatory capture and increased heterogeneity in regulation across sectors. Because of these risks, the government should ensure that the selection of top sectors and the establishment of top teams does not become a vehicle for favouring particular industries or firms within the top sectors through earmarking of R&D funds/activities or other preferential treatment. A particular concern is that larger firms and existing industries are better organised than SMEs and emerging industries, and thus benefit from a "first-mover" advantage in dealing with public support schemes. A balanced approach can be achieved by requiring that findings from the top teams are backed up by independent evidence and that their policy prescriptions are evaluated against alternatives.

Another element in the top sector approach is the increased attention to economic diplomacy, including the active involvement of representations abroad, to foster investment and trade linkages. Economic diplomacy has the potential for helping smaller firms break into export markets in the emerging economies, where doing business can be relatively complicated because of linguistic, bureaucratic, and political barriers. To ensure an appropriate allocation of public resources in economic diplomacy and avoid excessive demand for such services, it is important that the prices for these services, to some degree, reflect costs.

Better framework conditions are key to promote performance

Strengthening broad framework conditions will secure a market based promotion of comparative advantages. The government is pursuing this approach through its economic agenda, which focuses on improving the general business environment. The key elements are reducing administrative and regulatory burdens, establishing a new innovation framework to counter low and declining private R&D spending and improving the access to risk capital for small innovative firms. The approach of improving the general business environment should be broadened to include related policies. In particular, competition policies should receive greater attention, with a focus on highly concentrated sectors (such as financial and telecommunication services) and on business service sectors with relatively high entry barriers particularly when compared with low barrier countries, such as retailing, legal and road freight business. Bankruptcy procedures remain long and costly, pointing to a need for streamlining legislation in this area, as recommended in the 2006 *Survey*.

An important aspect of the reform of the innovation framework is to replacing direct subsidies with broader tax incentives. This is combined with a move towards evidence-based policy by establishing an indicator and monitoring system to guide innovation policies. This shift is commendable as it is move away from "picking winners" to a broader policy framework. However, the planned doubling in the number of R&D tax credits is likely to make the framework more complex. Thus, the policy framework could be further simplified by reducing the number of R&D tax credits. Moreover, innovation policies have been changed quite frequently.

A long-term political commitment is necessary for the new innovation policy framework to become effective to support firms' multi-year research programmes. The government is entering an agreement with universities to foster research being brought to the market. However, university staff have little economic incentive for these activities as they often neither enjoy higher salaries nor share patents rights. To enhance researchers' incentives to market the result of their research, clear and more generous rules for sharing patents rights should be established. Another issue is that the new innovation policy will tend to direct resources to traditional research oriented industries without necessarily promoting innovation in services, where new approaches to design, marketing, organisational structures and other intangibles are becoming increasingly important.

The new policies for the business sector are commendable for focussing on framework conditions. Whether the policies, however, will deliver the expected results in the context of globalisation is unclear. Most export and innovation activities are undertaken by large firms, while the aggregated contribution of SMEs in these areas is modest. Thus, policies to address market failures for smaller firms are unlikely to have much effect on the ability to benefit from globalisation unless they work in this direction.

> Box 7. **Main business sector policy recommendations**
>
> Taking advantage of the top team approach, similar teams for other sectors of the economy, especially services, should be created to improve sector regulation.
>
> Broaden the approach of improving the general business environment by giving more attention to competition policies.
>
> Establish clear and more generous rules for sharing patents rights to enhance researchers' incentives to market the result of their research.

Preparing the labour market for further globalisation and population ageing

The Dutch labour market has been one of the strongest in the OECD, characterised by low unemployment and high employment rates (including a female labour participation rate of nearly 75 per cent – the ninth highest in the OECD). However, looking ahead it is unlikely that the organisation of the labour market into a relatively small flexible segment and a much larger rigid segment within the context of an ageing labour force will allow the Netherlands to continue reaping the benefits of globalisation. That would require a more flexible labour market that can reallocate increasingly scarce labour resources to their most optimal use (Figure 15). A key factor behind the successful labour market performance is the early labour market debut for many young people, facilitating later transition into full time position and permanent contracts (OECD, 2011). On the other hand, the utilisation rate in terms of hours worked is low, which particularly reflects a high rate of part-time employment among relatively high-skilled women and a relatively low – but rising – effective retirement age (OECD, 2010). The main issues with respect to whether the labour market can reallocate labour resources across sectors to fully benefit from continued globalisation are: whether the ageing of labour force leads to higher wage costs because of the strong seniority element in wages and possible increases in health and pension premiums; and whether sufficient available labour resources can be mobilised to counter the ageing related contraction of the labour force.

Figure 15. **Job mobility is low**

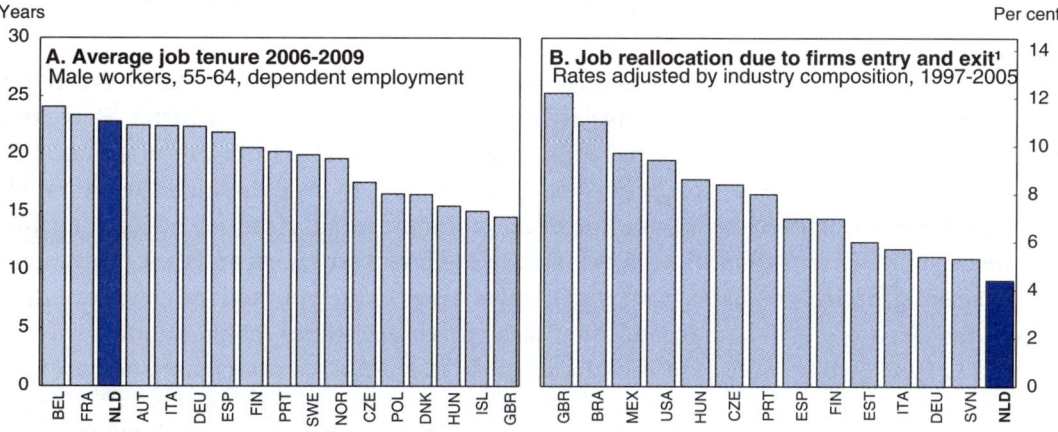

1. Adjusted reallocation rates are estimated averages rates of job creation and destruction by entry and exit to total dependent employment that would be observed in each country if it had the same industry composition as the average country.

Source: OECD (2012), *OECD Employment Outlook Database*.

StatLink http://dx.doi.org/10.1787/888932614206

A relatively small part of the labour market can easily be reallocated

About a quarter of the labour market consists of workers on temporary contracts (typically young people) and self-employed individuals. This group has a higher unemployment risk and lower social protection in the form of lower severance pay and unemployment benefits, and often a lack of sickness coverage. As a result, the effects of negative shocks fall disproportionally on this group. The rest of the labour market consists of (often older and higher skilled) workers with permanent contracts and high social protection that increases with tenure, giving few incentives for changing employment and thus often denying expanding sectors easy access to experienced high-skilled workers. Looking ahead, the labour supply is set to contract with population ageing, so by 2040, the working age population will have contracted by 10%. Moreover, a large part of the retiring labour force will be males employed in manufacturing.

Wage developments have contributed relatively little to reallocate labour resources, as relative wages between sectors have remained fairly constant, although globalisation has contributed to increasing the demand for high-skilled workers and the wage premium on education. Moreover, globalisation is making tax bases more mobile, which implies that risk sharing via the tax-benefit system may become more difficult if taxpayers react to high tax rates. In the context of continued and possibly accelerating globalisation, a relatively traditional export market structure and an export sector that relies on relatively few large firms, the necessary speed of adjustment to maintain the Dutch export position is likely to increase.

The reduction in labour resources can be mitigated by mobilising currently underutilised labour resources, such as older and female part-time workers, and encouraging immigration of skilled workers. As recommended in the 2008 *Survey*, female labour market participation can be encouraged by improving access to child care (subsidies as well as availability), by reducing the marginal effective tax rate faced by second earners – a measure that is being phased in with the gradual phasing out of the transferability of tax credits for second earners – and by conditioning work-related entitlements and tax credits on hours worked. Given the current bias towards female part-time work, the effects of such measures may only materialise over the medium-term. An important factor in this respect is that policies should be predictable for households to organise their work and family choices.

As also discussed in the 2008 *Survey*, immigration policies are essentially driven by employer demand, mainly benefiting larger internationally oriented firms. However, smaller firms without the international connections would benefit from a re-orientation of immigration policy towards expanding the available supply of high-skilled workers, by allowing them into the country via, for example, job search visas, or at least easing entrance conditions in the current system. Hence, income restrictions and time limitations on job-seeking foreign graduates from Dutch universities or recognised foreign universities should be eased or abolished. In addition, foreign representation could support this by promoting Dutch workplaces at international job fairs, special job search assistance, etc.

The labour market lacks sufficient flexibility to fully benefit from globalisation

The main impediment to greater mobility on the labour market to meet changing demands arising from globalisation is that employment protection for workers with permanent contracts is stricter than in many other countries. The cost of firing for employers is predictable but high if they bring cases to court, or lower but less predictable and more time consuming if they use the administrative route. In particular, the combination of a large seniority element in wages and the severance pay formula used in courts to establish the level of severance pay means that it increases relatively fast with age and income. The result is that the incentives for older workers to change jobs are very limited. This gives older workers few incentives for investing in life-long learning as long tenures reduce the return on (non-job specific) human capital accumulation – an unfortunate situation when globalisation has shifted labour demand towards higher skill workers. The key problem is that older workers can use a combination of severance pay and unemployment benefit as a pathway into early retirement – a move that is further facilitated by the generous tax treatment of housing and pension that facilitate the accumulation of capital.

Over the years, several attempts to reform the EPL system have been made, such as establishing an upper ceiling on severance pay of EUR 75 000, but to no avail. On the other hand, a revised formula has been adopted by the courts, leading to a somewhat lower severance pay across the board without affecting the relative generous treatment of older workers. Renewed efforts to implement an upper ceiling on severance pay should be pursued. This would also reduce early retirement incentives as highlighted in the 2010 *Survey* – a measure that could become more effective if the cap declines as workers approach retirement. As raised in previous *Surveys*, the dismissal system should be made simpler, more predictable and less time-consuming. Court appeals should be possible only *ex post* as recommended in the 2008 *Survey*.

The current wage formation system is characterised by highly co-ordinated sectoral wage negotiations, originating from the 1982 Wassenaar Agreement that laid the foundation for the consensus-based Dutch labour market model. Dialogue among social partners sets wage increases, either at the central or at the sector level, which are in line with macroeconomic conditions. Collectively agreed wage increases are often extended administratively by the labour minister. As a result, wage differentials are relatively narrow and fairly constant over time, making it difficult for workers to use this signal to leave declining sectors for (better paid) jobs in expanding sectors, particularly those that have to react rapidly to opportunities from globalisation. Indeed, for older workers such wage differences would have to be fairly large to compensate the large tenure based element in their wages and for the loss of accumulated severance pay rights.

To enhance the signal value of relative wages, the wage formation process – as recommended by the Social and Economic Council – should become more decentralised. That would also facilitate an alignment between wages and productivity developments, enabling older workers to remain employed. Such a system would also increase job turnover, which would boost on-the-job life-long learning effects. One way of reorganising the wage formation system could be along the Danish model by maintaining negotiations for framework conditions (such as work time, pensions, etc.) at the central or sector level and having locally negotiated wages.

> **Box 8. Main labour market recommendations**
>
> Implement an upper ceiling on severance pay to reduce the incentives for using it as a pathway into early retirement.
>
> Make the dismissal system simpler, more predictable and less time-consuming.
>
> Decentralise further the wage formation process to facilitate the reallocation of increasingly scarce labour resources.

Promoting competition and cost control in the health care sector

Health outcomes are relatively good, with indicators ranging from about average to good outcomes when compared with other OECD countries (Joumard et al., 2010). Life expectancy at birth is similar to most other western European countries, but life expectancy at retirement is only just above the OECD average. Moreover, accidental death is rare, implying that relatively few potential years of life are lost. Infant mortality is well below the OECD average, but still twice that of the best OECD performer. Contributing to these favourable outcomes are relatively healthy lifestyles and a high use of preventive screenings. Moreover, inequalities in health outcomes are low, reflecting good access and one of the lowest co-payments in the OECD. However, regional variation is relatively high and some hospital outcomes are quite far away from best practice, pointing to the scope for efficiency improvements.

At the same time, health spending as a share of GDP is among the highest in the OECD. This is partly explained by a high reliance on expensive institutional long-term care. Spending growth was lower than in other European countries until 2008, but has since accelerated. Over the period 2011-15, the government plans increases in health spending that are more than twice as fast as the projected GDP growth. Moreover, population ageing is estimated to boost health care spending by about one-fifth by 2060 and to more than double expenditures on long-term care. Despite the high spending on health care, supply of health care services is relatively low, both in terms of doctor consultations per capita and in terms of hospital stays (measured in terms of discharge rates). Overall, the health sector comes across as effective, but costly.

Effects of the health care reforms

In the mid-2000s, the Dutch government embarked on a series of health care reforms designed to move the sector from central control to a more market-based system. The reforms centred on the introduction of mandatory private health insurance with a risk equalisation scheme to avoid adverse selection, and giving health insurers the role of health service purchasers. The reforms successfully introduced competition on premiums among health insurers, leading to an initial fall in health premiums, as reported in earlier *Surveys*. However, subsequent cost increases have more than reversed this initial success. Increased competition also forced health insurers to consolidate, leading to a high degree of concentration, leaving the largest four insurers with a market share of more than 90%.

Reforms to strengthen competition among health providers have also been less than fully successful. Indeed, a government commission has concluded that the health care system is "stuck-in-the-middle" between a centrally planned and a market-oriented system, preventing the government from controlling costs, and health insurers from being cost-effective purchasers of care. The transition of the hospital sector to a market-based system was predicated on creating a competitive market where prices are negotiated between health insurers and providers (the so-called segment B) and a regulated market (segment A, typically for complex services).

The positive effects of this reform have been the entry of a substantial number of freestanding clinics, boosting competition among providers, and a substantial decline in segment B prices. Alongside these developments, reform of drug regulation induced a significant decrease in drug prices and boosted the use of generics. These benefits, however, have not prevented hospital spending from increasing by an annual 4% in real terms, in part as the result of supplier-induced demand (providers boosting the number of treatments) and up-coding (the provision of more expensive treatments) (Hasaart, 2011). The increased volume of health care services has not directly led to an observable improvement in health care outcomes, but may have contributed to the ongoing and gradual reductions in waiting times and higher life expectancy (which started much earlier).

The reforms also boosted the cost of doctors. Nearly half of the specialists working in hospitals are self-employed and when their remuneration was changed from lump-sum into fee-for-service, their incentives to boost output increased considerably. Likewise, the remuneration system for general practitioners was changed to have a larger fee-for-service element. Thus, one of the main effects of the reform has been a considerable increase in the (already internationally high) annual remuneration of doctors. The government imposed lower prices, but spending continued to rise as the volume of services grew even faster. The relatively low supply of specialists and General Practitioners (GPs) together with information asymmetries gives them market power, which the government should counter by increasing the number of available training places in hospitals, the capacity of medical schools, and by facilitating the recognition of foreign diplomas. However, this cannot be a standalone measure and additional steps are required to prevent supplier-induced demand. A step in this direction is the planned introduction of a new system of remuneration of self-employed specialists, which should help to rein in costs as prices for their services will be subject to negotiations between hospitals and insurers – negotiations that will take place within the framework of newly introduced macrobudgets for specialists, with the hospitals being responsible for reimbursements of budget overruns.

The increase in hospital spending reflects an information asymmetry between health insurers and providers of health care, as insurers have difficulty determining what constitutes unnecessary treatment and thus cannot counter supplier-induced demand. Moreover, the lack of cost control reflects a lack of financial risk because of *ex post* compensation of incurred costs. In addition, health insurers are lacking adequate instruments as the government regulates prices, supply and new entry. The problems are compounded by the lack of an adequate system of product classification and reliable public quality information.

The government's 2012-15 reform programme

The government is implementing an extensive set of reforms over the period 2012-15 to strengthen the role of market forces in the provision of health services and to secure cost containment. The new reform is doubling the size of the hospital market with freely negotiated prices to 70% of hospital revenues (the B segment), while the segment with regulated prices moves from a budgeting system to an output-based payment system. In addition, the *ex post* compensation for health insurers will be phased out, requiring further improvement of the risk equalisation scheme. A more transparent and manageable system of product classification will reduce the number of hospital products from around 30 000 to 4 400. Cost control will be pursued by replacing individual hospital budgets with a global budget for the sector.

The reform will contribute positively to induce more competition in the hospital sector and partly address the fundamental conflict embodied in combining a market-based approach with measures to control expenditures as well as contributing to finding the best mix between free market measures to enhance efficiency and control costs. However, the reform does not remove the fundamental asymmetry between insurers and providers, which can only be addressed by establishing adequate performance indicators to enable performance based contracting and help consumers to make choices that take into account both quality and price of provided services. Hence, the government should make its plans to establish an institute to strengthen information gathering and dissemination a priority. This is particularly important in the context of the new system of product classification.

However, additional measures are needed to secure cost control. The global budget means that the budget of individual hospitals depends on the budgetary performance of other hospitals, giving hospitals incentives for overspending as they anticipate similar strategic behaviour by other hospitals. Cost control is an important objective, but the global budgets will, at a minimum, need to be supplemented with controls on individual hospitals to deter such strategic behaviour. This, however, would mean a step back from the use of market tools and would probably inhibit efficiency improvements. Instead, therefore, policies to raise competition among hospitals should be pursued.

Better information should be supplemented with measures to reduce supplier-induced demand by replacing the current activity-based payment system with performance-based payment systems. The exact design of the systems should be left to insurers, which should be allowed to use mixed payments systems, including ones based on performance and on financial risk sharing (*e.g.* risk adjusted capitation payments). This is particularly important in the context of the recommendation to expand the number of doctors, which may increase supplier-induced demand further. Alternative payment systems can help to counter such a development by giving hospitals incentives to reduce the share of self-employed medical specialists, for example by replacing vacancies with salaried specialists. Vertical integration between insurers and providers may be another effective measure to reduce information asymmetries. On the other hand, such integration could reduce insurers' incentives for providing transparent information on the quality of care. On balance, the government is proposing a prohibition of such vertical integration to prevent insurers from foreclosing by directing their customers to their own providers with temporary exemptions for starting a new innovative provider and for securing provision of essential services. However, the proposal would reduce the room for effective competition and limited vertical integration can allow insurers to gather valuable information from suppliers. Indeed, in terms of competition the proposal is unnecessary as the Competition Authority can already prohibit vertical mergers that lead to dominant positions. Having multiple merger assessment authorities increases regulatory uncertainty, reducing new entry and hampering efficiency-enhancing mergers. Rather, the Competition Authority should remain the sole arbiter in this area, but should issue a clear methodology for assessing hospital mergers, which would improve transparency in decision making, boost agency capacity, and prevent political interference.

In addition to strengthening the role of the health insurers as health purchasers, bottlenecks on the supply side need to be addressed to allow more efficient provider models to appear. However, the hospital market is reserved for non-profit providers, which have few incentives for adjusting their supply. For-profit hospitals should be allowed to enter the hospital market to spur competition and innovation. At the same time, the orderly exit of bankrupt hospitals should be secured, for example by securing access to essential facilities. The changing market circumstances will enhance merger and acquisition incentives, leading to considerations about giving healthcare authorities merger assessment responsibilities in terms of quality and access.

An additional tool for cost control is to increase the internationally low co-payments, which would encourage consumers to make cost-effective choices and induce them to use their private information to counter supplier-induced demand and up-coding. Insofar as such a measure leads to concerns over rising socio-economic inequalities, these could be addressed via income related subsidies or by differentiating co-payment levels.

More cost-effective long-term care

On current projections, long-term care spending will more than double to more than 8% of GDP by 2060 – a level three times higher than the EU average (Figure 16). Recent policy efforts have focussed on reducing the internationally high reliance on institutional care and decentralising home help (practical matters, such as cleaning) to municipalities, taking advantage of their financial incentives for cost-efficiency. However, overall spending has tended to exceed budgets in the past few years, notably because of large new demand attracted by the cash benefits scheme, which offers patients freedom to arrange their own care for three quarters of in-kind care costs.

In the long term, decentralisation of home care to municipalities could be completed and institutional patients should be able to choose their own care providers to push institutions to compete for patients. The government plans further decentralisation by giving municipalities more responsibilities for home care (*e.g.* assistance with daily activities and administrative tasks) and care for young people with light mental handicaps to reap further cost efficiency gains. For non-decentralised services, the current system of (centralised) regional purchasers – often the largest regional insurer – of home and institutional care will be replaced with a system where all insurers must purchase care for their own clients as in the health care system, with the aim of exploiting possible synergies

Figure 16. **Health care cost now and in 2060**
As percentage points of GDP

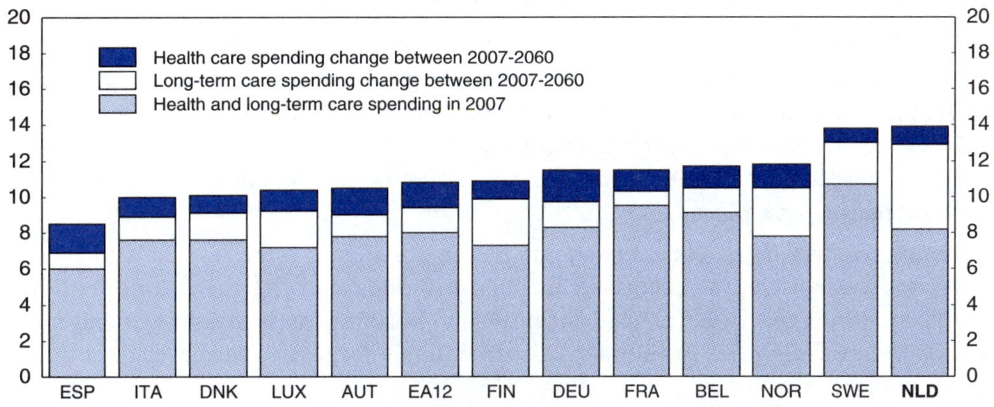

- Health care spending change between 2007-2060
- Long-term care spending change between 2007-2060
- Health and long-term care spending in 2007

ESP, ITA, DNK, LUX, AUT, EA12, FIN, DEU, FRA, BEL, NOR, SWE, **NLD**

Source: Commission Services, EPC, "2009 Ageing Report: Economic and budgetary projections for the EU-27 Members States (2008-2060)".

StatLink http://dx.doi.org/10.1787/888932614225

between health care and long-term care. The main problem with the latter measure is that the government will not let insurers bear any financial risks until a risk equalisation system is in place, thus insurers will have no incentives to pursue cost-efficient purchases.

However, designing a risk equalisation system is complicated, and may not even be feasible because of the lack of readily available data on potentially good predictors of individuals' future long-term care expenses. In the absence of a risk-equalisation system, insurers will have incentives to shift patients from insurer-paid cure to publicly-funded long-term care, resulting in higher overall spending (Besseling et al., 2011). Alternatively, the regional purchasers could be given financial incentives to become cost-efficient purchasers by financially rewarding the fulfilment of performance targets in terms of quality and efficiency of purchased care.

Home care should be encouraged further to reduce the more expensive and internationally high use of institutional care. This can be achieved by financially rewarding municipalities for lowering institutionalisation rates and by improving screening of patients entering institutional care. The latter could be combined with higher co-payments for accommodation costs. Access to cash benefits is being restricted to patients that are eligible for institutional care (about 10% of current recipients of cash benefits) to curb cost increases and address unintended use (and even fraud). As only patients with relatively modest requirements are denied access to cash benefits and some of these will claim (relatively expensive) in-kind care, the overall saving would be relatively limited. A more cost-efficient approach would be to replace the new access criteria with better screening and monitoring to avoid unintended use, e.g. by introducing vouchers directly payable to professionals. In addition, the system for assessing the individual patient's needs should be improved by further reducing regional discrepancies and allowing care purchasing agencies to make formal objections to supposedly inappropriate assessments. In this context, it is important to ensure that income related co-payments for in-kind home care are sufficiently high to encourage patients to make choices that take price and quality into consideration.

> **Box 9. Main health policy recommendations**
>
> Improve information gathering and replace the current activity-based payment system with performance-based payment systems to reduce supplier-induced demand.
>
> Limited vertical integration between insurers and providers should be allowed. Mergers assessments should solely be based on competition considerations, including consumer welfare concerns. For-profit hospitals should be allowed to enter the hospital market. This should be supplemented with measures on the demand side, such as increasing the internationally low co-payments.
>
> In long-term care, health insurers should not be transferred more responsibilities until they are given adequate incentives for cost-efficiency. In the meantime, regional purchasers could be given financial incentives to become cost-efficient purchasers by financially rewarding the fulfillment of performance targets in terms of quality and efficiency of purchased care.

Bibliography

Besseling, P., W. Elsenburg and C. van Ewijk (2011), "Risicodragende uitvoering AWBZ door zorgverzekeraars verhoogt de kosten", *Me Judice*, www.mejudice.nl/artikel/618/risicodragende-uitvoering-awbz-door-zorgverzekeraars-verhoogt-de-kosten.

CPB (2010a), "Actualisatie Economische Verkenning", *Document*, No. 213.

CPB (2010b), "Economische Verkenning 2011-2015", March.

CPB (2011a), "Houdbaarheidseffect sociaal akkoord AOW, witteveenkader envitaliteitspakket", *CPB Notitie*, December.

CPB (2011b), *Labour Market Flexibility in the Netherlands; The role of contracts and self-employment*.

CPB (2011c), *Macro Economische Verkenning 2012*.

Delta Commissie (2008), *Working together with water*.

De Vries, N., W. Liebregts and P. Vroonhof (2011), *Zelfbewurst een Zelfstandige Positie – Economische zelstandighedi van zzp'ers: resultaten zzp-panel meting I van 2011 EIM*.

DNB (2011a), "Overview of Financial Stability, Autumn 2011".

DNB (2011b), "Dutch residential mortgage risks unevenly distributed", *DNB Bulletin*.

European Commission (2009), "2009 Ageing Report: Economic and budgetary projections for the EU-27 Members States (2008-2060)", *European Economy*, No. 2, Brussels.

European Commission (2011), "Assessment of the 2011 national reform programme and stability programme of EU countries".

European Commission (2012), "Alert Mechanism Report – Report prepared in Accordance with Articles 3 and 4 of the Regulation on the Prevention and Correction of Macro-economic Imbalances", Brussels, COM(2012)68final.

Government (2010), *Budgetary framework. Annex to the Coalition agreement*.

Government (2011), *Miljoenennota 2012*.

Groot, S.P.T., H.L.F. de Groot, A.M. Lejour and J. Möhlmann (2011), "The rise of the BRIC countries and its impact on the Dutch economy", *CPB Background Document*.

Hasaart, F. (2011), *Incentives in the Diagnosis Treatment Combination payment system for specialist medical care. A study about behavioral responses of medical specialists and hospitals in the Netherlands*, PhD thesis, University of Maastricht, Maastricht.

Joumard, I., C. André and C. Nicq (2010), "Health Care Systems: Efficiency and Institutions", *OECD Economics Department Working Papers*, No. 769, OECD Publishing.

Kerdrain, C., I. Koske and I. Wanner (2010), "The Impact of Structural Policies on Saving, Investment and Current Accounts", *OECD Economics Department Working Papers*, No. 815.

KNMI (2006), "KNMI Climate Change Scenarios 2006 for the Netherlands", *KNMI Scientific Report*, No. WR 2006-01.

OECD (2010), *OECD Economic Surveys: Netherlands 2010*, OECD Publishing.

OECD (2011), *OECD Economic Surveys: Belgium 2011*, OECD Publishing.

OECD (2012), *OECD Economic Surveys: Euro Area 2012*, OECD Publishing.

Rabobank (2012), "Dutch mortgage market: a liability?", *Special Report*, No. 2012/02.

ANNEX A1

Progress in structural reform

This annex reviews actions taken to follow policy recommendations made in the 2010 OECD Economic Survey of the Netherlands. Recommendations that are new in this Survey are shown in the boxes at the end of each relevant chapter.

Recommendations in previous Survey	Actions taken and current assessment
A. Public finances	
Pursue the medium-term fiscal consolidation path.	The consolidation plan laid out in the 2010 Coalition Agreement is being implemented. An additional consolidation package is under negotiation.
Increase in the legal pension age to 67 and link it to life expectancy thereafter. Front-load the increase.	The legal pension age will increase to 66 in 2020 and is thereafter linked to life-expectancy.
Make permanent the exclusion of unemployment benefits from the expenditure rules.	Unemployment benefits have been included in the expenditure targets.
Use natural gas revenues (and other windfall gains) directly to reduce public debt.	Gas revenues (and other windfall gains) have been used to reduce the budget deficit and debt.
B. Financial markets	
Implement a credible and transparent exit strategy from the financial sector. The possibility of incurring capital losses should not prevent withdrawal of state involvement.	The 2011 exit strategy aims to reduce the government's stakes substantially over five years, conditionally to financial sector's stability and to full recovery of the government's participation costs.
Improve macro-prudential regulation and supervision of financial markets.	A macro-prudential advisory committee has been created.
Improve the awareness (among local governments) of the risks associated with deposits in banks not covered by the Dutch depositor protection scheme.	Local governments are encouraged to use the risk free treasury banking facility.
C. Labour market	
Strengthen job-search incentives of the unemployed by decreasing unemployment benefits more dynamically throughout their duration, shortening their duration and reducing their ceiling.	No action taken.
Focus on measures to increase activation and hours worked. Consider making active labour market policy (ALMP) spending more counter-cyclical. Relax employment protection legislation (EPL) and cap severance pay.	The double tax credits for people receiving social assistance will be reduced to avoid discouraging work.
Reconsider employers' obligation to pay up to two-year sick leave.	No action taken.
D. Pension system	
Use a more stable long-term interest rate as the discount rate to assess pension funds' solvency.	A three-month average of the yield curve has been used for end-2011.
Make permanent the extension of the recovery period (from three to five years) for funds to restore solvency.	The temporally extended recovery period has been brought back to three years.
Introduce longer contribution periods to structurally improve the funding ratios.	The age for future accrual of pension rights in the second pillar will be raised to 67 in 2014 and will be made dependent on the average life expectancy from thereon.
Provide greater information to support informed decisions on transfer of pension rights.	No action taken.

Recommendations in previous Survey	Actions taken and current assessment
Allow workers shifting to become self-employed to remain active members in their pension fund.	Since 2012, self-employed are allowed to remain active members in their pension funds for a maximum duration of ten years.
Allow members to leave persistently underfunded or underperforming funds.	No action taken
Strengthen the boards of the pension funds by increasing the representation of pensioners and sleepers and by making boards more professional.	No action taken.
Promote transparency of the performance of boards in terms of investment strategies and operating costs.	The Federation of Dutch pension funds has developed recommendations regarding operating costs, which are implemented in the regulatory reporting framework.

E. Transport system

Recommendations in previous Survey	Actions taken and current assessment
Streamline land release procedures and reconsider land use. Develop the secondary road system by giving local authorities part of the revenue coming from traffic and reducing the number of motorway entries and exits.	Spatial powers were further transferred to provinces in 2011.
Introduce systematic *ex post* evaluations for infrastructure projects and improve the cost-benefit analysis methodology. Require explicit justification in cases where CBA results are overruled.	Systematic *ex post* evaluations have been introduced.
Increase the amount of infrastructure projects available for private financing.	New private-public infrastructure projects are allowed to use road pricing as a financial instrument.
Implement the road pricing scheme.	No action taken.
The relative road prices should take into account existing charges through fuel taxation.	The tax exemption on the least polluting vehicles has been extended.
Focus the tax-free commuting allowance on low-wage workers.	No action taken.
If the road pricing scheme is not pursued, consider higher fuel taxes and congestion charges.	No action taken.
Taxation of diesel should be raised to better reflect the relative environmental costs of fuels.	No action taken.
Increase the flexibility of regional train contracts to better adjust to demand over time and space. Increase the scope of public tendering.	Regional governments will get more control over regional rail services, forcing the national railway operator to focus more on regional network effects.
Facilitate new entry in public transport.	No action taken.
Proceed with the tendering of public transport franchises in the main cities.	The main cities (Amsterdam, Rotterdam and The Hague) are now required to put their municipal/regional public transit systems up for public tendering.
The regulated ticket prices for public transport should better incorporate the marginal social and operational costs and benefits. The subsidies issued to public transport should be made transparent and should be clearly targeted at well-identified government objectives (*e.g.* universal services, equity, and mobility of specific groups).	Local public transit fares have become a regional government responsibility. The subsidies they receive for public transport will become part of their generic funding stream. The new concession of Dutch Railways (NS) provide for further differentiation of tariffs based on time of travel. User fees for the railway infrastructure have increased.

F. Housing market

Recommendations in previous Survey	Actions taken and current assessment
Adjust land use policies to facilitate a more responsive supply side, particularly in the Green Heart.	Development policies have been deregulated in 2012, including for the Green Heart.
Supplement planning needs by creating fiscal incentives for local municipalities to develop housing.	No action taken.
Replace the tax deductibility of mortgage interest payments with the principle of taxing net housing value.	No action taken.
Abolish (or lower) the property transfer tax.	The transfer tax has been temporarily lowered from 6% to 2% for a period of one year ending in the summer 2012.
Reduce income tax subsidies by increasing the taxation of imputed rent (and its scope).	The tax on imputed rent for houses with a value above EUR 1 million is increased to 2.35% in 2015.
Focus social housing associations on providing affordable housing for low-income households. Give incentives to housing associations to sell off dwellings. Transfer associated excessive capital gains to the government. Reduce the maximum rent of social dwellings.	Social rental housing has been restricted (for new tenants) to households with an income up to EUR 33.000. The sale of social housing stock to private investors and to tenants will be facilitated.
Liberalise rents in new constructions and deregulate rents for new contracts in existing dwellings. Index market based to reflect the cost of housing.	Higher regulated rents have been allowed in certain areas with strong scarcity. Furthermore, rents may now be increased by an additional 5% per year for households with an income above EUR 43 000.
Extend means testing to sitting tenants,	No action taken.
Give priority in social housing to households with employment related reasons.	No action taken.
Provide social housing through housing allowances.	No action taken.

Chapter 1

Reforming policies for the business sector to harvest the benefits of globalisation

The Netherlands has strongly benefited from globalisation, which boosted international trade, cross-border investment and economic growth over the latest decades. Looking ahead, the Netherlands needs to shift the trade and investment orientation from traditional slow-growing markets to faster growing emerging economies, in order to keep reaping the benefits from globalisation. In addition, the ongoing globalisation will push companies to become more innovative and search for new activities. Against this backdrop, the government is reforming its policies for the business sector. This includes a targeted approach, where the government is attempting to strengthen key sectors to become even stronger players on the international scene. This approach, however, carries some of the risks of more traditional industrial policy, making careful policy design and evaluation important elements for successful implementation. The other building block of the new policies is a strengthening of framework conditions, which promises a more market-based development of comparative advantages, and which could be further strengthened by broadening the approach to include other policies, such as competition policies.

The economy has been benefiting from accelerating globalisation and technology change. The increase in world trade has allowed the Netherlands to capitalise on Rotterdam's position as the main trade gateway to Europe. Both inward and outward foreign investment has increased, fostering the transfer of new technologies and efficiency-enhancing separation of production – ultimately supporting productivity growth. Moreover, consumers have benefited from downward pressure on prices via cheaper imports from emerging economies and greater choice. However, looking ahead, there is a need to strengthen export and investment linkages with emerging markets, while ongoing globalisation forces companies to innovate and search for new activities in which they can excel – partly as emerging markets quickly move up the value added chain. To capitalise on the opportunities and challenges from globalisation the Dutch government is reforming its policies for the business sector. The main thrust of the new policy approach is: to focus on areas of excellence, particularly in the form of a "top sector approach"; and to improve framework conditions for the entire private sector, referred to as the "economic agenda". The chapter first analyses how globalisation has shaped the Dutch economy and identifies major challenges. Then, the chapter assesses policies to strengthen the business sector in the context of globalisation and its interplay with other policies. The chapter concludes with a set of policy recommendations.

The benefits and challenges of globalisation

The Dutch position as a trading nation and gateway to Europe has allowed the economy to profit from globalisation for centuries. The golden age in the 17th century benefitted from skilled immigrants, innovations (*e.g.* the sawmill and freely transferable shares) and access to distant markets (*e.g.* Japan) allowing the economy to become a world leader (Barbour, 1950; Van Nieuwkerk, 2006). More recently, the latest decades of intensified globalisation has seen lower tariff barriers, technological progress, and a fall in transport and communication costs, which have fragmented production processes and strengthened the economic links to the rest of the world (Figure 1.1).[1]

Globalisation benefited Dutch trade

Exports have grown rapidly over the past decades on the back of faster world trade growth and the expansion and deepening of the European internal market. Since the early 1990s, the share of goods exports to GDP has increased from about 40% to 60%. Trade is highly concentrated with 1% of firms accounting for more than 70% of all exports (in value), while only around 11% of all firms are engaged in export activities (Statistics Netherlands, 2011). The exporting firms have in common that they tend to be larger, more productive and more skill and capital-intensive than non-exporting firms (Bernard et al., 2007; Van Bergeijk et al., 2011). The export market performance for goods has been stronger than in many other OECD countries (Figure 1.2). This reflects to a large degree a surge in re-exports of goods that often enter through the port of Rotterdam and which receive minor treatment (with value-added that is on average one eight of domestically produced goods) in the Netherlands before being re-exported (Box 1.1 and Figure 1.3) (Mellens et al., 2007; Kuypers et al., 2012). Particularly, the transport and logistics sectors are benefiting from this surge in the trade of

Figure 1.1. **Openness has increased**

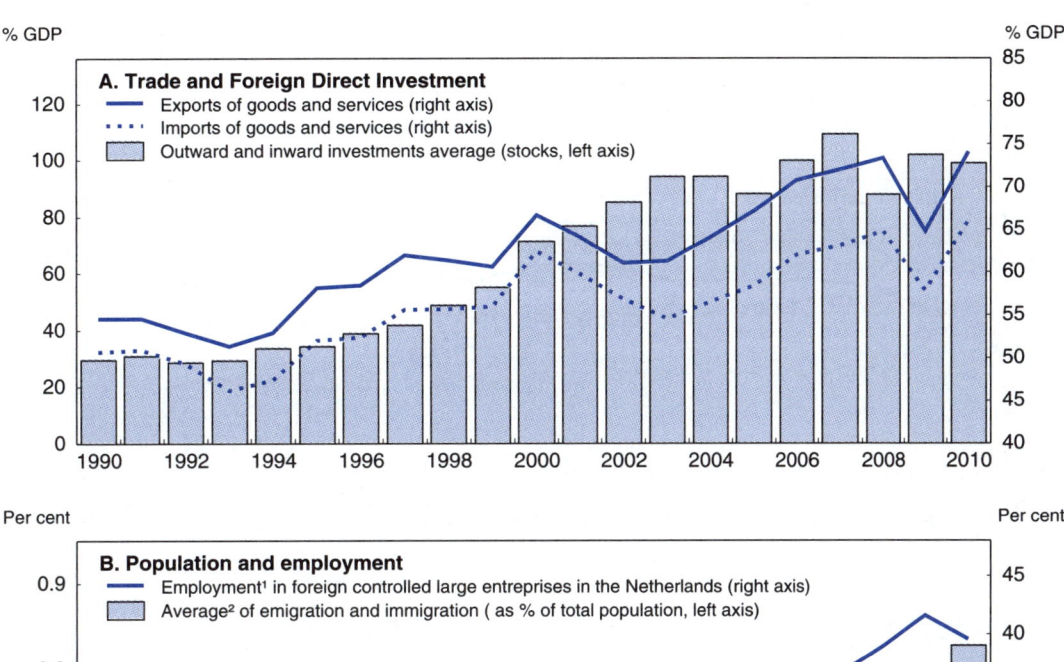

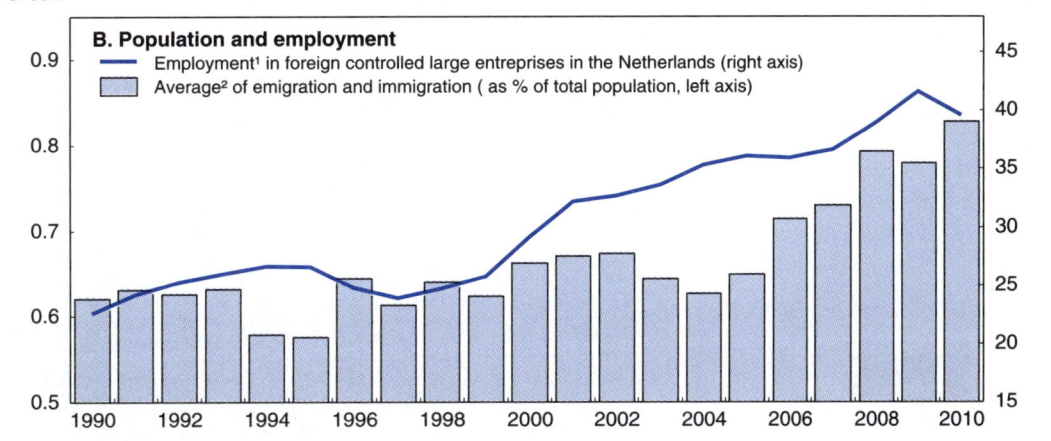

1. 2010 is preliminary data. Full-time equivalents employment as a percentage of total employment in large enterprises in the Netherlands. Based on survey among enterprises with a balance sheet over EUR 23 million, excluding financial sector.
2. Emigration and immigration are measured as flows, population as stocks, all on 31st December. Emigration includes net administrative corrections.

Source: OECD (2012), *OECD Economic Outlook* and *Foreign Direct Investment Statistics Databases*, CBS – Statline Database, March 2012.

StatLink http://dx.doi.org/10.1787/888932614244

goods. In this connection, a policy challenge is to ensure that infrastructure capacities keep up with private activity, where a road-pricing scheme would secure an efficient use of existing infrastructure as emphasised in the previous *OECD Economic Survey*.

Service trade has increased in line with goods exports, concerning activities like computer and information, financial and transport services. This reflects the increased services content in the economy, ongoing liberalisation of trade and investment, technological developments, as well as a related fragmentation of the international value added chain (OECD, 2005; OECD, 2007a; DNB, 2007). In total, service exports have remained stable at around 20% of total Dutch exports (Statistics Netherlands, 2011). However, this hides the fact that service trade is often in relatively high value added activities. Nowadays, about 40% of Dutch value added stemming from exports can be attributed to the exports of services, against 25% in 1990 (Kranendonk and Verbruggen, 2011).

1. REFORMING POLICIES FOR THE BUSINESS SECTOR TO HARVEST THE BENEFITS OF GLOBALISATION

Figure 1.2. **Competitiveness indicators**

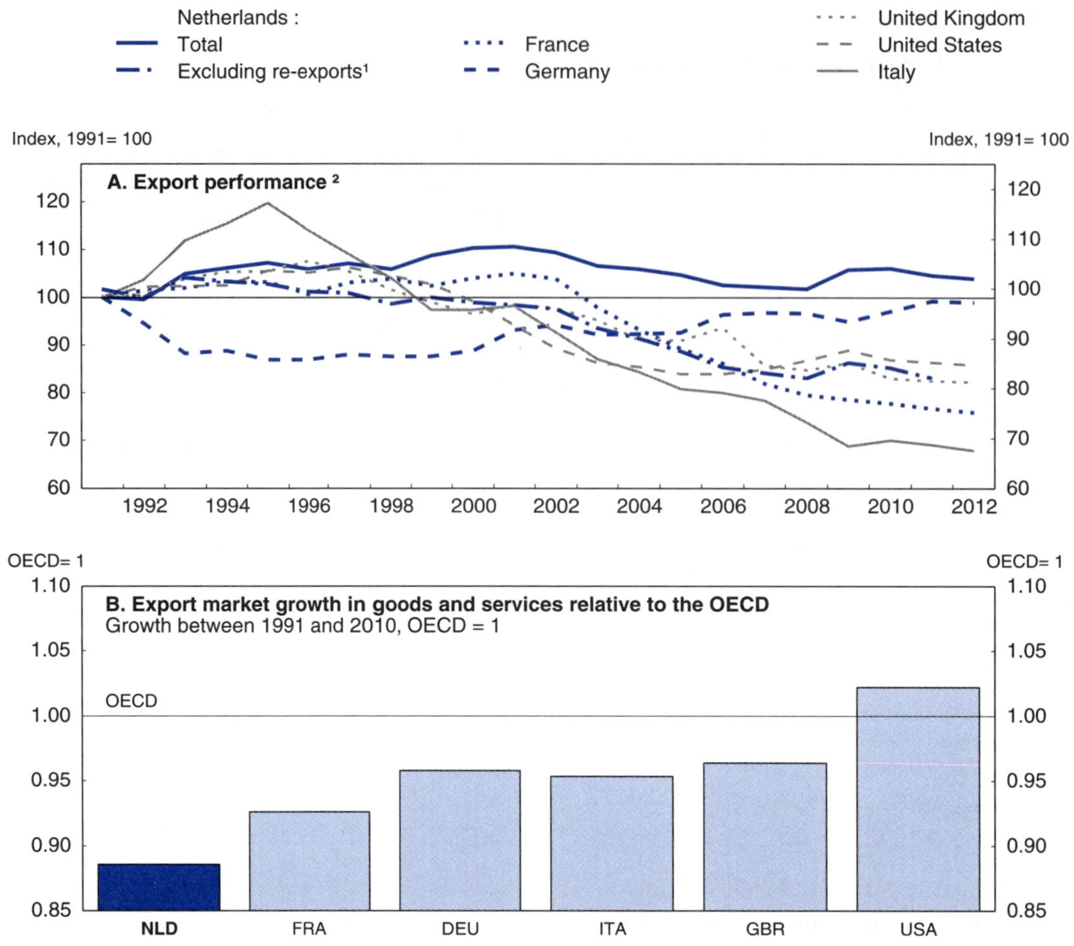

Netherlands:
— Total
—·— Excluding re-exports[1]
······ France
— — Germany
···· United Kingdom
– – United States
——— Italy

A. Export performance [2]

B. Export market growth in goods and services relative to the OECD
Growth between 1991 and 2010, OECD = 1

1. Re-exports according to Dutch classification.
2. Export performance is measured as actual growth in exports relative to the growth of the country's export market.

Source: OECD (2012), OECD Economic Outlook Database.

StatLink ⟶ http://dx.doi.org/10.1787/888932614263

Box 1.1. **The port of Rotterdam and the surge in re-exports**

The port of Rotterdam is, by far, the largest seaport of Europe, benefiting from easy access to ships with the deepest draughts. As gateway to the continent, the port and industrial complex stretches over 40 kilometres and covers some 10 thousand hectares. This excludes Maasvlakte 2, which is currently under construction and covers an additional 2 thousand hectares. The port handles about 430 million tons of cargo a year – corresponding to a 40% market share of North Sea port traffic (ports from Hamburg to Le Havre). Out of more than 18 thousand containers a day, Rotterdam ships on average over 4 thousand containers with China as the country of destination or origin. Reflecting bilateral trade volumes, about 40% of the containers from Rotterdam to China are empty, against 1% of the incoming ones.

> **Box 1.1. The port of Rotterdam and the surge in re-exports** (cont.)
>
> With an extensive network of hinterland connections – inland shipping, coastal shipping, rail, road and pipelines – Rotterdam facilitates the import and export of goods from and to the European market. Containers mainly go by road transport (57%), followed by inland shipping (33%) and rail transport (10%). Besides its role as distribution hub, the port offers facilities for the storage and handling of all kinds of commodities and products, while processing and chemical industries have a strong presence.
>
> For 2008, direct employment within the port and industrial cluster is estimated at about 90 thousand people, and indirect employment (*e.g.* suppliers, service providers) at 55 thousand. Activities related to the port of Rotterdam correspond to about 4% of GDP (Van den Bosch *et al.*, 2011). The Port Authority expects economic activity to increase rapidly, reflected by a projected increase of total throughput by up to 74%, to 750 million tons in 2030. Growth projections are especially strong for container shipment, while dry and liquid bulk handling is expected to grow more moderately. The expected expansion of activities poses considerable challenges related to *e.g.* spatial planning, the environment and hinterland connection.
>
> The port of Rotterdam plays an important role in the surge in re-exports. In the Netherlands, these exports are defined as goods that are imported and then leave the country without undergoing much processing. Re-exports represent about half of total exports of goods, and are (contrary to transit trade) included in the trade statistics as soon as a Dutch company temporarily becomes the owner of the goods. Europe is the most important destination with 85% of all re-exports, which concerns mainly items like machinery, computers, electronic devices and chemical products. The average value added content in re-exports (about EUR 7.5 cents per exported euro) is much lower than domestically produced goods (EUR 58.5 cents). Nonetheless, the surge in re-exports has been an important driver of growth in the Netherlands, accounting in net terms to an annual 0.2 percentage point to GDP growth over the last two decades (Kranendonk and Verbruggen, 2011).
>
> *Source:* Port of Rotterdam Authority (2011a, b, c); Mellens *et al.* (2007); Van den Bosch *et al.* (2011); Kranendonk and Verbruggen (2011); Kuypers *et al.* (2012).

Figure 1.3. **Re-exports have surged**[1]

Current prices

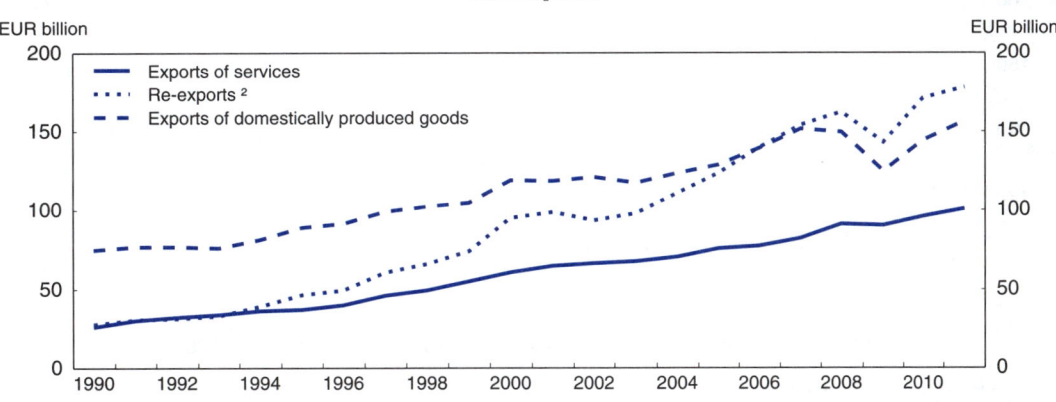

1. Data excludes energy.
2. Re-exports according to Dutch classification.

Source: CPB (2012), CPB Netherlands Bureau for Economic Policy Analysis.

StatLink ⬛⬛ http://dx.doi.org/10.1787/888932614282

Dutch exports have benefited from strong import growth in rapidly growing emerging market economies. Even though the Netherlands' market shares in these markets have not increased since the mid 2000's, they account for an increasing share of total exports (Figure 1.4). Exports, nevertheless, remain mainly concentrated in traditional and relatively slow growing markets in Europe and North America. Indeed, compared to other OECD countries, the Netherlands exports relatively little to the emerging economies (Figure 1.5), although distance, the composition of the export structure and the high share of re-exports can partly explain the difference.[2] The picture is unchanged when taking into account indirect exports to emerging economies (via Dutch goods used as inputs in other countries' exports to the emerging economies) (Groot et al., 2011a).[3] Given the more dynamic long-term economic outlook of emerging economies, it is important to secure better export penetration in these countries. However, doing business in emerging markets is relatively complicated, *e.g.* due to cultural differences, regulatory barriers (to trade and FDI), discriminatory procedures and government involvement in economic activity, which could justify public intervention.

Figure 1.4. **Export performance to the emerging economies**

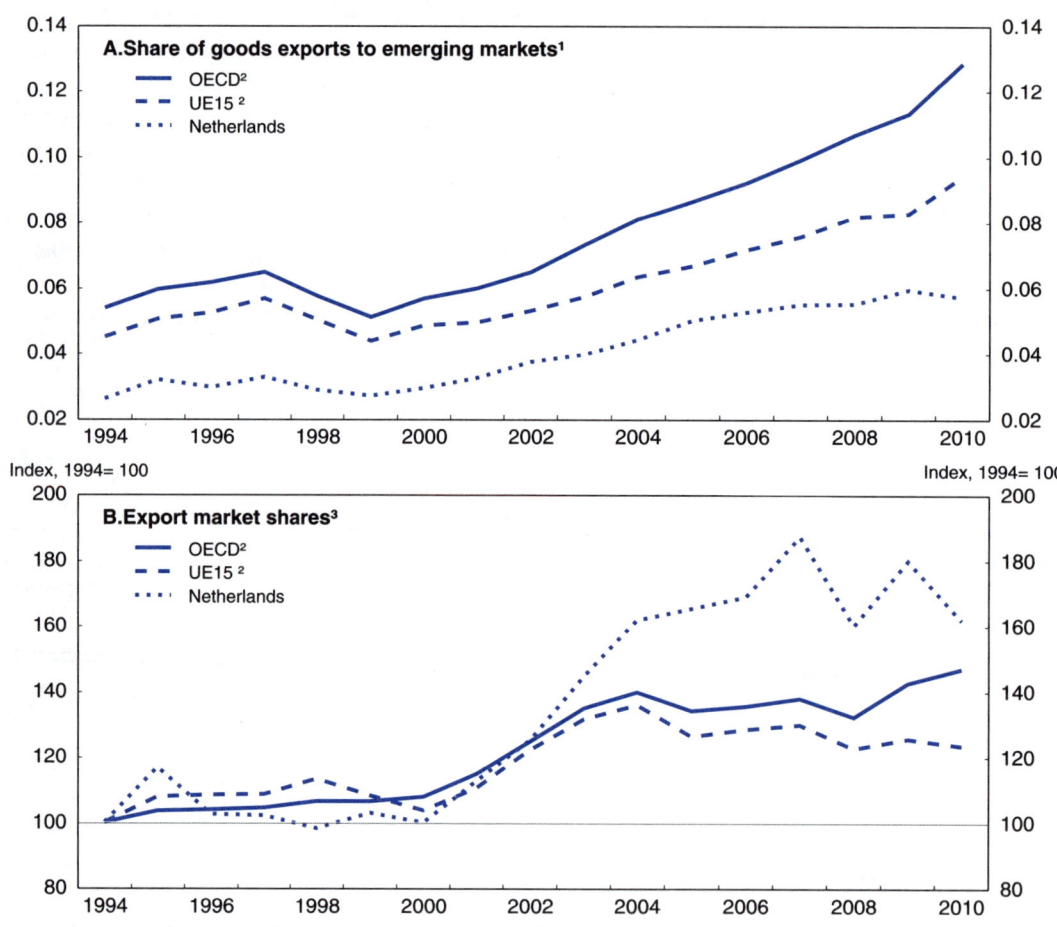

1. Exports to Brazil, Russian Federation, India, Indonesia, China, South Africa and Turkey over total exports.
2. OECD excludes Turkey. Estimated data for the Slovak Republic between 1994 and 1997, and for Luxembourg between 1993 and 1999.
3. Exports over emerging markets total imports.

Source: OECD, ITCS Database and IFS.

StatLink ⟶ http://dx.doi.org/10.1787/888932614301

Figure 1.5. **Modest exports to emerging markets**
Exports of goods to BRIC countries,¹ as percentage of total, 2010 or latest year available

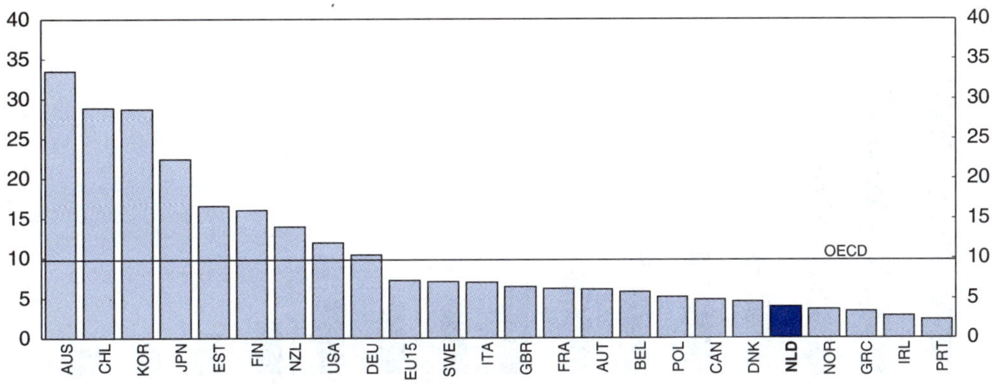

1. Total goods exports to BRIC countries as a percentage of total goods exports of presented countries.
Source: OECD (2012), International Trade and Commodities Statistics database.

StatLink ⟶ http://dx.doi.org/10.1787/888932614320

An important positive effect of globalisation is the increase in consumer welfare through greater choice of goods and lower prices (Groot et al., 2011b; Pain et al., 2008; Suyker et al., 2007). In addition, companies benefit from lower prices of intermediate goods. The share of goods imports from emerging economies has increased rapidly since 1990, particularly from China, and competition from low-cost foreign suppliers has dampened domestic inflation pressures. Conservative estimates suggest that globalisation has reduced Dutch inflation up to 0.3 percentage points per annum in the period 2000-05 (Pain et al., 2008). This calculation includes the emerging economies' role in the surge of energy and commodity prices. Looking ahead, the effect of globalisation on inflation is likely to weaken as the emerging markets converge towards more advanced economies, although the effect on choice should persist.

Globalisation spurred investment

Foreign direct investment (FDI) in the form of acquisitions and greenfield investment (i.e. opening a new subsidiary) have increased rapidly over the last few decades to the highest level in the OECD when measured by the value of inward and outward FDI positions. However, for the Netherlands, about three-quarters is accounted for by Special Purpose Entities, i.e. subsidiaries of foreign parent companies that function as financial turntables, benefit from the favourable Dutch tax regime and hardly affect the real economy (DNB, 2008; DNB, 2011; Statistics Netherlands, 2011).[4] Subtracting these, the share of in- and outward FDI remains relatively high (Figure 1.6). The inward FDI fosters technology spill-over, innovative activities as well as capital deepening and enhance competitive pressures on domestic firms (Nicoletti et al., 2003; Gelauff et al., 2010). Foreign affiliates account for a relatively large share of value-added, investment and turnover and, to a lesser extent, employment (Table 1.1). In addition, these enterprises are more innovative and productive and pay higher wages than domestically controlled counterparts (Statistics Netherlands, 2008; 2009; 2010a). Indeed, foreign controlled enterprises account for about a third of R&D investments and half of total trade (Statistics Netherlands, 2010a; 2010b). However, a small part of the inward FDI comes from emerging markets.[5] This might be influenced by the often very vocal public debate erupting in case

1. REFORMING POLICIES FOR THE BUSINESS SECTOR TO HARVEST THE BENEFITS OF GLOBALISATION

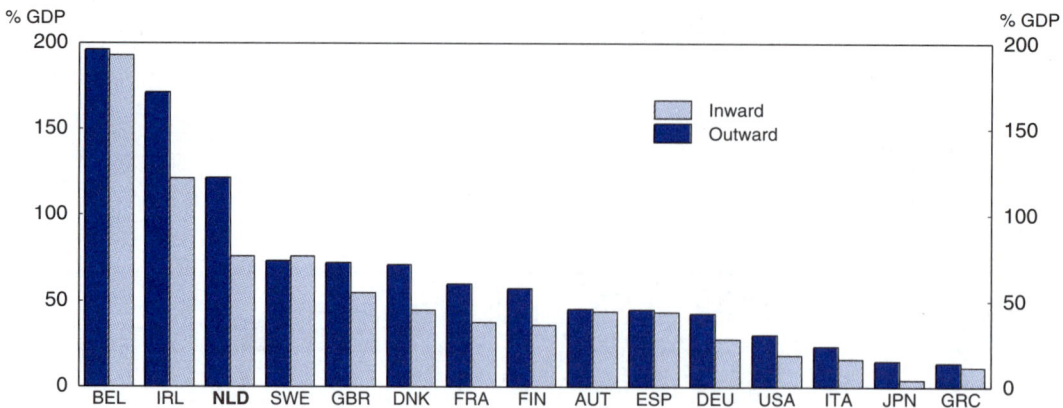

Figure 1.6. **Relatively high in- and outward FDI**
Stocks,[1] as a percentage of GDP, 2010

1. Excluding Special Purpose Entities (SPEs) for Austria and the Netherlands.
Source: OECD (2012), *International Direct Investment Statistics* and *National Accounts of OECD Countries* – online Databases, February.

StatLink ⟶ http://dx.doi.org/10.1787/888932614339

Table 1.1. **Foreign controlled enterprise activity**
% total private sector activity (except financial and insurance activities) of country, 2008

	Netherlands	France	Germany	Finland	Denmark	Sweden	EU15 average[1]
Number of enterprises	1.0	0.7	1.1	1.0	1.6	1.9	1.1
Number of persons employed	14.0	12.6	12.0	15.7	15.3	22.5	14.2
Value added at factor cost	24.4	19.5	20.2	19.4	24.2	26.9	20.7
Gross investment (tangible goods)	21.8	7.5	19.1	12.6	16.2	22.7	17.2
Turnover	31.4	21.8	26.7	20.9	23.9	32.5	24.9

1. Unweighted, excluding the Netherlands, available countries.
Source: Eurostat, Inward FATS.

of foreign takeovers – often centred on risks of job losses – despite that empirically such takeovers have little or no impact on employment growth in subsequent years (Urlings et al., 2011).[6]

The outward FDI position is even larger – mirroring the country's sustained current account surplus. Investment takes mainly place in other advanced economies, whereas the share in emerging markets is limited. Outward FDI allows firms to serve foreign markets and enhance the efficiency of production as well as helping multinationals to build global R&D networks to tap into local knowledge and develop new technologies (OECD, 2007a). Outward FDI also reflects the outsourcing of production, mostly to European countries although Asia is also a popular destination with about 30% of outsourcing activities (Statistics Netherlands, 2011). The labour market effect of outsourcing is modest; most studies find that relatively few jobs are involved in international outsourcing, especially compared to regular job turnover (*e.g.* Gorter et al., 2005; Heyma and Theeuwes, 2008). In particular, there appears to be no substantial difference between unemployed workers from off-shoring and non-off-shoring industries in terms of unemployment duration, reemployment probability and subsequent wages (Heyma and Theeuwes, 2008). A relatively new development is that outsourcing is increasingly affecting highly-skilled employees and services (OECD, 2005; Van Gorp, 2008 and 2010). Thus, looking ahead, outsourcing may expose a greater share of the workforce to international competition, increasing the need for reallocation of workers across and within sectors (see Chapter 2).

Globalisation, including stronger international competition, forces companies to innovate. In addition, as the population ages (see Chapter 3) economic growth must increasingly come from innovation-induced productivity growth. However, private R&D spending is well below the OECD and EU 15 averages and has been declining over the past decade (Figure 1.7) (Court of Audit, 2011).[7] The persistently low R&D ratio mirrors the difficulties various policies have had in boosting private R&D activities, though it can partly be linked to the specialisation of the Dutch economy in relatively less R&D intensive industries, particularly in services (Erken and Ruiter, 2005; EIM, 2011; Schmidt-Ehmcke and Zloczysti, 2011). Moreover, little is known about the relative effectiveness and efficiency of various public innovation schemes (Government, 2010; CPB, 2010; Lanser and Van der Wiel, 2011), calling for greater reliance on "evidence-based policy making", i.e. putting more emphasis on monitoring and evaluations to guide policies.

Figure 1.7. **Private R&D spending is low**
Business enterprise expenditure on research and development, as a percentage of GDP

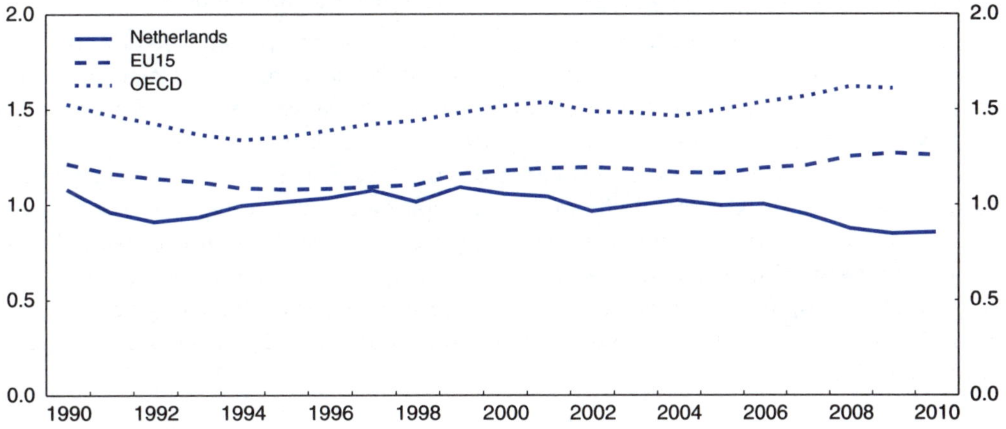

Source: OECD (2012), Main Science and Technology Indicators Database.
StatLink http://dx.doi.org/10.1787/888932614358

Globalisation is set to continue and the Netherlands has, as discussed above, profited considerably from the associated opportunities. This has been supported by factors such as a well-educated labour force, a strong business environment, sound access to other markets, and existing agglomeration and location advantages. In addition, there has – so far – been limited overlap between the revealed comparative advantages of the Netherlands and emerging countries (Groot et al., 2011b; Rae and Sollie, 2008; SER, 2008). However, companies may face tougher competition in the future from emerging economies, as these are quickly moving up the value-added chain. Indeed, the integration of these new players is challenging existing comparative advantages of countries, forcing companies to search for new activities in which they can excel and to enhance their productivity by being more innovative (OECD, 2007a). At the same time, the likely shift in global economic activity, notably towards Asia and Latin America, makes it important to establish strong export and investment positions in these new zones of economic activity. In all, it is important that policies for the business sector are continuously evaluated and updated to address these challenges.

Benefiting from globalisation by strengthening the business environment

The government seeks to improve the competitiveness of the business sector, meet the challenges from globalisation, and boost innovative activities by implementing a new policy for the business sector (Box 1.2) (Ministry of EL&I, 2011a, 2011b, 2012). The policy combines targeted support with an improvement in general framework conditions, and consists of two main planks. One plank is a broad "economic agenda" with a focus on framework conditions to reduce the regulatory burden, strengthen the innovation framework, and improve access to risk capital.[8] The other plank is a targeted "top sector approach" focussing on nine key sectors in the economy. The rationale for the new policy

---

Box 1.2. New policies for the business sector

In February 2011, the government presented a new policy to foster business sector competitiveness' and prepare the economy to face challenges and opportunities from globalisation. In addition, the new policy intends to help to address economic and social goals related to population ageing, climate change and pressure on global resources. Specifically, the government has set three targets: to be one of the top five knowledge economies in the world by 2020 (using the World Economic Forum as a yardstick); increase R&D spending to 2.5% of GDP (currently 1.8% of GDP); boost public-private co-operation in knowledge and innovation activities to more than EUR ½ billion by 2015 (Ministry of Economic Affairs, Agriculture and Innovation, 2011b).

The new policy has two planks: an "economic agenda" for the entire private sector and a "top sector approach" with specific attention to nine economic sectors of the economy. In February 2011, the general framework and ideas were outlined, after which an interactive process between public and private stakeholders progressively specified the new policies (Table 1.2). Important building blocks are the demand driven approach – policies are mainly based on input from the private sector – the reduction in innovation subsidies in exchange for tax credits, broader access to corporate finance, and fostering the clustering of economic and research activities. Moreover, an important element is the stronger reliance on "evidence-based policy making", i.e. putting more emphasis on monitoring and evaluation to guide policies. Against the backdrop of the need to consolidate public finances, the fiscal scope of the new enterprise policies is limited (gradually increasing to about 0.3% of GDP by 2015), and mainly involves a reallocation of different existing outlays to support business and innovative activities.

Table 1.2. **The main dates in the formulation of the new policies of the business sector**

September 2010
Coalition agreement stipulates an improvement of the business climate and selects nine economic "top sectors".

February 2011
Presentation of general framework by government and announcement of first policies.

June 2011
"Top teams" present first proposals and objectives as requested by government.

September 2011
Response by government to first proposals and further specification of generic policies.

January/April 2012
"Top teams 2.0" present "innovation contracts", "human capital" and "internationalisation agenda's".

2012 – beyond
Further development and implementation of policies.

Source: Ministry of Economic Affairs, Agriculture and Innovation, 2011a, 2011b, 2012.

> **Box 1.2. New policies for the business sector** *(cont.)*
>
> The *economic agenda* involves a range of policies to improve the business environment for the entire private sector. It aims to cut substantially the administrative and regulatory burden. In addition, subsidies for innovative activities are largely being replaced by tax credits and an investment fund has been created to provide innovation credits and seed capital, mainly for starting, innovative and/or rapidly growing SMEs. Moreover, the agenda intends to foster the application of new knowledge in products or processes, increase the use of ICT and improve spatial economic conditions for economic clusters (*e.g.* related to the port of Rotterdam and Schiphol airport), among others.
>
> For the *top sector approach* the government has identified nine economic sectors (agro-food, crops, water, high-tech, life sciences, chemicals, energy, logistics and the creative industry) plus "headquarters" (for internationally operating firms) as key areas of competence, where investments should be prioritised and bottlenecks identified. According to the government, these sectors are knowledge intensive, export-oriented, usually with specific legislation and regulation, and could make an important contribution to solving societal issues. In total, an annual EUR 1.5 billion (0.2% of GDP) is to be (re-) allocated to the top sectors by 2015.
>
> To facilitate a demand driven "bottom-up" process, multidisciplinary teams (the so-called "top teams") were formed for each top sector. The teams include sector experts (typically well-known business figures), a high-ranking civil servant, an SME entrepreneur and a representative from a research institution. The tasks of the teams were to identify opportunities and challenges for the respective sector and formulate proposals to address sector-specific problems, mainly related to research and innovation, foreign policy, sector specific regulation, and education/human capital. Besides having identified sector specific bottlenecks, the teams stressed that some of the challenges ask for (a top sector) overarching policies (*e.g.* related to elements of education, innovation, and availability of risk capital), thereby further shaping the economic agenda relevant to the entire private sector. The first interactive phase of establishing objectives and policies has mostly been finalised, while implementation is gradually taking place.

is to address information asymmetries and co-ordination failures by linking the business sector, knowledge institutions and the government. Indeed, a key feature is strong private sector involvement to facilitate demand driven policies. The policy is still being developed.

An important issue in the literature is to what extent such policies can strengthen the economy. An improvement of general framework conditions can foster innovation and productivity performance, allowing market forces to shape comparative advantages over time. More controversial is the role for targeted intervention supporting specific sectors or activities (Naudé, 2010a). Targeted support could be justified by positive externalities (*e.g.* knowledge spillovers via economic clustering or innovation in clean technology), information asymmetries (*e.g.* leading to capital market imperfections) and co-ordination failures (*e.g.* lack of co-ordination between different actors that leads to underinvestment in projects with high initial costs) (Rodrik, 2008; Lin and Chang, 2009; Aghion *et al.*, 2011; OECD, 2011a). However, targeted support also has potential drawbacks, such as wrong sector selection and rent-seeking behaviour from economic agents (Rodrik, 2008; Lin and Chang, 2009; Naudé, 2010a and 2010b). Hence, insofar as more targeted interventions are successful in correcting market failures they should benefit the economy, though it is a policy challenge to design governance procedures to detect and correct market failures and manage vested interests. Moreover, it is important to recall that national economies do not "compete" like corporations (Krugman, 1994). If industrial policy succeeds in altering comparative advantages by increasing activity in promoted sectors, it will also draw economic resources away from other sectors without necessarily boosting overall economic performance. In this respect, a possible pitfall is that governments often lack the information and capability to select and promote the sectors that may have a latent comparative advantage.

Targeted policies pose challenges

While having abandoned old-style industrial policies in the 1980s, the Netherlands is moving to an alternative form of targeted support. The rationale is to address market and government failures at the sector level for nine areas of expertise as well as to prioritise research and development activities in these "top sectors" – i.e. agro-food, crops, water, high-tech, life sciences, chemicals, energy, logistics and the creative industry, plus "headquarters" (for internationally operating firms). These failures are particularly a limited knowledge transfer from universities, a co-ordination failure among different branches of the government, overly detailed sector regulation, and an insufficiently supply of skilled workers. The selection criteria included the sectors that are knowledge-intensive and export-oriented, usually with sector-specific regulation, and that can potentially make an important contribution to solving societal issues (Ministry of Economic Affairs, Agriculture and Innovation, 2011b).

The top sector approach follows up on earlier initiatives – mostly in the area of innovation – that aimed to strengthen the competitiveness of roughly the same sectors of the economy (Court of Audit, 2011). However, the new approach is to be broader and more integrated, covering different aspects of the business environment related to sector specific regulation, innovation, human capital and internationalisation. Another important new element is that the private sector has been leading and shaping the new policies. This demand driven approach was facilitated by the creation of "top teams" for each sector, which typically included a well-known business figure, a high-ranking civil servant, an SME entrepreneur and a representative from a research institution. The government asked the teams to identify opportunities and challenges for the respective sector and subsequently formulate agendas to address sector-specific bottlenecks, notably related to research and innovation, human capital, regulation and internationalisation, both at the government level and by the sectors themselves. Moreover, the new approach stipulates a move towards more "evidence-based policy making", by using targets, monitoring and evaluations to guide policies in the different top sectors.

The demand driven process is commendable as it could help address policy makers' information constraints. Indeed, to design effective policies governments need to elicit information from the market, which often requires close co-operation between different private and (semi) public stakeholders – tough in the discussion with the private sector it is a challenge to sufficiently involve SMEs and notably innovative start-up firms that may face very different bottlenecks than incumbents (Rodrik, 2008). In addition, the focus on evidence-based policy making is a welcome move as it is key in the design of sound industrial policy and likely to support accountability for the successes and failures of it. In this respect, very clear criteria for success and features such as conditionality, sunset clauses, programme reviewing, and benchmarking should be developed (OECD, 2011a; Rodrik, 2008).

Gauging the overall size and scope of the selected sectors is difficult as the sectors are not strictly defined and sometimes overlap (Koster and Edzes, 2011). In addition, as the individual top sectors are relatively broad and often encompass completely different industries (e.g. logistics could include services as diverge as road haulage, air transport and taxis to warehousing and packaging), it is unclear to what extent all relevant industries are indeed covered and represented by the top sector approach. This complicates the linking of instruments and objectives as well as the general move to "evidence-based policy making". Hence, to ensure an efficient use of public funds and enable evidence-based policy making by linking instruments and objectives, the scope of the top sectors should become more clearly defined.

The selected top sectors are to a large extent representing the traditional manufacturing sectors, while the presence of services is relatively limited. This seems somewhat counterintuitive given the large services content in the economy, their role as an important input for the manufacturing sector and the importance of services exports, which make the services sector key to fully reap the benefits from globalisation (Figure 1.8). Hence, as a mean to identify sector bottlenecks and further improve sector regulation, the government should consider establishing similar teams (or alike initiatives) for other sectors, notably in the service sectors, without necessarily making them top sectors.

Figure 1.8. **Services exports specialised in professional business, communication as well as royalties**[1]

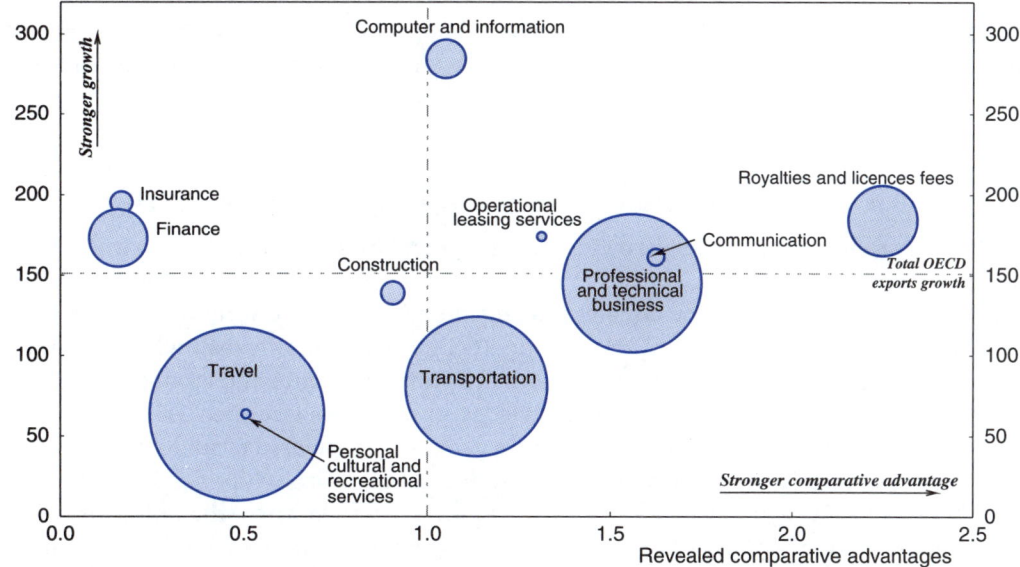

1. The graph shows the relative export specialisation of the Netherlands compared to other OECD countries (for which data are available). The RCA (or Balassa) index of revealed comparative advantage is a measure of a country's export market share of a services category compared to the world's (here OECD) export share of that category. A value above 1 suggests that a country is relatively specialised in the category. The bubbles give an indication of the size of the total (OECD) export market: the bigger the bubble the bigger the size of the export market. The high value of royalties and license fees is likely to reflect the position of the Netherlands as a financial turntable (e.g. the Netherlands has also a high import share in this category).
2. Growth of export market calculated in nominal USD.

Source: OECD, Trade in Services Database.

StatLink ⟶ http://dx.doi.org/10.1787/888932614377

In addition, to capitalise on new opportunities from globalisation, the top sector approach should remain open to accommodate rising sectors or industries in the future, reflecting changes in comparative advantage over time. Similarly, the approach should be able to let structurally declining sector go, which may be politically more difficult. To this respect, a swift and broad implementation of the planned move towards evidence-based policy making would facilitate future sector selection.

Research and innovation are to be strengthened via "innovation contracts" for the top sectors. The contracts are based on public private partnership agreements at the sector level, aiming at reaching a balanced mix of fundamental research, applied research and the application of knowledge in private activity. The top teams developed different research projects for the innovation contracts that fulfil their sector's need for which about EUR 1 billion of public support was made available from already existing (partly from fundamental and applied) research activities. Hence, there are no additional public resources available, but part of them is now explicitly allocated to the top sectors and private sector demand is given a larger role in the work of the research institutions. Moreover, long-term partnership between industry and research bodies within top sectors is promoted via a planned additional tax credit for participation in Top Consortia for Knowledge and Innovation (TKIs) (Box 1.3). In the context of scarce public resources, the prioritisation of research activities in the areas of the top sectors could be justified, insofar as these earmarked activities are to create relatively large positive (knowledge) spillovers. However, the government should ensure that the earmarked activities do not become a vehicle for favouring particular industries or firms within the different top sectors. A particular concern is that larger firms and existing industries are better organised than SMEs and emerging industries, and can thus gain from a "first-mover" advantage in dealing with public support schemes. A balanced approach can be achieved by requiring that findings from the top teams are backed up by independent evidence and that their policy prescriptions are evaluated against alternatives.

> **Box 1.3. Top Consortia for Knowledge and Innovation (TKIs)**
>
> The establishment of Top Consortia for Knowledge and Innovation (TKIs) is an important element of the innovation contracts to secure long-term public-private research co-operation. The TKIs build on already existing initiatives in some sectors (*i.e.* the virtual "Technologische Top Instituten" or Leading Technological Institutes), where several research and private parties work on demand driven fundamental and strategic research as well as the application of scientific knowledge in processes (see the 2006 *Survey* for a more detailed description). As the institutes are generally considered to successfully foster long-term public-private research co-operation, the idea is to introduce similar institutes in other sectors. Being under construction, the exact scope and form of the TKIs is likely to vary among the top sectors, while some sectors might have more than one consortium to sufficiently cover sector's activities.
>
> To foster participation in TKIs, a fiscal incentive on R&D activities is to be put in place as of 2013 (see below), and comes on top of the generic tax credits to support R&D. Thereby, the government makes an exception in the approach that R&D support should be provided via broad framework conditions. Although the exact format of the tax credit has yet to be determined, the government plans to allocate EUR 90 million on an annual basis, which needs to benefit enterprises as well as knowledge institutions like universities. The government's vision is that more than EUR 0.5 billion will be involved in the TKIs by 2015, of which at least 40% will be financed by the business sector.

The top teams proposed more plans than are possible with available public funding. The final allocation is being partly determined by the private sector's own contributions (EUR 1½ billion, mostly based on letters of intent). However, it remains to be seen whether the new approach leads to additional private R&D activities. The demand driven approach may encourage companies to provide additional funds as research becomes more oriented towards their needs. On the other hand, there is also a risk that the new format crowds out current private R&D activities as companies bring in-house research activities under the innovation contracts to benefit from associated public support.

The top teams also prepared education and training agenda to strengthen the link between education and the top sectors' human capital needs (Rae and Sollie, 2008; Baldwin, 2006). The proposed initiatives focus on fostering qualification of pupils, life-long learning and linkages between supply and demand of human capital. Thereby, the top teams suggested putting stronger (financial) incentives in place to stimulate studies that are considered more valuable to the private sector and society (Government, 2012). Specifically, there is a strongly perceived shortage of employees with a science and technology background – including lower skilled technical staff. However, it is hard to find strong evidence of a skill gap in this area (Jacobs and Webbink, 2004; Noailly et al., 2005; De Graaf et al., 2007). For instance, this group of workers only have an average entry salary and they have not seen their relative wages increase over time despite the decreasing supply of workers in the area of science and technology (Figure 2). In addition, more than half of the workers trained in this area work in other economic sectors (Cornet et al., 2006). These findings suggest that the shortage is smaller than perceived, or impediments in the wage formation process that prevent wages to sufficiently reflect relative shortages.

Advice was also sought from the top teams about how to reduce the regulatory burden at the sector level. Such involvement helps to pinpoint market (and government) failures. However, it could also lead to regulatory capture and too much heterogeneity in regulation across sectors, making it potentially harder for investors, including foreign ones, to identify and comply with Dutch sector regulation. This would weaken the positive effects of the attempt to reduce the administrative burden for the entire private sector by 20% (see below). For instance, some sectors consider the income threshold to allow foreign qualified workers (see Chapter 2) to be too high, thereby acting as a sector specific bottleneck. However, such a bottleneck should be addressed at the general level (i.e. not at the sector level) to avoid too much heterogeneity in regulation across sectors. Hence, the establishment of the top teams is a welcome move to address sector bottlenecks, but it is important this does not lead to unnecessary differences in regulation across sectors.

Support for internationalisation of firms is to be given via "economic diplomacy". This involves activities like trade missions, providing advice and information for doing business abroad as well as removing barriers to international trade and investment. Activities in this area are already well established, but the new approach gives more attention to establishing business links with (larger) emerging economies (with again a focus on the nine top sectors), increasing the number of internationally operating SMEs, and attracting (high-tech) FDI from emerging markets (Ministry of Economic Affairs, Agriculture and Innovation, 2011a, 2011b and 2011c).[9] Foreign representations are mobilised to support internationally operating firms. Most services are provided at a fraction of provision costs, though at times a private contribution in the order of EUR 250-500 is in place.

The rationale for economic diplomacy is the existence of market failures, e.g. related to positive international knowledge spillovers, incomplete markets or enforceability of property rights (Harris and Li, 2005; Veenstra et al., 2010). Indeed, doing business in emerging markets is complicated by linguistic, cultural, bureaucratic and political issues,

Figure 1.9. **The share of graduates with a science or engineering degree is low**[1]
As a percentage of total new degrees in 2008

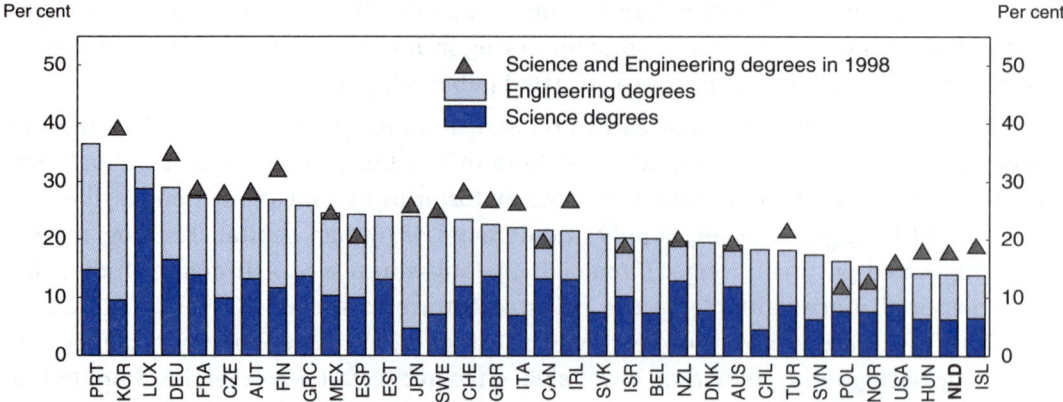

1. Data includes tertiary type-A degrees and advanced research programmes (ISCED 5A and 6).
Source: OECD (2012), Education Database, March.

StatLink http://dx.doi.org/10.1787/888932614396

Figure 1.10. **High explicit barriers to trade and investment in emerging markets**
From 0 least restrictive to 6 most restrictive, 2008[1]

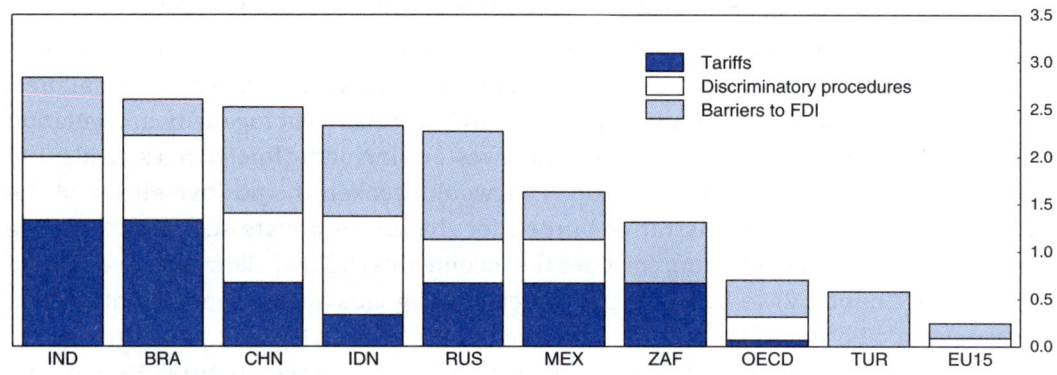

1. IND refers to India and IDN to Indonesia.
Source: OECD (2012), International Trade and Commodities Statistics Database.

StatLink http://dx.doi.org/10.1787/888932614415

explaining why exporting firms often move slowly to the most distant markets (Creusen and Lejour, 2011). In addition, firms are subject to information problems. This concerns particularly SMEs, as they tend to have relatively small information-networks and gathering capacity (Figure 1.10). For the Netherlands, empirical work points to economic diplomacy as an effective tool to remove impediments to international trade and investment (e.g. Van den Berg et al., 2008; Creusen and Lejour, 2011; Moons and Van Bergeijk, 2011).[10]

The increased emphasis on economic diplomacy, notably on doing business with emerging markets, is likely to support trade and investment linkages with the increasingly important players in the world market. However, Dutch exports are concentrated in a small number of larger firms that can generally enter and expand in foreign markets without specific government support. Hence, economic diplomacy efforts that support these firms could displace similar private efforts without boosting internationalisation. In addition, this is an area where developing evidence to form policy is important, as little is known about the cost-efficiency of the different elements that support the internationalisation of firms. In any case, to secure the cost-efficient use of scarce public resources, it is important that the prices for these services reflect some of the costs. For example, the Danish Trade Council's hourly charge is EUR 120 and the council is subject to a cost coverage target of 25%, which together with customer satisfaction evaluations aims at securing relatively efficient demand driven activities.[11]

Improving framework conditions should be key

Over the last two decades, the main focus of industrial policy in the Netherlands has been the improvement of framework conditions, which is reflected in low barriers to entrepreneurship (Wölfl et al., 2009; and WEF, 2011). However, weaknesses remain in the Netherlands' ability to respond to globalisation. These include the relatively low innovation activity, the limited number of fast growing innovative SMEs and entry and exit barriers that hamper economic growth via the process of "creative destruction". The government intends to improve framework conditions for the entire private sector via the economic agenda part of the new policies for the business sector.

Public expenses on stimulating R&D is projected to increase from EUR 3.2 billon (0.5% of GDP) in 2008 to about 4 billion in 2015 (0.6% of GDP) (Ministry of EL&I, 2011d).[12] To increase innovative activities, various direct innovation subsidies will be replaced by R&D tax incentives. The fiscal costs of the tax incentives are projected to more than double over the government's term, partly reflecting the doubling in the number of schemes (Table 1.3). These costs are partly offset by lower direct subsidies to innovation and lower spending on applied research institutions. Another important element of the adjusted innovation framework is the stronger focus on "evidence-based" policy, which follows up on the 2006 *Survey* recommendation, to enable evaluation of policies. Implementing such monitoring and measuring the effects of innovation policies is difficult, but at least the establishment of some indicators and individual targets per policy instrument could better guide innovation policies.

The policy shift towards tax incentives and evidence-based innovation policy may improve the business environment, make innovation policies simpler and strengthen policy guidance. The shift could make the system more effective, as empirical studies show that tax incentives tend to have a relatively higher impact on private innovation than direct R&D subsidies, although at the cost of subsidising activities that would have been undertaken anyway (Jaumotte and Pain, 2005; OECD, 2010a) (Box 1.4). Tax incentives have the advantage that they can potentially benefit all firms, reduce the temptation to "pick winners" and are more flexibility regarding the range of R&D activities undertaken (OECD, 2006a).[13] Additionally, in the context of the growing internalisation of R&D activities, stronger tax incentives might also attract R&D activities of multinationals.[14] Finally, the new innovation policy reduces the strong focus on SMEs, which used to receive five times more direct subsidies per invested R&D euro than larger firms, despite the lack of a correspondingly sized market failure to justify such a strong focus (Government, 2010; CPB, 2010) (Figures 1.11 and 1.12).

Dutch innovation policies have often shifted over time. For example, the 2006 OECD *Economic Survey* reported a shift from generic towards more specific support for business R&D – an approach that is now being reversed. Such policy volatility may damage R&D activity since expectations that R&D incentives are permanent should strengthen R&D

Table 1.3. **Tax measures to foster innovative activities (main features per scheme)**
Fiscal costs in 2015

	EUR billion
Promotion of Research and Development Act ("WBSO", existing scheme)	0.7
Tax credit for wage costs of employees directly involved in R&D activities:	
• Reduces company wage tax and social security contributions (or income tax if self employed).	
• Deduction of 42% of the first EUR 110 thousand in R&D wage costs (2012). And of 14% for the remaining R&D wage costs.	
• Tax benefit capped at EUR 14 million per company (2012), and 8.5 million in 2013, relatively benefitting SMEs.	
• In case of under- or overshooting of the estimated fiscal costs, the % deductibility will be adjusted accordingly in the next year.	
• Directly improves liquidity positions of companies.	
RDA scheme (New scheme: part of the new policies for the business sector)	0.5
Tax credit for non-salary expenses and investment in R&D (*e.g.* consumables and R&D equipment):	
• Reduces corporate tax payments (or personal income tax if the company is not listed).	
• Deduction of 40% of R&D costs (2012), implying a net benefit of 10% (given the corporate tax rate of 25%).	
• Tax benefit not capped, implying that the RDA tax credit serves SMEs and large companies equally well.	
• In case of under- or overshooting of the estimated fiscal costs, the % deductibility will be adjusted accordingly in the next year.	
• If there is no taxable income, the credit can be carried forward or backward in time.	
RDA+ scheme (New scheme: part of the new policies for the business sector)	0.1
Tax credit to promote public private partnership in Top Consortia for Knowledge and Innovation (TKIs):	
• Measure still to be specified (before budget 2013).	
• Only for the identified "Top sectors" of the economy.	
Innovation box (existing scheme)	0.6
Tax incentive for corporate income derived from patented know how, or R&D activities under the WBSO scheme.	
• Over this income the corporate tax rate is 5% (instead of 25%).	
• Tax incentive not capped.	
• No adjustment in case of over- or undershooting of the estimated fiscal costs ("open ended" policy).	
Total	**1.9**

Source: Ministry of Economic Affairs, Agriculture and Innovation (2011d); Agentschap NL; Dutch tax administration; Authorities.

Box 1.4. **The design of R&D tax credits**

R&D tax credits can be part of a balanced policy mix to increase innovation. Their benefit relatively to direct R&D subsidies is that they can potentially benefit all R&D activities, ensuring a more market-based selection of research projects. On the other hand, tax credits are not targeted, which means that the government cannot use such credits to steer research resources into areas with (perceived) high social returns. Moreover, tax credits involve significant deadweight losses in the sense that they notably support research projects that would have been undertaken anyway. Finally, tax credits tend to benefit incumbent firms more than young SMEs, which often lack taxable income to take advantages of tax reliefs.

The deadweight loss could be partly addressed by making R&D tax incentives incremental, *i.e.* being based on the increase in R&D activity, rather than volume based (applied to all R&D spending). For instance, combining volume and incremental tax incentives would support the level of R&D investment and reward higher investment growth. However, incremental-based support systems are relatively complex to design and implement: a reason why most OECD countries are moving towards volume-based incentive schemes.

Source: OECD (2011b), Criscuolo et al. (2009), Jaumotte and Pain (2005).

Figure 1.11. **Dutch R&D tax incentives have strong SME focus**
Tax subsidies rate for USD 1 of R&D, 2008

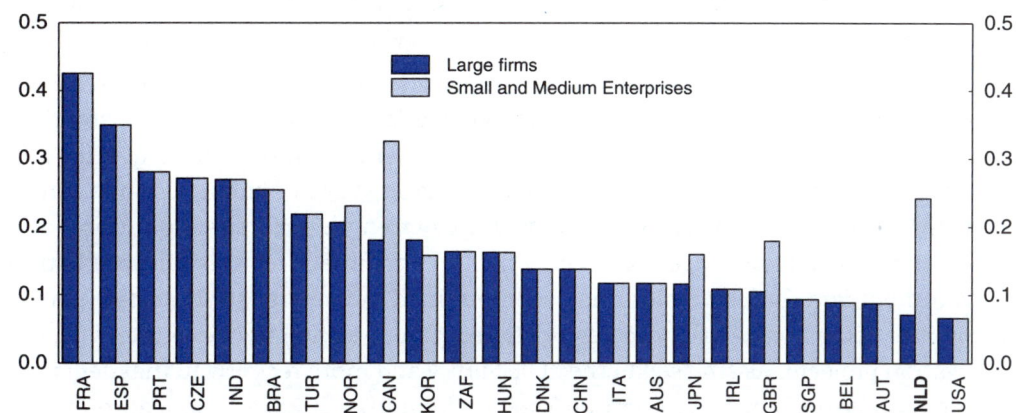

Source: OECD (2009), OECD Science, Technology and Industry Scoreboard 2009.

StatLink http://dx.doi.org/10.1787/888932614434

Figure 1.12. **Business R&D by size class of firms**
As a percentage of total BERD, 2009[1]

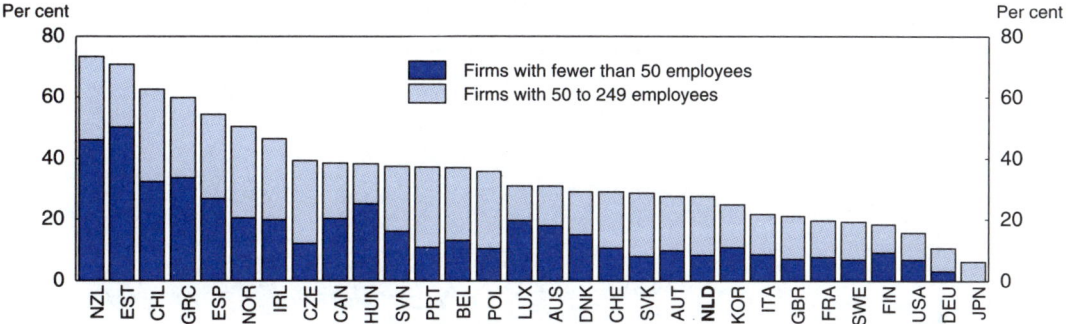

1. Or latest year available. 2008 for Australia, Canada, Chile, France, Korea, Portugal, Poland, Switzerland and the United Kingdom. 2007 for Austria, Belgium, Germany, Italy, Luxembourg, Spain, Sweden, and the United States. 2005 for Denmark, New Zealand and Ireland. Small firms (fewer than 50 employees): for the United States, 5-49 employees; for Luxembourg, the Netherlands and Sweden, 10-49 employees. Medium-sized firms (50-249 employees): for Japan, fewer than 299 employees. For Japan, the survey excludes firms with a capital of less than JPY 10 million.

Source: OECD (2011), OECD Science, Technology and Industry Scoreboard 2011.

StatLink http://dx.doi.org/10.1787/888932614453

investment (Guellec and Van Pottelsberghe de la Potterie, 2003). This point to the need for long-term political commitment to the new R&D support framework. By the same token, the new policy increases the number of R&D tax incentives from two to four, possibly raising company transaction costs and increasing overlap and interaction between the schemes. Hence, the policy framework could be further broadened by reducing the number of R&D tax credits.

The government's ambitious goal to boost R&D spending from 1.8% to 2.5% of GDP depends strongly on raising private sector spending, given that public spending is to remain broadly stable in relation to GDP. The policy goal might gradually become more difficult to attain over time as the services content of the economy is likely to increase further, as the R&D intensity of the services sector is relatively low. It should also be noted that the new innovation framework is focussing on "traditional" R&D activities, such as science and technology research. However, globalisation is likely to increase the value of investing in other innovative activities, such as new approaches to design, databases, marketing and organisational structures (OECD, 2010b; OECD, 2011c). In fact, investment in such intangible assets is likely to become increasingly important for service-oriented economies.

To complement the innovation policy approach, the 2006 OECD Economic Survey showed that business application of new knowledge is only average, notwithstanding a very strong research system (Figure 1.13). The government intends to make greater use of private demand to direct university research by allocating 2.5% of public research funds to convert knowledge into applied innovations and by strengthening the monitoring of the application of public knowledge. However, while an agreement for this purpose between the government and the universities has been outlined, university staff has few personal financial incentives (e.g. in salary scales or shared patent rights) to co-operate with firms on innovation projects. As stressed in the 2006 Survey and more recently in the media, such incentives are important to strengthen science-business linkages. Hence, to enhance researchers' incentives to market the results of their research, clear and more generous rules for sharing patent rights should be established.

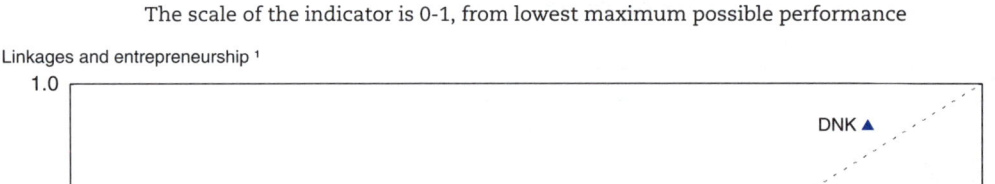

Figure 1.13. **Excellent research system but mediocre business linkages**

The scale of the indicator is 0-1, from lowest maximum possible performance

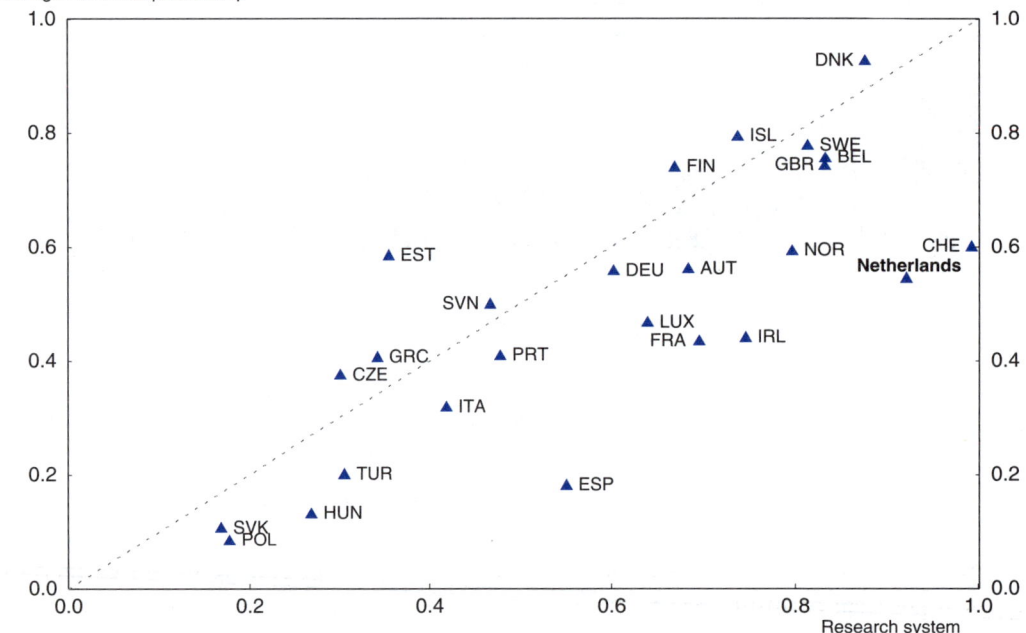

1. Linkages and entrepreneurship concerns the items: Public-private co-publications per million population. Innovative SMEs collaborating with others as per cent of SMEs; SMEs innovating in-house as per cent of SMEs. Research system concerns the items: International scientific co-publications per million population; Scientific publications among the top 10% most cited publications worldwide as per cent of total scientific publications of the country; Non-EU doctorate students as a per cent of all doctorate students.

Source: European Commission (2011), Innovation Union Scoreboard 2010.

StatLink ⟶ http://dx.doi.org/10.1787/888932614472

Structural funding bottlenecks for young innovative and fast growing SMEs hamper innovation and growth (Boot and Schmeits, 2004; Ministry of EL&I, 2011e; AWT, 2011). As in other OECD countries, these issues are mostly related to information problems – on the part of the entrepreneur or among the financers of innovative SMEs – as well as the dominance of traditional banking finance in the Netherlands (OECD, 2006b). Consequently, these SMEs have limited access to risk capital. The associated restricted growth of innovative SMEs means that the economy is not fully capitalising on this important driver of employment creation and productivity growth (OECD, 2010d; AWT, 2011; Bos and Stam, 2011). Moreover, young innovative SMEs have a higher probability to come up with radical innovations contributing to the process of "creative destruction" (Stam and Gerritsen, 2009).

The government is creating a new SME+ Innovation fund to back innovative and fast growing SMEs as an umbrella for different (partly existing) finance schemes in this area (Ministry of EL&I, 2011a and 2011b). This fund aims at avoiding interferences in the segments of the private market that work appropriately. The fund, with an annual budget of EUR 120 million, has three pillars. The first is direct credits for R&D projects, which are converted into subsidies in the case of project failure. The second and third pillars concern respectively early-stage and later-stage capital and notably take the form of public participation in investment funds (via public-private investment funds as well as a "fund of funds"). The aim is to mobilise private capital to close a perceived equity gap for investments of between EUR 0.2 and 3 million. The SME+ fund is designed as a "revolving fund", where on average about 80% of the invested money should return for new investments. It is open to the entire private sector, though part of its spending is earmarked for the top sector "creative industry".

The new SME+ innovation fund has the potential to contribute to the development of the (small) venture capital market, which is often a key financial source for innovations (Figure 1.14) (Van Ark et al., 2009). Indeed, venture capitalists bring sector specific knowledge, access to relevant networks and may help raising additional financing at a later stage (Boot and Schmeits, 2004; Da Rin et al., 2005). Moreover, the fund is complementary to the innovation tax credits, which benefit relatively less to young innovative SMEs (as these firms often lack taxable income). However, there are several risks to the approach. First, the targeted recovery rate on investments (80%) risks leading the SME+ fund to avoid financing the most risky projects, even though these projects are potentially the most radically innovative. There is also a risk of crowding out private financing for the less risky projects. Another potential issue with the target recovery rate is that assessing returns on investment takes time, as investments from private venture capital funds typically take 5 to 10 years to materialise (Lerner, 2009; Murray and Lingelbach, 2009; Nesta, 2009). Moreover, there can be an issue of potentially "over-engineering" of the venture capital market, where public programmes could create artificial funding barrier between successive phases of the development of the company that requires an evolving funding process (Lerner, 2009; Nesta, 2009). Finally, deviations from the fund's generic nature – like the earmarked funding for the "creative industry" – risk hindering strict project selection.

Greater emphasis on competition policy is an area where policies to improve the business environment could be broadened. A robust competition framework supports entrepreneurship and an efficient allocation of production, and may strengthen possible positive effects of more targeted support as well as innovation (Jaumotte and Pain, 2005; OECD, 2010d; Aghion et al., 2011). In the Netherlands, unnecessarily high regulatory barriers still harm competition by discouraging new firms from entering markets, notwithstanding the relaxation of barriers to entrepreneurship since the mid-1990s (Kocsis et al., 2009). Monetary costs of starting a business and the time delay caused by entry regulations are associated with lower entry rates (Fisman and Sarria-Allende, 2009; Klapper et al., 2006;

Figure 1.14. **Venture capital market is relatively small**
Venture capital as a percentage of GDP, 2009

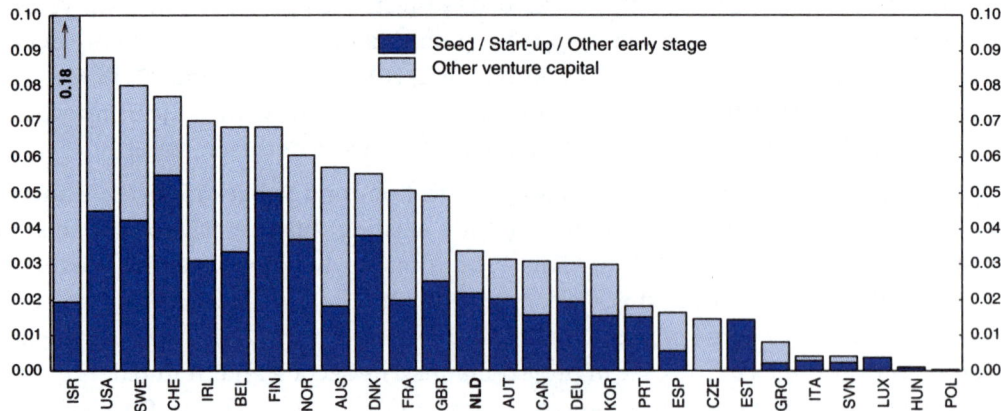

Source: OECD (2011), Entrepreneurship at a Glance.

StatLink ⌸ http://dx.doi.org/10.1787/888932614491

Ciccone and Papaioannou, 2007). Against this backdrop, the planned further reduction in red tape is a welcome move (Box 1.5) (Figure 1.15). Moreover, a number of network and services sectors, like retail distribution, legal services, accounting and road freight business, remain relatively sheltered from entry (Figure 1.16), while concentration in some sectors, such as financial and telecommunication services, is quite high. Likewise, streamlining *exit procedures* could further facilitate the process of creative destruction. As covered in the 2006 *Survey*, bankruptcy procedures in the Netherlands remain long and costly, pointing to a need for reform. Hence, the new policies for the business sector should be broadened by giving greater attention to competition policies, in particular to lower entry and exit barriers.

The different elements of the economic agenda are likely to improve framework conditions, which – together with stronger competition policies – should foster entrepreneurial activity. However, business policies cannot be a standalone measure, particularly if the Netherlands is to reach the government's ambition of becoming one of the

---

Box 1.5. Reducing red tape

The economic agenda has ambitious targets to reduce the administrative burden for businesses (Ministry of EL&I, 2011a). Based on Standard Cost Model calculations – a method for measuring and pricing the administrative burden imposed by regulation by assessing time spend on compliance – the burden has to decrease by 10% in 2012 (compared to 2010) and by an annual 5% in the years after. The targets are a continuation of the significant reductions of administrative burdens over the latest decade (OECD, 2010c). Besides cutting red tape, the government aims at reducing compliance and supervisory costs as well as improving government services. The specific measures include simplifying payroll taxes, reducing bureaucracy formalities for starting limited private companies, scrapping chambers of commerce levies, lowering reporting requirements (such as tax returns and financial statements), creating an administrative "one-stop-shop" for all entrepreneurs and reducing inspection for companies that consistently comply with existing rules. Better regulation is an important contribution to improve broad framework conditions.

Figure 1.15. **Administrative burdens on start-up**
The scale of the indicator is 0-6 from least to most restrictive, 2008

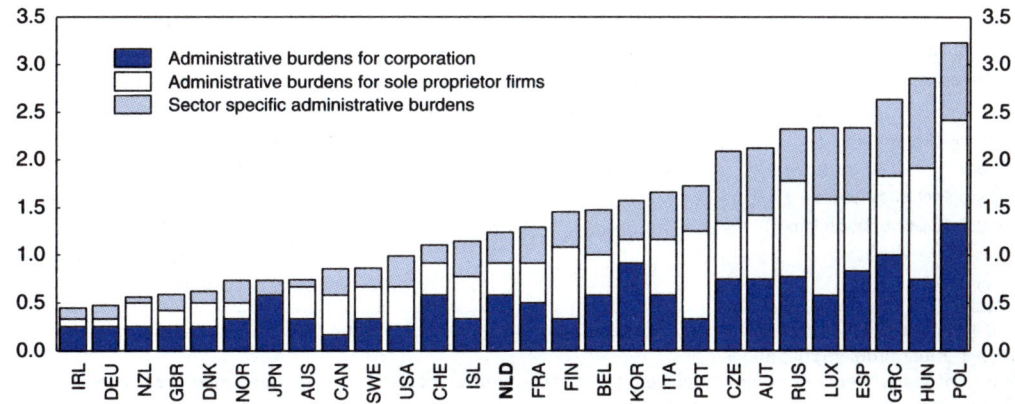

Source: OECD (2011), Product Market Regulation Database, www.oecd.org/economy/pmr.
StatLink ⟶ http://dx.doi.org/10.1787/888932614510

Figure 1.16. **Entry regulation for a selection of sectors**
The scale of the indicator is 0-6 from least to most restrictive, 2008[1]

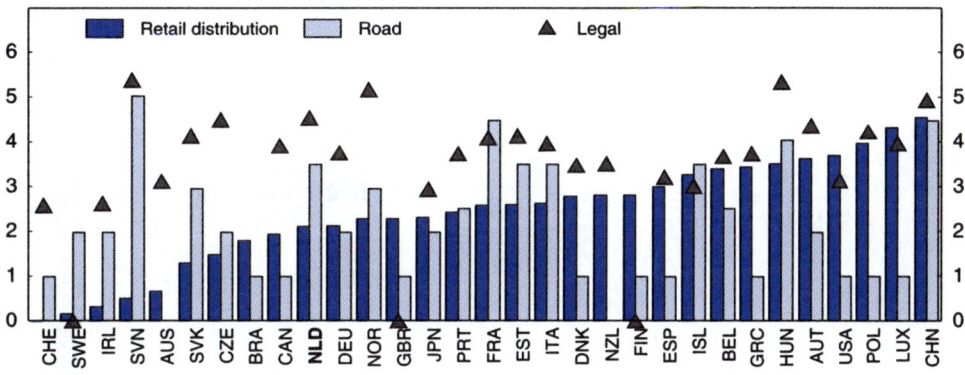

1. 2007 for Road.
Source: OECD (2011), Product Market Regulation Database, www.oecd.org/economy/pmr.
StatLink ⟶ http://dx.doi.org/10.1787/888932614529

top five knowledge economies by 2020 (Box 1.2). Surveys notably point to problems with the labour market and tax issues (Table 1.4 and Chapter 2), areas that receive far less attention in the new policies for the business sector. Reforms that increase the flexibility of the Dutch labour market would be complementary to the new business policy, as such reforms are likely to foster innovative activities and the diffusion of knowledge (Bovenberg and Theeuwes, 2004). High-risk innovative sectors tend to be smaller in countries, like the Netherlands, with strict employment protection legislation (Bartelsman et al., 2010). Also, more flexible labour markets lower the necessary wage premium to attract high skilled workers to fast growing sectors (Van Ark et al., 2009). A related issue is that there are relatively few "growth-oriented" innovative SMEs in the Netherlands; an observation that is in part linked to labour market rigidities and the high protection of workers (e.g. Stam and Gerritsen, 2009; OECD, 2010d; AWT, 2011) (Figure 1.17). Hence, the policies to improve the business sector environment should be backed by reforms that address labour market rigidities.

Table 1.4. **Top 10 problematic factors for doing business in the Netherlands**

	World Economic Forum[1]		Business climate survey Ernst and Young[2]		Employer organisations[3]
1	Restrictive labour regulations	1	Labour costs	1	Labour market flexibility
2	Inefficient government bureaucracy	2	Real estate costs	2	Legal obligations entrepeneurship[4]
3	Access to financing	3	Labour market flexibility	3	Administrative burden wage bill
4	Tax rates	4	Tax benefits and subsidies	4	Access to financing
5	Inadequately educated workers	5	Availability and quality of R&D	5	Barriers to international trade and investment
6	Tax regulations	6	Expertise in own industry	6	Innovation policy
7	Inadequate supply of infrastructure			7	Procurement: SME involvement
8	Poor work ethic in national labour force			8	Zoning and planning regulation
9	Inflation			9	Local supervisory burden
10	Policy instability			10	Local licence and permits system

1. From a list of 15 factors, respondents were asked to select the five most problematic for doing business in their country and to rank them between 1 (most problematic) and 5.
2. Based on share of respondents (among key players in internationally operating firms) that judge the mentioned elements of the business climate "little attractive", or not attractive at all.
3. Top 10 business bottlenecks that hamper companies to expand according to MKB-Nederland and VNO-NCW.
4. For instance, mandatory wage payments for workers who are sick or disabled beyond the control of the employer.

Source: World Economic Forum (2011), Ernst and Young – Barometer Nederlands vestigingsklimaat (2011), Ministry of Economic Affairs, Agriculture and Innovation – Zelfstanding ondernemerschap (2009).

Figure 1.17. **Fast growing (innovative SME) enterprises**
Share of high-growth enterprises[1] in 2007

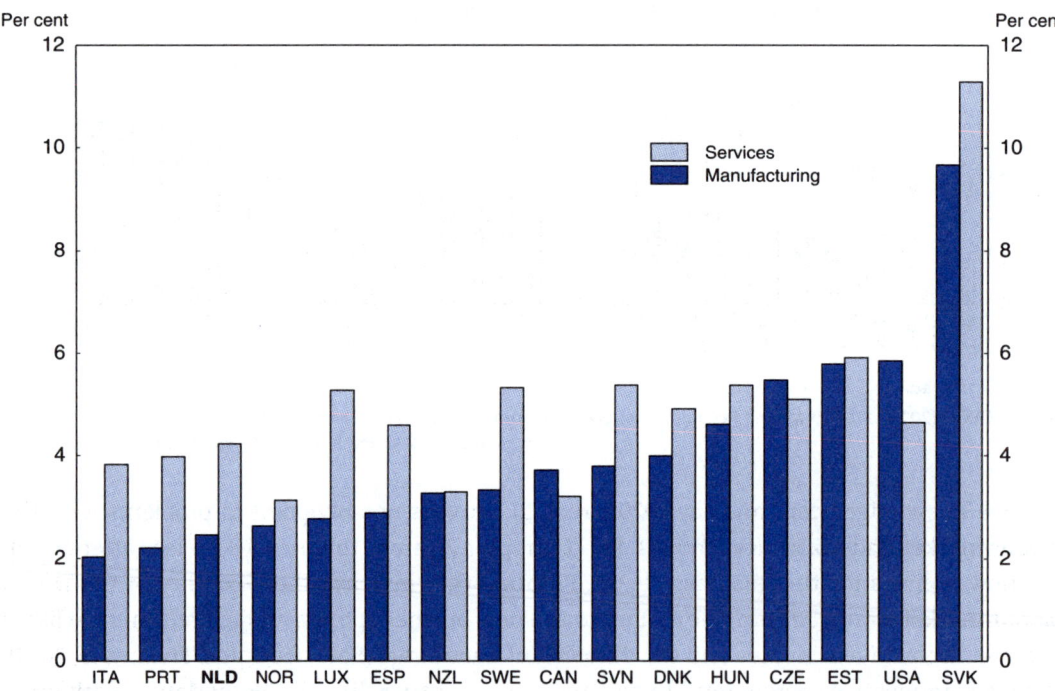

1. The share of high-growth enterprises is compiled as the number of high-growth enterprises as a percentage of the population of enterprises with ten or more employees, 2006 for Norway.

Source: OECD (2011), *Entrepreneurship at a Glance*.

StatLink ⇒ http://dx.doi.org/10.1787/888932614548

> **Box 1.6. Recommendations to strengthen the business environment**
>
> **Broaden targeted support to different sectors**
>
> - The scope of the top sectors should be more clearly defined in order to ensure an efficient use of public funds and enable evidence-based policy making.
> - To take full advantage of the top team approach to improve sector regulation, similar teams should be created for more sectors of the economy, especially services.
> - The government should ensure that the funds earmarked to top sectors in the area of research do not become a vehicle for favouring particular firms, especially as incumbents may benefit from a first mover advantage.
> - The top sector approach should remain open to future emerging sectors and industries as well as to let any declining ones go. A swift and broad implementation of the planned move towards evidence-based policy-making would facilitate future sector selection.
> - Regarding economic diplomacy, the public services offered should reflect at least some of the costs, in order to secure the cost-efficient use of scarce public resources.
>
> **Further enhance framework conditions**
>
> - The stability of the new R&D support framework should be backed by long-term political commitment to support firms' multi-year research programmes.
> - The R&D support framework should be simplified by reducing the number of tax credits.
> - To strengthen the relatively weak science-business linkages, researchers' incentives to market the results of their research should be enhanced by establishing clear and more generous rules for sharing patents rights.
> - The government should further promote framework conditions by giving greater attention to competition policies. In particular, lower entry and exit barriers will support the process of "creative destruction".
> - The policies to improve the business sector environment should be backed by reforms that address labour market rigidities.

Notes

1. Globalisation may be defined as the process whereby domestic product, capital and labour markets become more integrated across borders (OECD, 2007a).
2. In 2009, 3.8% of total goods exports had Brazil, Russian Federation, India or China (BRIC countries) as destination, against 4.3% of domestically produced exports goods (Statistics Netherlands, 2010c).
3. A notable exception is the export of services: about 6% of Dutch services exports find their way to the BRIC countries, compared to about 5.5% for the OECD as a whole.
4. The favourable tax regime concerns the relatively low statutory corporate tax rate, the possibility of advance tax ruling to give certainty about the level of taxation, the broad tax treaty network, a favourable "participation exemption" regime, and a zero statutory withholding tax rate on outbound royalty payments, among others (Top team Head Offices, 2011; NFIA, 2011).
5. Although FDI data do not suggest a substantial establishment of firms from emerging market economies in the Netherlands, microdata in firm ownership indicate that the Netherlands seem to be an attractive location in Europe for firms with their origin in the BRIC countries. The latter could be related to the large distribution and logistics sectors (Groot et al., 2011b).
6. An unfortunate development is the sometimes less positive public and political approach towards the acquisitions of Dutch companies by foreign parties, especially when the investors find their origin in non-OECD countries. See, for instance, the discussions surrounding the acquisition of ECT by Hutchinson Whampoa in 1999, Hoogovens/Corus by Tata Steel in 2007 and the attempted takeover of Draka by Xinmao in 2011.

7. Country rankings of innovation performance – that take into account a wide range of indicators to capture a country's performance both on the output and input side of innovation – usually show the Netherlands in the middle to upper range of OECD/EU countries. See the Synthetic Innovation Indicator by Rae and Sollie (2008); the Innovation Union Scoreboard by the European Commission (2012) and the innovation pillar of the Global Competitiveness Index by the World Economic Forum (2011).

8. Other elements – which are outside the scope of the present discussion – include the improvement of spatial economic conditions for economic clusters (*e.g.* related to the port of Rotterdam and Amsterdam Schiphol airport), and the application of information and communication technology (ICT).

9. Furthermore, part of the programmes for international development co-operation will be linked to the areas of the top sectors.

10. However, some instruments appear to be more effective than others. For instance, the presence of embassies and high level trade missions appear to create stronger results than other policy instruments.

11. Some (basic information) services are free of charge, or against discount rates (usually applied to SMEs with fewer than 50 employees and with a maximum annual turnover of less than DKK 50 million).

12. Spending of central government, *i.e.* excluding local governments.

13. In general, R&D tax incentives are found to contribute to R&D investment, innovation output and welfare in a country, although the responsiveness is greater in the long run and the empirical evidence is scattered (OECD, 2011b).

14. Although other factors such as market access and the country's knowledge base tend to be more important (OECD, 2011b).

Bibliography

Aghion, P., J. Bulanger and E. Cohen (2011), "Rethinking Industrial Policy", *Breugel Policy Brief*, Issue 2011/04, June.

AWT (2011), "Kapitale kansen", February, Zoetermeer.

Baldwin, R. (2006), "Globalisation, the great unbundling(s)", Secretariat of the Economic Council, Finnish Prime Minister's Office, Helsinki.

Barbour, V. (1950), *Capitalism in Amsterdam in the Seventeenth Century*, Johns Hopkins Press, Baltimore.

Bartelsman, E.J., P.A. Gautier and J. de Wind (2010), "Employment Protection, Technology Choice, and Worker Allocation", *Tinbergen Institute Discussion Paper*, No. TI 2010-042/3, Amsterdam/Rotterdam.

Bernard, A.B., J. Bradford Jensen, S.J. Redding and P.K. Schott (2007), "Firms in International Trade", *Journal of Economic Perspectives*, Vol. 21, No. 3.

Boot, A. and A. Schmeits (2004), "Imperfecties in de vermogensmarkt en overheidsbeleid", in *Innovatie in Nederland: De markt draalt en de overheid faalt, Koninklijke Vereniging voor de Staathuishoudkunde*, Preadviezen.

Bos, J. and E. Stam (2011), "Gazelles, Industry Growth and Structural Change", *Discussion Paper Series*, No. 11-02, Tjalling C. Koopmans Research Institute, Utrecht.

Bovenberg, L. and J. Theeuwes (2004), "Arbeid en Innovatie", in *Innovatie in Nederland: De markt draalt en de overheid faalt, Koninklijke Vereniging voor de Staathuishoudkunde*, Preadviezen.

Ciccone, A. and E. Papaioannou (2007), "Red Tape and Delayed Entry", *Journal of the European Economic Association*, No. 5(2-3), April-May.

Cornet, M., F. Huizinga, B. Minne and D. Webbink (2006), "Kansrijk kennisbeleid", *CPB Document*, No. 124, Centraal Planbureau, The Hague.

Court of Audit (Algemene Rekenkamer) (2011), "Innovatiebeleid", *Algemene Rekenkamer*, 28 September, The Hague.

CPB (2010), *Keuzes bij innovatiebeleid: Bouwstenen voor heroverwegingswerkgroep Innovatie en Toegepast Onderzoek*, 2010/13.

CPB (2011), *Reactie op Research en Development aftrek*, CPB notitie, Centraal Planbureau, The Hague.

Creusen, H. and A. Lejour (2011), "Uncertainty and the Export Decisions of Dutch Firms", *CPB Discussion Paper*, No. 183, Centraal Planbureau, The Hague.

Criscuolo, C., D. Czarnitzki, C. Hambro and J. Warda (2009), "Design and Evaluation of Tax Incentives for Business Research and Development: Good Practice and Future Development", *Final Report*, submitted by the Expert Group on Impacts of R&D Tax Incentives to the European Commission, Directorate General – Research, 15 November.

Da Rin, M., G. Nicodano and A. Sembenelli (2005), "Public Policy and the Creation of ActiveVenture Capital Markets", *ECB Working Paper Series*, No. 430, European Central Bank, Frankfurt am Main.

De Graaf, D., A. Heyma and C. van Klaveren (2007), "De arbeidsmarkt van hoger opgeleide bèta's", *SEO-rapport*, No. 992, Amsterdam.

DNB (De Nederlandsche Bank) (2007), "Dutch competitiveness in international services trade", *Quarterly Bulletin*, December, Amsterdam.

DNB (De Nederlandsche Bank) (2008), *Statistical Bulletin*, September, Amsterdam.

DNB (De Nederlandsche Bank) (2011), "Netherlands Leads the Field in Direct Investment", *DNB Bulletin*, August, Amsterdam.

EIM (2011), "Analyse sectorstructuur en private R&D: Verklaring van de relatieve positie van Nederland", Zoetermeer.

Erken, H.P.G. and M.L. Ruiter (2005), "Determinanten van de private R&D-uitgaven in internationaal perspectief", Ministry of Economic Affairs and Dialogic, The Hague.

Ernst and Young (2011), Barometer Nederlands vestigingsklimaat.

Gelauff, G., A. van der Horst and B. ter Weel (2010), "The Netherlands of 2040", *CPB Document*, No. 88, Centraal Planbureau, The Hague.

Gorter, J., P. Tang and M. Toet (2005), "Verplaatsing vanuit Nederland", *CPB Document*, No. 76, Centraal Planbureau, The Hague.

Government (2010), *Innovatie en Toegepast Onderzoek. Rapport brede heroverwegingen*, April, The Netherlands, The Hague.

Government (2012), "Aanbieding Samenvatting Innovatiecontracten en Human Capital Agenda's", Letter by the Chairmen of the Top Teams to the Minister of Economic Affairs, Agriculture and Innovation, January, The Hague.

Groot, S.P.T., A. Lejour and M. Gerritsen (2011a), "Uitvoer Naar Opkomende economieën", *Economische Statistische Berichten*, No. 96(4601).

Groot, S.P.T, H.L.F. de Groot, A.M. Lejour and J. Möhlmann (2011b), "The rise of the BRIC countries and its impact on the Dutch economy", *CPB Background Document*, Centraal Planbureau, The Hague.

Guellec, D. and B. Van Pottelsberghe De La Potterie (2003), *The impact of public R&D expenditure on business R&D*, Economics of Innovation and New Technology, No. 12:3, pp. 225-243.

Fisman, R. and V. Sarria Allende (2009), "Regulation of Entry and the Distortion of Industrial Organization", *Journal of Applied Economics*, Vol. XIII, No. 1, May.

Harris, R. and Q. Cher Li (2005), "Review of the Literature: The Role of International Trade and Investment in Business Growth and Development", *Report to UK Trade and Investment*.

Heyma, A. and J. Theeuwes (2008), "Offshoring and the Worker", *SEO-Report*, No. 2007-94, Amsterdam.

Jacobs, B. and D. Webbink (2004), "Onderwijs, innovatie en productiviteit", in *Innovatie in Nederland: De markt draalt en de overheid faalt*, Koninklijke Vereniging voor de Staathuishoudkunde, Preadviezen.

Jacobs, B. and J. Theeuwes (2004), *Innovatie in Nederland: De Markt Draalt en de Overheid Faalt*, Koninklijke Vereniging voor de Staathuishoudkunde, Preadviezen, Amsterdam.

Jaumotte, F. and N. Pain (2005), "Innovation in the Business Sector", *OECD Economics Department Working Papers*, No. 459, OECD Publishing.

Klapper, L., L. Laeven and R. Rajan (2006), "Entry Regulation as a Barrier to Entrepreneurship", *Journal of Financial Economics*, No. 82.

Kocsis, V., R. Lukach, B. Minne, V. Shestalova, N. Zubanov and H. van der Wiel (2009), "Relation Entry, Exit and Productivity. An Overview of Recent Theoretical and Empirical Literature", *CPB Document*, No. 180, Centraal Planbureau, The Hague.

Koster, S. and Arjen Edzes (2011), "Topsectoren behoeven eenduidige definiëring", *Economische Statistische Berichten*, No. 96(4601).

Kranendonk, H. and J. Verbruggen (2011), "Het belang van uitvoer en binnenlandse bestedingen voor productie en werkgelegenheid in Nederland", *Achtergronddocument bij CEP*, Centraal Planbureau, The Hague.

Krugman, P. (1994), "Competitiveness: A Dangerous Obsession", *Foreign Affairs*, Vol. 73 No. 2, March/April.

Kuypers, F., A. Lejour, O. Lemmers and P. Ramaekers (2012), "Kenmerken van Wederuitvoerbedrijven", Centraal Planbureau/Centraal Bureau Voor de Statistiek, The Hague/Heerlen.

Lanser, D. and H. van der Wiel (2011), "Innovatiebeleid in Nederland: De (on)mogelijkheden van effectmeting", *CPB achtergronddocument*, Centraal Planbureau, The Hague.

Lerner, J. (2009), "Boulevard of Broken Dreams: Why Public Efforts to Boost Entrepreneurship and Venture Capital Have Failed – and What to Do About It", Princeton University Press.

Lin, J. and H.J. Chang (2009), "Should Industrial Policy in Developing Countries Conform to Comparative Advantage or Defy it?", *Development Policy Review*, No. 27(5), A Debate Between Justin Lin and Ha-Joon Chang.

Maastricht Economic and Social Research Institute on Innovation and Technology (2011), European Commission, Innovation Union Scoreboard, February.

Mellens, M.C., H.G.A. Noordman and J.P. Verbruggen (2007), "Re-exports: International comparison and implications for performance indicators", *CPB Document*, No 143, Centraal Planbureau, The Hague.

Ministry of Economic Affairs (2009), "Zelfstandig ondernemerschap", September, The Hague.

Ministry of Economic Affairs, Agriculture and Innovation (EL&I) (2011a), "To the Top. Towards a New Enterprise Policy", February, The Hague.

Ministry of Economic Affairs, Agriculture and Innovation (EL&I) (2011b), "To the Top, the Enterprise Policy in Action(s)", September, The Hague.

Ministry of Economic Affairs, Agriculture and Innovation (EL&I) (2011c), "Buitenlandse Markten, Nederlands kansen", June, The Hague.

Ministry of Economic Affairs, Agriculture and Innovation (EL&I) (2011d), "Rijksbreed overzicht innovatiemiddelen", October, The Hague.

Ministry of Economic Affairs, Agriculture and Innovation (EL&I) (2011e), "Naar een gezonde basis: bedrijfsfinanciering na de crisis", *Advies van de expertgroep bedrijfsfinanciering op verzoek van de minister van Economische Zaken, Landbouw en Innovatie*, June, The Hague.

Ministry of Economic Affairs, Agriculture and Innovation (EL&I) (2012), "Eerste Reactie op Innovatiecontracten en Human Capital Agenda's van de Topsectoren", January, The Hague.

Moons, S. and P. van Bergeijk (2011), "De Effectiviteit van Economische Diplomatie", *Economische Statistische Berichten*, No. 96(4616).

Murray, G. and D. Lingelbach (2009), "Twelve Meditations on Venture Capital: Some Heretical Observations on the Dissonance between Theory and Practice When Applied to Public/Private Collaborations on Entrepreneurial Finance Policy", *Working Paper*, No. 09/06, University of Exeter Business School.

Naudé, W. (2010a), "Industrial Policy", *Working Paper*, No.2010/106, United Nations University, World Institute for Development Research.

Naudé, W. (2010b), "New Challenges for Industrial Policy", *Working Paper*, No. 2010/107, United Nations University, World Institute for Development Research.

Nesta (2009): "From funding gaps to thin markets, UK Government support for early-venture capital", *Research Report*, with BVCA.

NFIA (2011), "Why Invest in Holland?", Netherlands Foreign Investment Agency, January.

Noailly, J., D. Waagmeester, B. Jacobs, M. Rensman and D. Webbink (2005), "Scarcity of science and engineering students in the Netherlands", *CPB Document*, No. 192, Centraal Planbureau, The Hague.

Nicoletti, G., S. Golub, D. Hajkova, D. Mirza and. K. Y. Yoo (2003), "Policies and International Integration: Influences on Trade and Foreign Direct Investment", *OECD Economics Department Working Papers*, No. 359, OECD Publishing.

OECD (2005), "Growth in Services – Fostering Employment, Productivity and Innovation", *OECD Digital Economy Papers*, No. 94, OECD Publishing.

OECD (2006a), *Going for growth*, OECD Publishing.

OECD (2006b), "The SME Financing Gap", OECD Publishing.

OECD (2007a), Staying Competitive in the Global Economy, Moving up the Value Chain, OECD Publishing.

OECD (2007b), "Making the Most of Globalisation", *OECD Economic Outlook*, Chapter 3, Vol. 2007/1, No. 81, June, OECD Publishing.

OECD (2010a), *OECD Economic Survey: Germany 2010*, OECD Publishing.

OECD (2010b), *The OECD Innovation Strategy: Getting a Head Start on Tomorrow*, OECD Publishing.

OECD (2010c), *Better Regulation in Europe: Netherlands 2010*, OECD Publishing.

OECD (2010d), "The Role of High Growth Firms in Catalysing Entrepeneurship and Innovation", No. DSTI/IND(2010)9, OECD Publishing.

OECD (2011a), "Fostering New Sources Of Growth – Is There a Role For 'Industrial' Policy in the 21st Century?", *Background Paper*, No. STI/IND/AH(2011)1, OECD Publishing.

OECD (2011b), "Tax Reform Options: Incentives for Innovation. The International Experience with R&D Tax Incentives", Testimony by the OECD, United States Senate Committee on Finance, 20 September.

OECD (2011c), *OECD Observer*, No. 284, Q1, OECD Publishing.

OECD (2011d), "New Sources of Growth: Intangible Assets, Preliminary Evidence and Policy Issues", No. DSTI/IND(2011)2, OECD Publishing.

Pain, N., I. Koske and M. Sollie (2008), "Globalisation and OECD Consumer Price Inflation", *OECD Economic Studies*, No. 44, 2008/1.

Port of Rotterdam Authority (2011a), *Haven in Cijfers*, May, Rotterdam.

Port of Rotterdam Authority (2011b), *Annual Report 2010*, Rotterdam.

Port of Rotterdam Authority (2011c), *Port Compass: Port Vision 2030*, December, Rotterdam.

Rae, D. and M. Sollie (2008), "Globalisation and the European Union: Which Countries are Best Placed to Cope?", *OECD Economics Department Working Paper*, No. 586.

Rodrik, D. (2008), "Normalizing Industrial Policy", *Commission on Growth and Development Working Paper*, No. 3, Washington, DC.

Schmidt-Ehmcke, J. and P. Zloczysti (2011), "Industries at the Wold Technology Frontier: Measuring R&D Efficiency in a Non-Parametric DEA Framework", *GRASP Working Paper*, No. 16, August.

Sociaal-Economische Raad (SER) (2008), "On sustainable globalisation: A world to be won", *Advisory report*, Sociaal-Economische Raad, The Hague.

Stam, E. and D. Gerritsen (2009), "Gazellen in de Lage Landen", Universiteit Utrecht.

Statistics Netherlands (2008), "Internationaliseringsmonitor 2008", The Hague.

Statistics Netherlands (2009), "Internationalisation Monitor 2009", The Hague.

Statistics Netherlands (2010a), "Internationalisation Monitor 2010", The Hague.

Statistics Netherlands (2010b), "Helft Nederlandse internationale handel door buitenlandse bedrijven", *Webmagazine*, November.

Statistics Netherlands (2010c), "Half of Dutch good exports to Germany manufactured in the Netherlands", *Webmagazine*, June.

Statistics Netherlands (2011), "Internationalisation Monitor 2011", The Hague.

Suyker, W., H.L.F. de Groot and P. Buitelaar (2007), "India and the Dutch economy: Stylised facts and prospects", *CPB Document*, No. 155, Centraal Planbureau, The Hague.

Top team Head Offices (2011), *Met Hoofdkantoren Naar de Top*, June.

Urlings, N., F. Fortanier and M. Korvorst (2011), "Inkomende investeringen en werkgelegenheid in Nederland", Statistics Netherlands, The Hague/Heerlen.

Van Ark, B., J.X. Hao, C. Corrado and C. Hulten (2009), "Measuring intangible capital and its contribution to economic growth in Europe", in *R&D and the financing of innovation in Europe*, EIB Papers, Vol. 14, No. 1.

Van Bergeijk, P.A.G., F. Fortanier, H. Garretsen, H.L.F. de Groot and S.J.V. Moons (2011), "Productivity and Internationalization: A Micro-Data Approach", *De Economist*, No. 159, pp. 381-388.

Van den Berg, M., M. de Nooij, H. Garretsen and H.L.F. de Groot (2008), "Een onderzoek naar de maatschappelijke kosten en baten van het financieel buitenlandinstrumentarium van het Ministerie van Economische Zaken", *SEO-Report*, No. 2008-64.

Van den Bosch, F.A.J., R. Hollen, H.W. Volberda and M.G. Baaij (2011), "De strategische waarde van het Haven- en Industriecomplex Rotterdam voor het internationale concurrentievermogen van Nederland".

Van Gorp, D.M. (2010), "Offshoring by manufacturing and service firms in the Netherlands, Offshoring behavior in times of a financial crisis", Nyenrode Business University.

Van Gorp, D.M. (2008), "Offshoring in the Service Sector: An empirical investigation on the offshoring behavior of service firms and its influence on their foreign entry mode choice", Nyenrode Business University.

Van Nieuwkerk, M. (2006), *Dutch Golden Glory*, Becht Press, Haarlem.

Van Veenstra, M.L.E., M. Yakop, and P.A.G. van Bergeijk (2010), "Economic Diplomacy, the Level of Development and Trade", *Discussion Papers in Diplomacy*, The Netherlands Institute of International Relations, Clingendael.

Wölfl, A., I. Wanner, T. Kozluk and G. Nicoletti (2009), "Ten Years of Product Market Reform in OECD Countries: Insights from a Revised PMR Indicator", *OECD Economics Department Working Papers*, No. 695, OECD Publishing.

World Economic Forum (WEF) (2011), *The Global Competitiveness Report 2011-12*, World Economic Forum, Geneva.

Chapter 2

The Dutch labour market: Preparing for the future

The well performing labour market has delivered low unemployment and relatively stable wage developments. However, it is divided into a small flexible segment and a large more rigid segment, where the adjustment burden of external shocks falls disproportionally on the first group. At the same time, labour utilisation is relatively low, despite a relatively high overall participation rate, due to a high frequency of part-time employment, a low effective retirement age and a high use of disability benefits. Looking ahead, it is unlikely that the organisation of the labour market will allow the economy to continue reaping fully the benefits of globalisation. That would require a labour market that facilitates the allocation of increasingly scarce labour resources to their best use and mobilises underutilised labour resources to counter the ageing related contraction of the labour force.

At the overall level, the labour market has adapted well to globalisation as reflected by prolonged periods of low unemployment. However, this strong performance masks a labour utilisation rate (defined as hours worked relative to working age population) that is about 7½ per cent lower than the European average. The positive effect of a high participation rate is offset by the highest rate of part-time employment in the OECD, an effective retirement age that, despite recent increases, is still several years lower than the mandatory retirement age and an extensive use – despite a reduction in enrolment – of disability benefits. Moreover, the labour market is characterised by a small flexible segment (often younger workers on temporary contracts or self-employed) and a large more rigid segment (often older and better skilled workers with strong social protection). The adjustment to external shocks falls disproportionally on the first group, positively as well as negatively. Possibly more worrying in the context of globalisation is that productivity growth has been lower than in other OECD countries, indicating that the labour market may not be sufficiently effective in transferring labour resources to new and fast growing sectors. Looking ahead, a concern is whether the organisation of the labour market facilitates the transfer of increasingly scarce labour resources at a time of continued globalisation and an ageing labour force. The first section of this chapter shows how the labour market so far has adjusted to globalisation. This is followed by an examination of avenues to foster efficient allocation of labour and mobilise additional labour resources.

The effect of globalisation on labour demand

Globalisation is leading to greater integration of national labour markets. Emerging economies have provided an unprecedented pool of labour, which, together with technological progress and continued liberalisation of international trade and capital flows, have allowed an unbundling of the production process of goods and services. As a result, advanced economies have benefited from access to these labour resources via imports, off shoring of production, and immigration (IMF, 2007). The internationalisation of the production chain has driven up wages for higher skilled workers in the advanced economies relative to lower skilled workers. In addition, technical changes have proved a powerful driver of increased wage dispersion (OECD, 2007a). Moreover, overall employment should benefit as the competition enhancing effect of globalisation boosts demand for final products, increasing labour demand at given real wages, and as greater external competition reduces wage pressures at given employment levels. However, whether this leads to a reduction in unemployment depends on whether labour resources are successfully reallocated from declining to expanding industries (OECD, 2007a).

The Dutch labour market has benefited from globalisation and skilled-biased technical change over recent decades, as reflected in higher employment, low and declining unemployment and modest structural mismatches (Figures 2.1 and 2.2). At the same time, a more efficient international division of labour has moved production up the value-added chain, fostering higher labour productivity and real wage growth (DNB, 2005; SER, 20008; Heyma and Theeuwes, 2008). Employment in sectors like agriculture, textile

Figure 2.1. **Labour market indicators**[1]

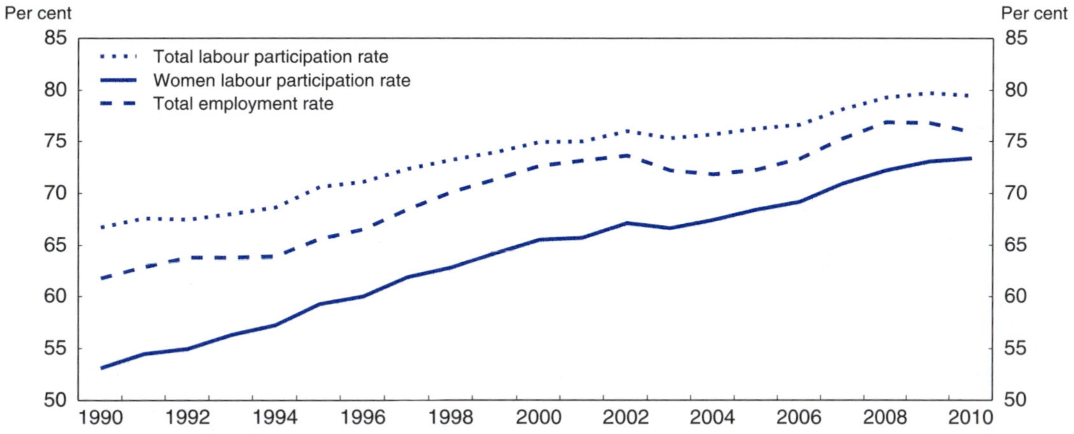

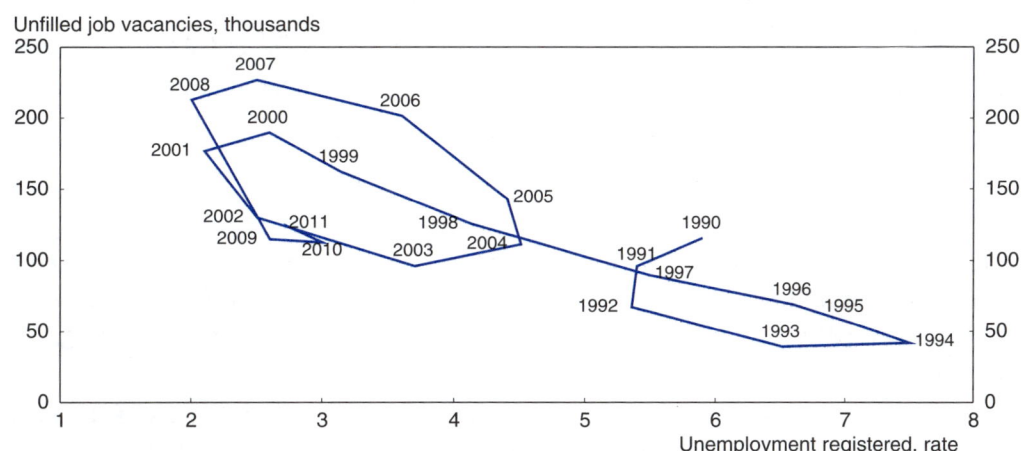

1. As a percentage of working-age population.
Source: OECD (2012), Labour Force Statistics Database.

StatLink ⟶ http://dx.doi.org/10.1787/888932614567

Figure 2.2. **Beveridge curve**

Source: OECD, Main Economic Indicators Database and CBS Statline.

StatLink ⟶ http://dx.doi.org/10.1787/888932614586

and (low-tech) manufacturing industries has fallen, while the share in business services has increased (Figures 2.3 and 2.4). Further specialisation took place within sectors, e.g. shipbuilders moved from producing heavy large-scale ships to high-tech vessels (SER, 2008). The shift towards knowledge intensive work was enabled by an increase in the overall skill level of employees (Figure 2.4).

Lower-skilled workers as a group have benefited from globalisation and skilled-biased technical change, mirrored in an increase in their real wages and an unemployment rate that is less than half the EU15 average.[1] On the other hand, they have benefited less than high-skilled workers, as there has been a concurrent shift in relative labour demand in the favour of the latter (outpacing the substantial increase in supply). This has led to an increasing rate of return on investment in human capital (and higher earning dispersion) since the early 1990s (Jacobs, 2004; Jacobs and Webbink, 2006; CPB, 2008; OECD, 2008a).[2] Nonetheless, wage dispersion remains compressed compared to most OECD countries

Figure 2.3. **Employment shifts to knowledge intensive services**
1990-2009, as percentage of total employment

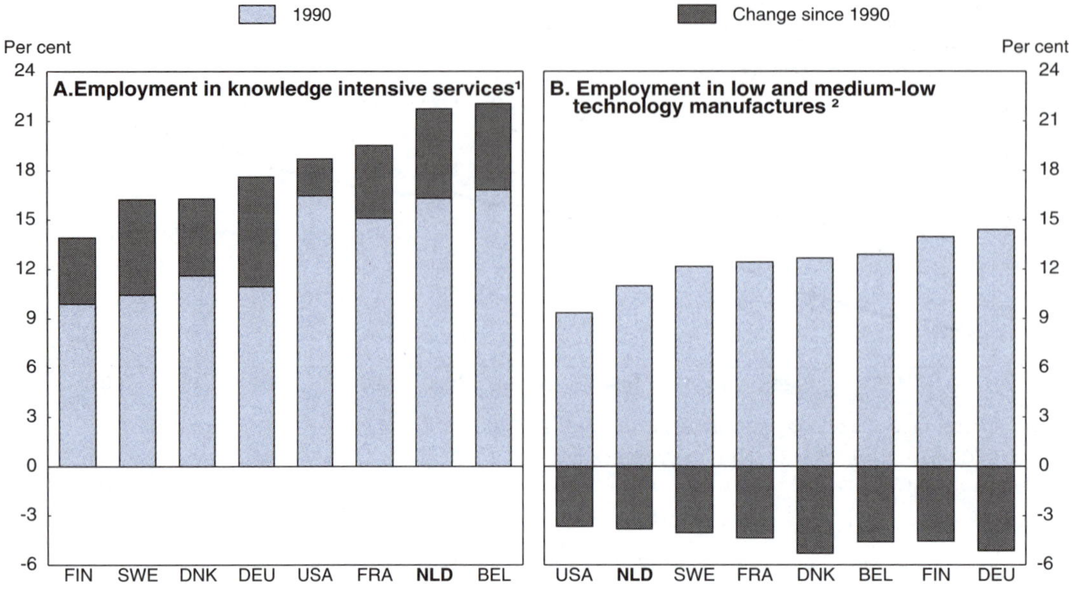

1990 — Change since 1990

A. Employment in knowledge intensive services[1]
FIN SWE DNK DEU USA FRA **NLD** BEL

B. Employment in low and medium-low technology manufactures[2]
USA **NLD** SWE FRA DNK BEL FIN DEU

1. Knowledge-intensive market services refers to Post and Telecommunications (ISIC Rev.3, division 64), Finance and insurance (division 65-67), and business activities (division 71-74).
2. Low and medium-low technology manufactures refers to manufactures excluding chemicals and chemicals products (ISIC rev.3, division 24), manufactures of machinery and equipment, n.e.c (division 29), electrical and optical equipment (division 30-33), and transport equipment (division 34-35).

Source: OECD (2012), *STAN Structural Analysis Database*.

StatLink ⟶ http://dx.doi.org/10.1787/888932614605

(Figure 2.5). Moreover, there are no strong indications that globalisation has threatened the jobs and wages of middle-skilled workers (CPB, 2008; Groot and De Groot, 2011), in contrast with findings for the United Kingdom and the United States (Goos and Manning, 2007; Autor *et al.*, 2008).

Over the past decades, there has been an increase in the flexible part of the labour market, which may have facilitated the reallocation of labour resources. Nowadays, about a quarter of the Dutch labour market consists of workers on temporary contracts and self-employed individuals, who are typically younger and lower skilled (Cörvers *et al.*, 2011). This part of the labour market faces higher unemployment risk and lower social protection as this is positive related to job tenure (*e.g.* lower severance pay, unemployment benefits as well as sickness coverage). The implication is that the adjustment burden from external shocks falls disproportionally on this group. At the same time, globalisation is making tax bases more mobile, making risk sharing via the tax benefit system more difficult. It should noted, though, that part of the group with short-term contacts consists of students that combine studies with small hour jobs, facilitating school-to-work transition (OECD, 2008 and 2010). In addition, the rest of the labour market (often older and high-skilled workers with permanent contracts) typically has high social protection (in terms of severance pay and unemployment benefit) that increases with tenure, giving few incentives for changing employment and thus often denying expanding sectors easy access to experienced high-skilled workers. Moreover, employers of this group of workers have incentives to provide (job-specific) training.

Figure 2.4. **Employment of high-skilled workers increased**
As a percentage of total employment

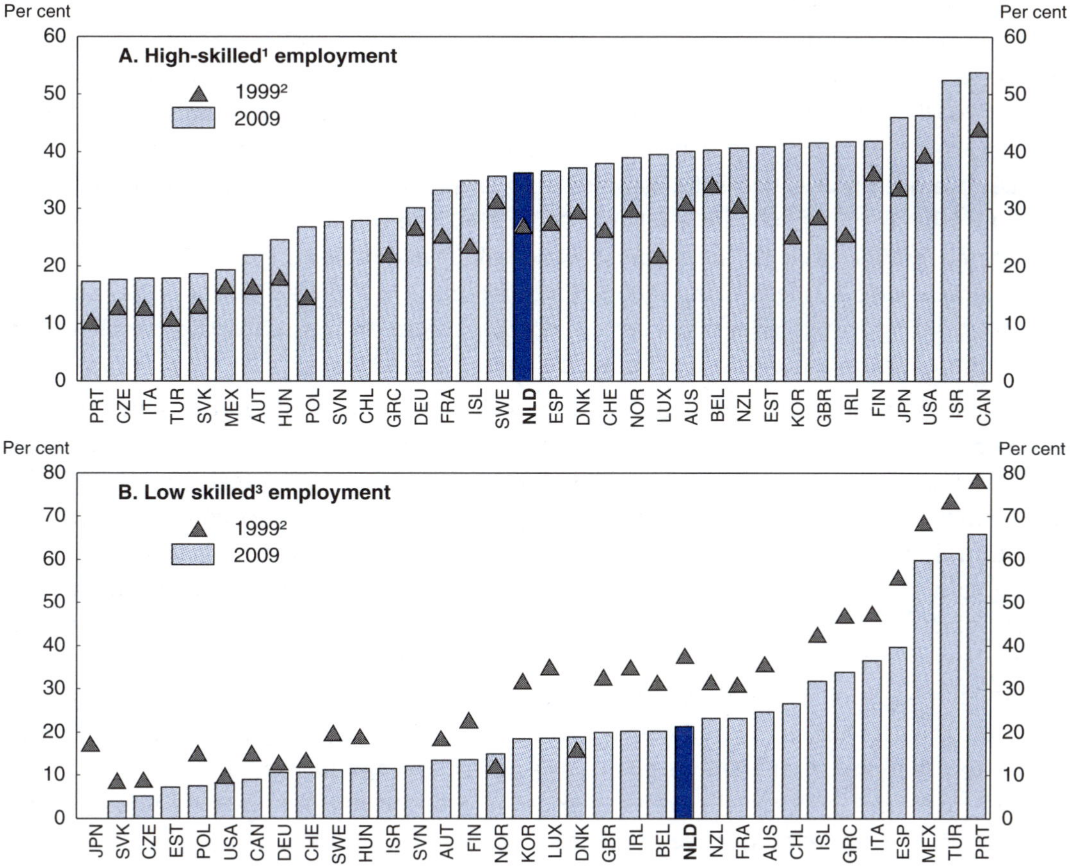

A. High-skilled[1] employment
▲ 1999[2]
2009

B. Low skilled[3] employment
▲ 1999[2]
2009

1. High-skilled workers are defined as workers with tertiary education or higher.
2. 1999 not available for Chile, Estonia, Israel and Slovenia.
3. Low skill workers are defined as workers with pre-primary, primary and lower secondary education.

Source: OECD (2012), *Education at a Glance Database*.

StatLink ⟶ http://dx.doi.org/10.1787/888932614624

Figure 2.5. **Wage dispersion is relatively small**
High skilled earning to low skilled earnings ratio, 2008[1]

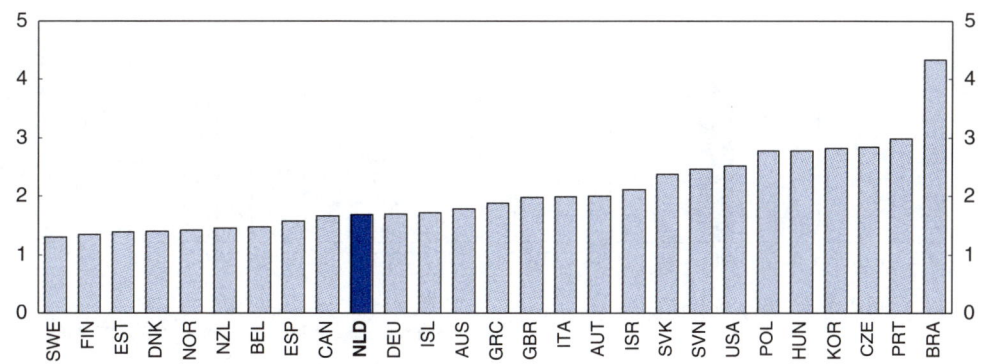

1. 25-64 year-old population. 2005 for Australia, 2006 for Austria, Belgium, Denmark, Greece, Iceland, Italy, the Netherlands, Poland, Portugal, Sweden and Slovenia, 2007 for Canada, Finland, Korea and Spain.

Source: OECD (2010), *OECD Education at a Glance*.

StatLink ⟶ http://dx.doi.org/10.1787/888932614643

Looking ahead, it is unlikely that the organisation of the labour market into a relatively small flexible segment and a much larger rigid segment within the context of an ageing labour force will allow the economy to fully reap the benefits of future globalisation. That would require a labour market that can reallocate increasingly scarce labour resources to their best use, particularly in sectors where the economy enjoys a comparative advantage (OECD, 2007b and c). Such reallocation would raise (a relatively low) productivity growth (Figure 2.6).[3] A possible contributing factor to low productivity growth is that the labour market has been more successful in preserving employment for low-skilled workers than in many other countries (Figure 2.4, Panel B). By 2040, the working age population will have contracted by 10%, while the dependency ratio will have doubled (Figure 2.7). In addition, a considerable part of the retiring labour force is employed in traditional manufacturing sectors, adding to the necessary speed of adjustment to maintain the Dutch export performance at the same time as population ageing accelerates.

Accelerating globalisation increases the premium on flexibility in the sense that the reallocation of resources across sectors, firms and occupations allows firms to make the necessary move up the value-added chain and boost productivity growth (Rae and Sollie, 2007). Moreover, globalisation is becoming increasingly complex, moving from the traditional trade in products, to "trade in tasks" as different stages and tasks of the production process are outsourced to various countries (Baldwin, 2006; Akçomak et al., 2010; Gelauff et al., 2010). In this respect, the Dutch labour market is not well adapted to such changes as labour mobility is relatively low with long average job-tenures and unemployment spells, especially among older workers (where the incidence of long-term unemployment is 46% compared with 43% for the OECD average) (Figure 2.8). Even in terms of job-to-job mobility, the Dutch position is about average in the OECD (OECD, 2010a). Indeed, there is a concern that older workers are becoming increasingly misallocated, i.e. they could be more productive in other jobs (Euwals et al., 2009).

Figure 2.6. **Labour productivity growth**
Measured as annual compound growth of GDP per hour worked between 1990 and 2010

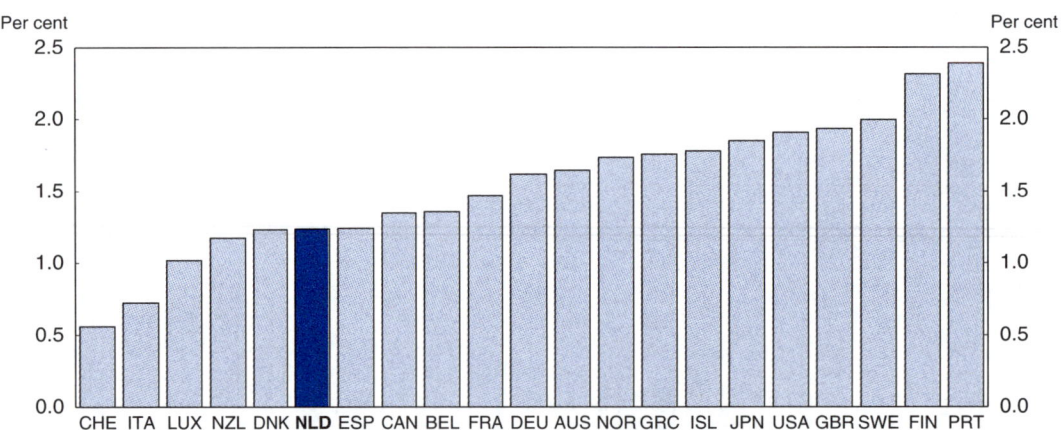

Source: OECD (2012), Productivity Database.

StatLink http://dx.doi.org/10.1787/888932614662

Figure 2.7. **Population ageing**

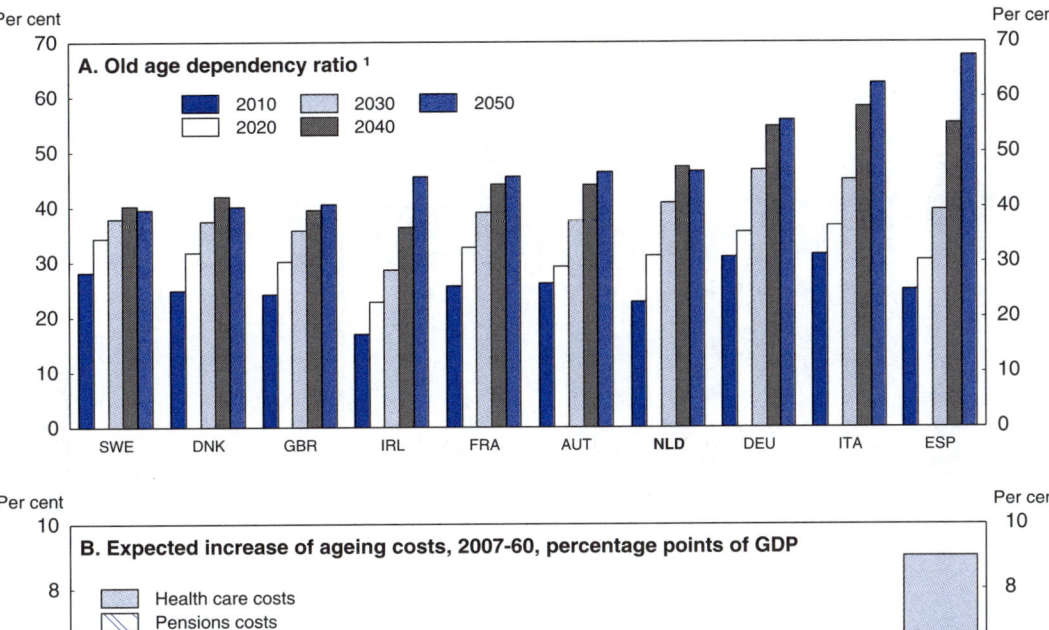

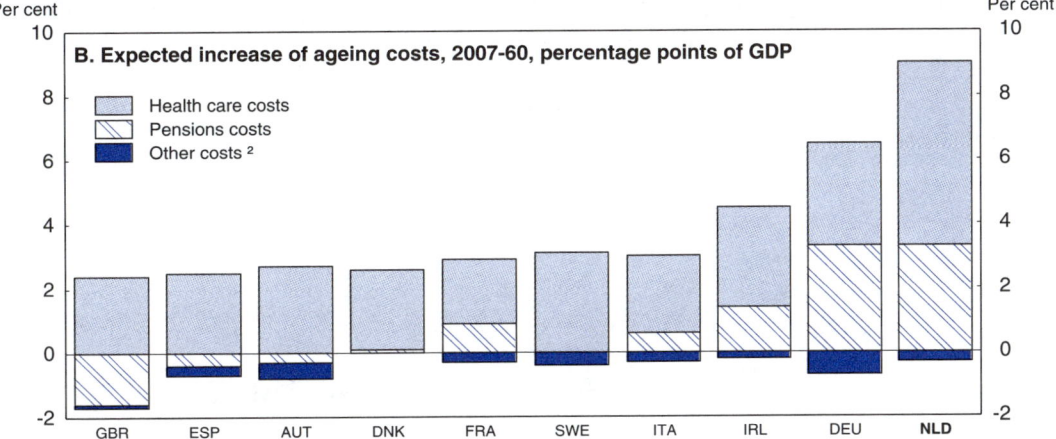

1. Population 65 years and over divided by 15-64 years population.
2. Unemployment benefits and education costs.

Source: OECD (2011), *Historical Population Data and Projections Database (1950-2050)*, and European Commission (2009), "2009 Ageing Report: Economic and budgetary projections for the EU-27 Members States (2008-2060)".

StatLink ⟶ http://dx.doi.org/10.1787/888932614681

Policies to foster labour mobility

Easing employment protection legislation

The main impediment to the reallocation of labour is strict employment protection legislation (EPL) for workers with permanent contracts (Figure 2.9). In the Dutch system, there are two routes to terminate open-ended contracts: the costly but predictable court route or the cheaper but less predictable and lengthier administrative route (via the public employment service body – "UWV") (See also the 2008 *Survey* for a detailed description). The system benefits workers with a strong labour market position as severance pay increases relatively fast with age and with income, giving increasing incentives for remaining in the same job.[4]

As discussed in the 2010 *Survey*, strict EPL for workers with permanent contracts reduces labour turnover, hampering productivity-enhancing reallocation of labour resources. This is particularly relevant in the context of globalisation, as internationally exposed firms often need to reorganise workplaces and move/attract employment to new economic activities. A

Figure 2.8. **Job mobility is low**

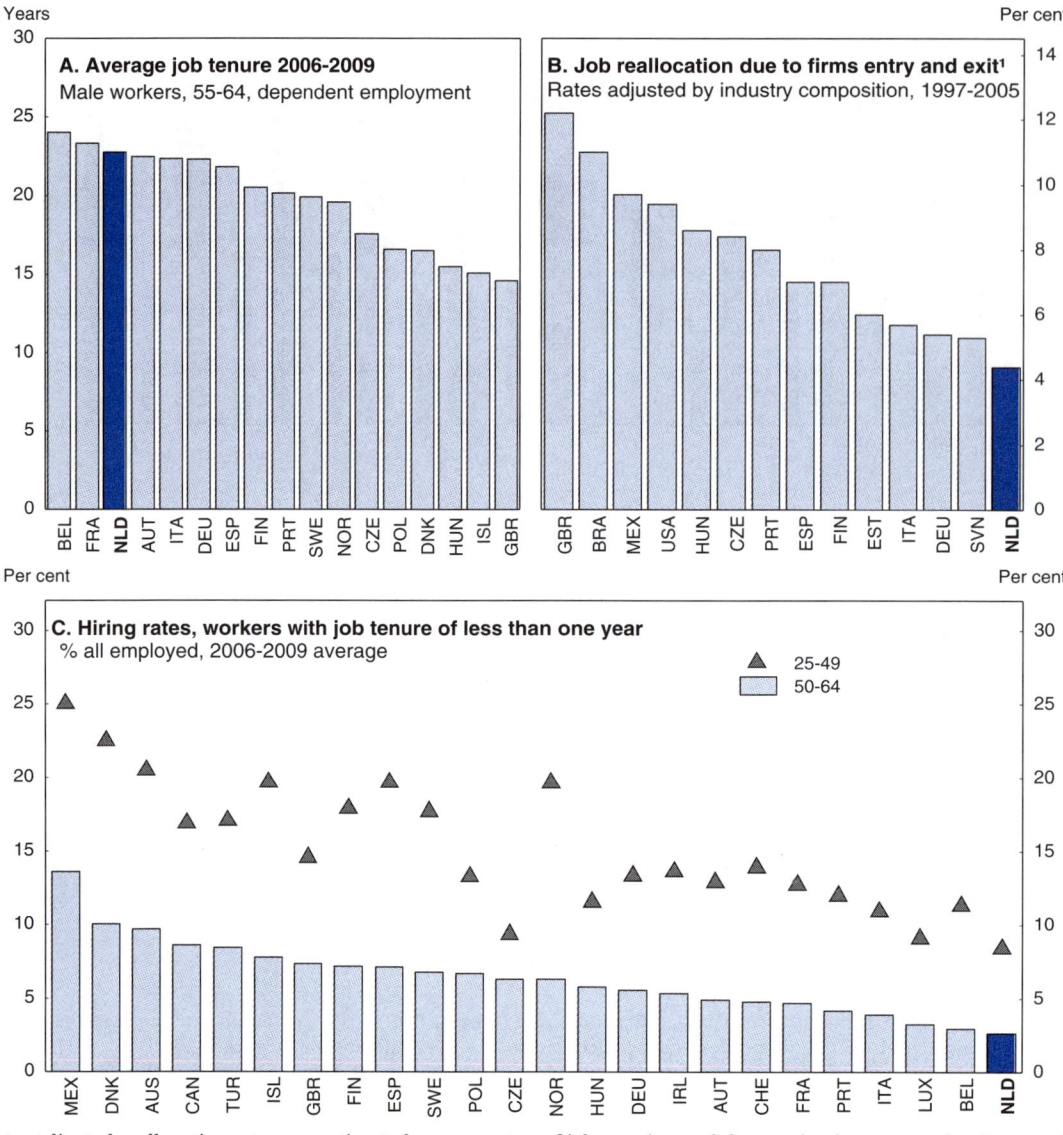

1. Adjusted reallocation rates are estimated average rates of job creation and destruction by entry and exit to total dependent employment that would be observed in each country if it had the same industry composition as the average country.

Source: OECD (2012), *OECD Employment Outlook Database* and OECD (2009), *OECD Employment Outlook*.

StatLink ⟹ http://dx.doi.org/10.1787/888932614700

particular problem is that accumulated severance pay rights are lost when changing jobs, severely reducing the incentives for older workers with substantial accumulated rights to change jobs (Euwals et al., 2009). In addition, older unemployed have high reservation wages, resulting from a combination of their often generous severance pay and generous unemployment benefits as well as strong seniority element in wages (see below).

Easing EPL for workers with permanent contracts can contribute to an improved allocation of labour by increasing job flow via more exit and entry in and out of unemployment, reduced incidence of long term unemployment, more job creation and destruction, and higher job-to-job flows (OECD, 2004; Deelen et al., 2006; Haltiwanger et al.,

Figure 2.9. **Employment Protection Legislation (EPL) for workers with permanent contracts remains high**

Index scale of 0-6 from least to most restrictive, 2008[1]

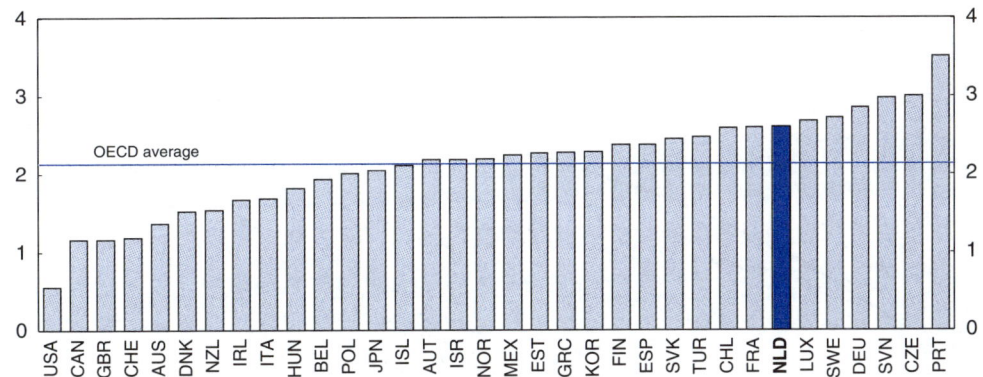

1. 2009 for France, the Netherlands and Portugal. This indicator refers to version 3 as defined in the methodology.
Source: OECD (2012), OECD Employment Protection database.

StatLink http://dx.doi.org/10.1787/888932614719

2008; Bassanini et al., 2008).[5] For example, reducing EPL to the level of Denmark would shorten average unemployment duration by 5 months to 15 months and reduce the share of long-term unemployed by 3 percentage points (Deelen and Jongen, 2009). Moreover, a less strict and more predictable EPL system could make the Netherlands a more attractive country for foreign direct investment – a government objective (see Chapter 1). Over the years, several attempts aimed at reforming the EPL system, such as the effort to establish an upper ceiling on severance pay of EUR 75 000, have failed. Smaller changes to the system, however, have been introduced. The Last-In-First-Out firing principle has been replaced by the principle of collectively dismissed workers reflecting the overall age composition of the firm's employees, moving some of the unemployment risk to older workers. More recently, there has been an adjustment of the general court guidelines for severance pay, reducing somewhat severance pay across the board, but especially for younger workers.

The small successes in reducing severance pay do not suffice and renewed efforts to implement an upper ceiling on severance pay are needed. Moreover, there is a need to make the dismissal system simpler, more predictable and less time-consuming, as recommended in previous OECD *Surveys* and *Going for Growth*, including clearly specifying the rules governing layoffs in law and marking court appeals only possible *ex post*. Such reform would promote productivity-enhancing reallocation of labour and enhance older workers' job-to-job mobility, particularly if combined with reform of the generous unemployment benefits (see below).

Reducing tenure-based pay

The return to tenure in the Netherlands is relatively high, making it unattractive for older workers to switch jobs, as this often implies lower wages (Deelen, 2011; Van Vuuren and De Hek, 2009; Borghans et al., 2007).[6] Male employees between 55-59 earn almost 160% of the level at the age 25-29: a profile that is roughly comparable to Belgium and Germany, but much higher than in the UK, the US and the Nordic countries, where the wage-tenure profiles tend to decline after 60 (Figure 2.10). The increasing tenure profile can be explained

Figure 2.10. **High tenure premia for men**[1]
Salary of 25-29 year old = 100

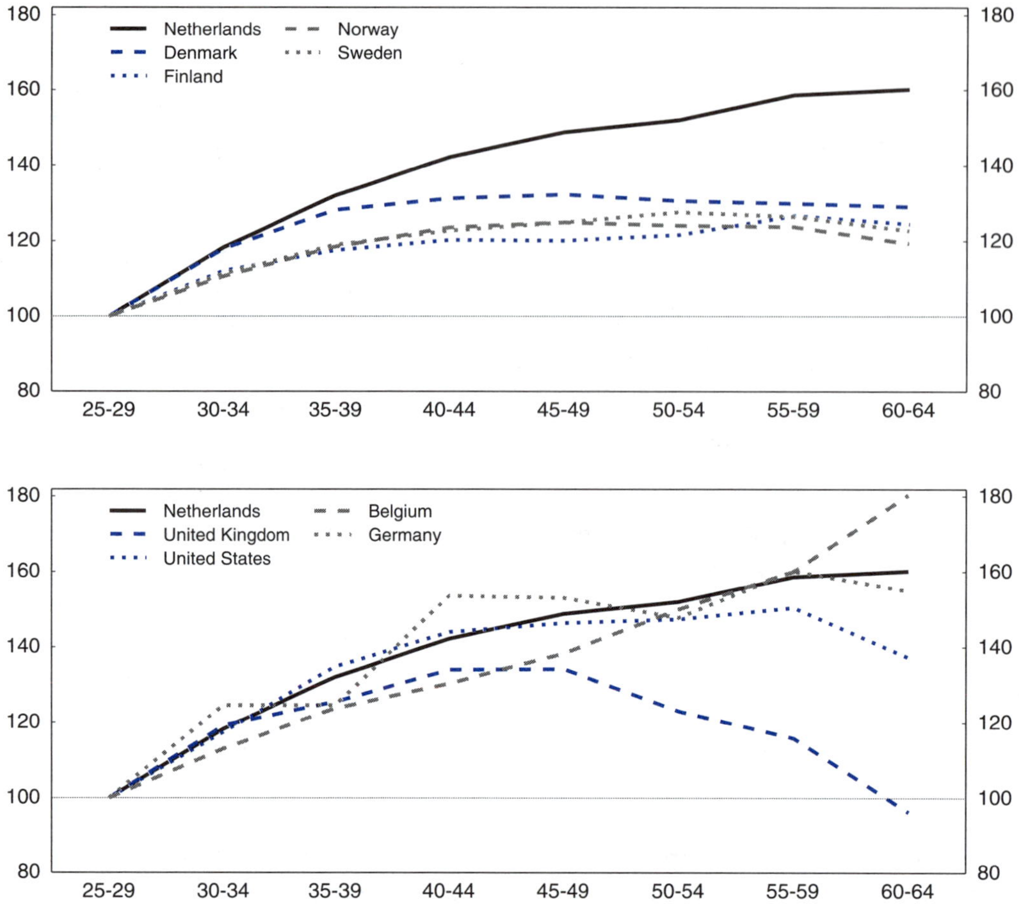

1. The data refer to full-time workers and to various years over the period 1998-2003, and to median salaries for Denmark and the Netherlands.

Source: OECD, *Earnings Database*, unpublished data.

StatLink ⟶ http://dx.doi.org/10.1787/888932614738

to some extent by the strict employment protection legislation, which tightens with increasing seniority and boosts insiders' bargaining power (Deelen, 2011). In recent years, the social partners have tried to move away from tenure-based pay by basing wage increases more on individual performance (see below). This has had a positive effect on labour mobility for the concerned companies (Gielen *et al.*, 2006). Nonetheless, around 70% of the collective agreements provide an automatic yearly salary increase (Ministry of Social Affairs and Employment, 2011a). Moreover, for older workers who have often reached the highest grade of their wage scale, wage reduction is still very unusual (Van Vuuren and De Hek, 2009). Thus, the reallocation of older workers can be further supported if social partners would reduce the automatic tenure element in wages. In addition, such a measure may enhance reemployment chances of the older unemployed.

Another reason why social partners should address the issue of tenure based wage is that the current wage formation system may drive up wage costs, eroding external competitiveness. The strong tenure element in wage means that population aging leads to an automatic wage increase that is not related to productivity developments (OECD, 2008b). Additional pressures on total wage costs may arise from the need to finance increasing ageing related costs, particularly in the area of health care (Chapter 3). Indeed, the great majority of employers expect ageing to push up wage costs (Van Dalen *et al.*, 2008). These issues can be addressed by changing the wage formation system to secure a closer link between wage and productivity developments.

Greater wage flexibility can support better allocation of increasingly scarce labour resources

Nominal labour costs in the Netherlands have developed broadly in line with most euro area competitors over the latest decade, notwithstanding the relatively tight labour market. This has been supported by the highly co-ordinated and broad wage-setting framework (including administrative extension of agreements) that takes into account the macroeconomic situation, reduces transaction costs, and secures common standards for working conditions (Box 2.1). However, the system also often delivers relatively high wage increases after the economy is slowing down, damaging cost-competitiveness at an unfortunate point in the business cycle (Leering, 2007; OECD, 2008b; SER, 2006). Indeed, there has been upward pressure on unit labour costs (Figure 2.11). In addition, strong

---

Box 2.1. Wage bargaining and a shift to decentralisation

Compared to other EU countries, a higher share of the labour force in the Netherlands is covered by collective agreements (about 80% of the dependent labour force against 60% for the EU27), although the union density (of about 20%) is somewhat below average (European Commission, 2011). The high collective coverage results from the relatively high enrolment in employers' organisations and is complemented by the ministerial extension of collective agreements within an industrial sector to employers who are not members of an employer's organisation (*Algemeen Verbindend Verklaren*) (SER, 2007a).

The bargaining takes predominantly place at the sector-level: sector agreements account for about 90% of all employees covered, against 10% at the company level (Ministry of Social Affairs and Employment, 2011a). The lower level bargaining is accompanied by co-ordination at the central level. In some years, this involves agreements between federations on wage developments, or – occasionally with involvement of the government – the settlement of other working conditions or social pacts (*e.g.* on pensions, working hours, disability benefits) (Leering, 2007; Ministry of Social Affairs and Employment, 2008). In years where employers and union federations do not set common wage recommendations at the central level, trade union federations tend to set a maximum for wage bids, thereby taking into account macroeconomic conditions (Leering, 2007; SER 2007a). The ceiling serves as a guideline for associated trade unions when negotiating (contract) wages at the industrial or company level. Upward deviations from the rule are mainly via "incidental wage" growth (*i.e.* wage drift), including *e.g.* promotions, allowances, bonuses and dividend payments.

In recent decades, decentralisation and wage differentiation have been promoted. For instance, more collective agreements contain performance-based pay arrangement (like profit sharing, individual bonuses, or a salary increase depending on performance) or other flexible pay arrangements (like one off payments being independent of any performance) (SER, 2006 and 2008). Most collective arrangements at the sector level provide "opt-out" clauses (*dispensatiebepalingen*), allowing firms to (partly) deviate from branch agreements under certain conditions, although these are seldom used (SER, 2007a; Basis en Beleid, 2007; Regioplan 2008). At the lower end of the wage distribution, the real statutory minimum wage has been reduced, and the lowest adult salary in collective agreements has been brought close to the statutory minimum wage level (SER, 2007a; Ministry of Social Affairs and Employment, 2011a).

Figure 2.11. **Unit labour costs have increased relatively fast**

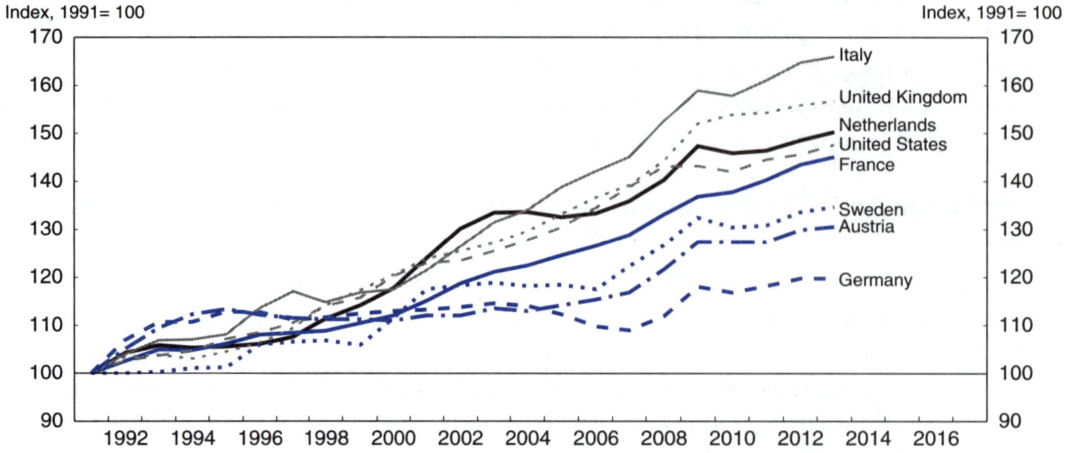

Source: OECD (2012), OECD Economic Outlook Database.

StatLink ⟶ http://dx.doi.org/10.1787/888932614757

centralisation/co-ordination tends to preserve relative wage structures, distorting wage signals between declining and expanding sectors and thus hampering labour reallocation, putting the Netherlands at a disadvantage in a globalised world (OECD, 2007b; OECD, 2004).[7]

In the future, it will become increasingly important to align wage and productivity developments, both to preserve external competitiveness and to assure the proper allocation of increasingly scarce labour resources. The Wassenaar Agreement from 1982 (the founding document for the current wage formation process) included an objective of more decentralised wage agreements – a move reinforced in a 1993 agreement (SER, 2006; Ministry of Social Affairs and Employment, 2008). The social partners have stated that decentralisation should be pursued and could include collective agreements at the company level, fewer detailed rules and regulations in collective agreements, further emphasis on performance-based pay and a degree of macroeconomic policy co-ordination (SER, 2007a; SER, 2008). So far, decentralisation measures include wider use of performance-based pay arrangements and greater availability of (seldom used) opt-out clauses (Box 2.1). However, sector level wage agreements still dominate, and have even been increasing (Table 2.1).

Decentralisation of wage negotiations would enhance the signal value of relative wages and the productivity enhancing reallocation of labour resources. In this respect, a continued good employment record would depend on not only moving away from the strong co-ordination, but also moving wage setting to the local level as otherwise there is a risk that the wage determination system would neither take into account macroeconomic conditions nor local productivity developments (Bassanini and Duval, 2006; OECD, 2004). In addition, the increase in job turnover is likely to boost on-the-job life-long learning effects, furthering productivity growth (Box 2.2). Indeed, more relative wage flexibility sends clear signals for human capital investment (OECD, 2004). At the same time, more decentralised wage formation would facilitate that tenure-based wage profiles are in line with productivity developments, enabling older workers to remain employed.

Reforming the wage determination system requires action from the government and social partners. The government should as a first step towards more decentralised wage setting limit or abolish ministerial extensions of sector collective agreements, as they

Table 2.1. **Workers covered by collective agreements**[1]

	Collective agreements	Covered workers	Share of workers covered at:	
			Sector level	Company level
	Total number	Millions	% of all covered workers	
2003	712	5.8	88.7	11.3
2004	759	6.1	88.2	11.8
2005	748	6.2	86.1	13.9
2006[2]	538	4.8	81.4	18.6
2007	715	5.8	89.9	10.1
2008	716	5.9	90.7	9.3
2009	748	6.1	90.3	9.7
2010	709	6.4	91.0	9.0
2011	688	6.1	91.3	8.7

1. Concerns regular, notified collective agreements.
2. Outlier because of lower registration.
Source: Voorjaarsrapportages CAO-afspraken.

Box 2.2. Life-long learning incentives

In a globalised world, high human capital is key to create greater mobility as it facilitates life – long learning, boosting the ability to change jobs (Baldwin, 2006; Rae and Sollie, 2008). However, Dutch workers have few incentives for investing in life-long learning. Only about 40% of all employees are involved in training, whereas the share is double that in Denmark, Finland and Sweden (Euwals *et al.*, 2009). The combination of EPL that tightens with seniority and the strong seniority elements in wages gives strong incentives to keep the same job as long as possible thereby reducing the return on (non-firm specific) human capital accumulation. The effect of limited investment in human capital on mobility is exacerbated by the fact that the sector training funds ("O&O-fondsen") mainly focus on acquiring sector specific skills, instead of general training that can facilitate labour mobility between sectors and particularly out of declining sectors (Government, 2010a; SER, 2011). Using the funds collectively for more general training should be promoted but may be complicated by the fact that the size of the funds differs substantially among sectors. The 2013 Vitality scheme contains training budgets specifically targeted to facilitate mobility between sectors.

---

restrict the scope for local wage setting. At the same time, social partners should facilitate the use of op-out clauses to allow firms to deviate from sector agreements – a little known option (especially among SMEs) as almost three-quarter of companies are unaware of the possibility, which is thus hardly ever used despite that most agreements contains such clauses (Regioplan, 2007; Regioplan, 2008; Basis en Beleid, 2007). This implies that social partners should ensure that collective agreements contain clear procedural guidance for judging opt-out requests, which is often lacking (Basis en Beleid, 2007). Even better would be to mandate that opt-out clauses are solely determined by the directly involved parties at the local level, doing away with sector approvals.

More importantly would be for the social partners to reorganise the wage formation system to move wage negotiations to the local level. This could, for example following the Danish model, be achieved by maintaining central or sector negotiations for framework conditions (such as work time rules, pension, etc.) while wages are determined at the local level. The government could contribute to this process with a reform of the strict employment protection legislation to counter the potentially strong bargaining position of older workers, particularly in SMEs.

Mobilising underutilised labour resources

The flows of skilled workers across national borders and the global competition for talent have become important aspects of globalisation (OECD, 2008c and 2009a). The Netherlands benefits from non-EU high-skilled immigrants, reflecting their substantial contributions to economic and innovative activities and their minor demands on the education and social welfare systems (Theeuwes, 2011; Roodenburg et al., 2005; Muysken and Ziesemer, 2011). Compared to other countries, however, the share of highly educated immigrants in high-skill jobs is relatively low, despite the admission policy for such immigrants being relatively liberal (Berkhout et al., 2010) (Figure 2.12). Various – mostly demand-driven – admission policies are in place to support entrance of non-EU high-skilled workers (Box 2.3). Not all of these policies reflect the fact that the decision of a high-skilled person to settle abroad depends on a broad range of factors, including career and financial opportunities, the presence of highly ranked research institutions, attractive living conditions or personal reasons (OECD, 2009a; Berkhout et al., 2010). Moreover, demand for immigrant workers is often for low-skilled workers, for instance in agriculture and construction, in part reflecting problems of mobilising these workers domestically.[8]

The "knowledge worker" scheme is driven by (mainly larger) firms' demand for high-skilled workers and is based on long-term work relationships between the employer and employee. It does not allow for short time assignments that are often required in a globalised world and thus hampers employment of foreign staff, or complicates training of employees of foreign companies in the Netherlands (for instance on their latest purchase of Dutch equipment) – an issue also identified in the new policies for the business sector (Chapter 1) (Top-team High Tech, 2011). To address part of this problem, a short stay (i.e. less than 3 months) work permit for high-skilled workers was introduced in early 2012 as a two-year pilot.[9] As such a scheme enables a better match of labour supply and demand, it should be made permanent. Another issue on the demand side is the income

Figure 2.12. **Immigrants in high-skill jobs**
As a percentage of all persons in high-skill jobs, 2009

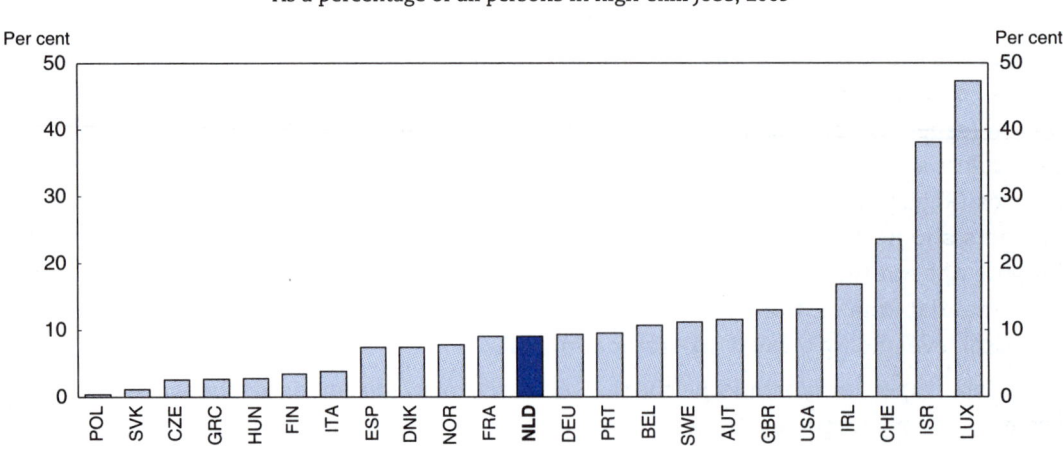

Source: OECD (2011), International Migration Outlook.

StatLink ⟹ http://dx.doi.org/10.1787/888932614776

> **Box 2.3. Polices to attract high-skilled workers**
>
> The Netherlands has implemented policies to attract high-skilled workers from outside the EEA. On the demand side, the "knowledge workers scheme" exempts workers from work permit requirements if their yearly income meets the gross annual income criterion of EUR 51 239 (in 2012) or about 10% more than an average full time gross wage. Young workers below 30 have to earn at least EUR 37 575 (the average wage for the 25-30 year olds is about EUR 33 000); while no income requirements are in place for scientific researchers and doctors in training. Besides the fact that the employer has to be enrolled in the high-skilled workers programme, income is essentially the only criterion, making the scheme more straightforward than the EU "blue card" scheme. Since its introduction in 2004, the number of immigrants under this scheme has increased from 2 200 in 2005 to 6 570 in 2010, and accounts for about a third of all work permits distributed to workers from outside the EEA (and Romania and Bulgaria). Moreover, to facilitate the entrance of high-skilled workers for a short stay, a short-term work permit for high-skilled workers has been introduced in January 2012 (in the form of a pilot project).
>
> The Netherlands has also implemented policies to increase the supply of high-skilled workers: International Bachelor and Master students from outside the EEA are entitled to find a job within a year of graduation from a Dutch University (Zoekjaar Afgestudeerde Buitenlandse Studenten), which pays at least EUR 26 931. The government plans to explore possibilities to increase the retention rate of international students, for example by encouraging students to learn Dutch and fostering connections between students and the private sector (Ministry of Education, Culture and Science, 2011).* Similarly, Master and PhD graduates from internationally highly ranked universities are allowed to stay for one year in the Netherlands to search for a job that pays as well as in the knowledge workers scheme (*Regeling Hoogopgeleiden*). In addition, there is a scheme for self-employed, whose access is granted based on personal skills and experience, a business plan and the potential contribution to the Dutch economy. In practice, few immigrants enter the Netherlands via these supply side measures (roughly one out of five high-skilled workers), of which the recent graduates are the most important group.
>
> Moreover, tax incentives are in place to attract high-skilled foreign workers via the "30% ruling", which is a tax-free allowance of 30% of the employee's salary for up to 10 years. To qualify for the allowance the foreign employee has to have specific expertise not readily available in the Dutch labour market, a criterion that is linked to the minimum income level of the knowledge workers scheme. The ruling has recently been revised to include foreign PhD candidates who graduated in the Netherlands and to exclude employees living in neighbouring countries within a short distance to the Dutch border.
>
> The most important country of origin for non-EEA high-skilled workers in the Netherlands is India (30% of recent yearly inflows), followed by the US (15%), and thereafter China, Turkey and Japan (INDIAC, 2010). Surveys suggest that most knowledge workers are employed in financial and business services (33% of total). Other important sectors are research and education (17%), manufacturing and utilities (13%), and transport and communication (11%) (Berkhout *et al.*, 2010).
>
> * A proxy for stay rates as calculated by the OECD suggest that the "stay rate" in the Netherlands is somewhat above the OECD average (OECD, 2011c).

criterion in the knowledge workers scheme, which some sectors, like creative industries (concerning sectors like art, entertainment, fashion design and architecture), consider too high, weakening their international competitiveness (Top-team Creative Industries, 2011). To address this particular bottleneck, the current income restrictions should be eased substantially. This should take the form of a general reduction (i.e. not sector specific) to avoid overly heterogeneous regulation among sectors (Chapter 1).

Further options to enhance the available pool of high-skilled workers should be explored. As recommended in the 2008 Survey, the (firm) demand-driven scheme should be supplemented by a scheme to expand the available supply of high skilled immigrants, who should be granted job-search visas to make themselves available on the Dutch labour market. Under such a scheme (for example in the form of a points based system to determine the relevant skill level) workers with desired characteristics would be granted a job-search visa without the *ex ante* requirement of a job contract – the latter should automatically lead to a work permit. Such a scheme has the advantages of expanding the availability of high-skilled workers for SMEs and of increasing their mobility between different employers (SER, 2007b; OECD, 2008b). Another – easy to implement – measure to boost the availability of high-skilled immigrants is to make it easier for non-EEA graduates from Dutch universities or internationally recognised foreign universities to seek employment by relaxing or abolishing current income restrictions and time limitations. Another avenue to explore is to be more active in recruiting high-skilled foreign workers through participation in international job fairs, more multilingual job postings and special job-search assistance to high-skilled immigrants who might lack host-country-specific knowledge (Chaloff and Lemaitre, 2009). For instance, Denmark has set up a "work in Denmark" centre in India to attract high-skilled immigrants, such as health care workers, engineers and IT and communications specialists (OECD, 2009b).

A large underutilised labour resource is the large number of high-skilled part-time female workers. Almost two-thirds of female workers hold part-time jobs, contributing to low average hours worked (Figures 2.13 and 2.14). As covered in the 2008 Survey, the high share of part-time work is partly linked to labour market policies that promote part-time employment, insufficient provision of child care services as well as high effective marginal taxes – in some specific cases even exceeding 100% (Ministry of Social Affairs and Employment, 2011b). Moreover, the tax benefit system is fairly complicated in this area, with for example no less than twelve different tax and subsidy measures in place to support parental income and/or labour participation, which are partly overlapping and countering each other (Government, 2010b; Ministry of Social Affairs and Employment, 2012a). Plans are being made to reduce the number of child benefits from 12 to 4 in 2014.

Efforts to raise hours worked have been stepped up. Child care related spending increased in the second half of the 2000s by more than 40% to reach 1.7% of GDP in 2010, including participation supporting measures as well as income support.[10] Moreover, the transferability of the tax credit for second earners is being phased out over 15 years to enhance employment incentives – a measure that was recently strengthened by abolishing the exception for families with young children. In addition, the double tax credit will be phased out of the reference minimum wage for calculating social assistance benefits in 20 steps from 2012 onwards to prevent the benefits from being higher than the minimum wage. Also from 2012 onwards, child care support provisions depend on the number of hours worked by the least-working parent. The government aims at streamlining supporting measures to make the system more transparent and effective (Ministry of Social Affairs and Employment, 2012a). As

Figure 2.13. **High incidence of female part-time employment**
Share of employed women working part-time, 2010

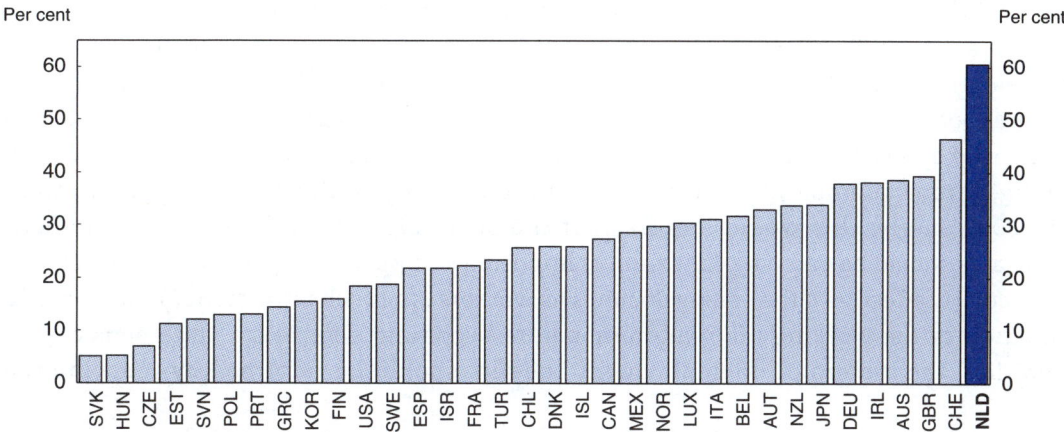

Source: OECD (2012), *Incidence of FTPT Employment – Common Definition Database.*
StatLink http://dx.doi.org/10.1787/888932614795

Figure 2.14. **Low average annual hours actually worked per worker**
2010 or latest year available[1]

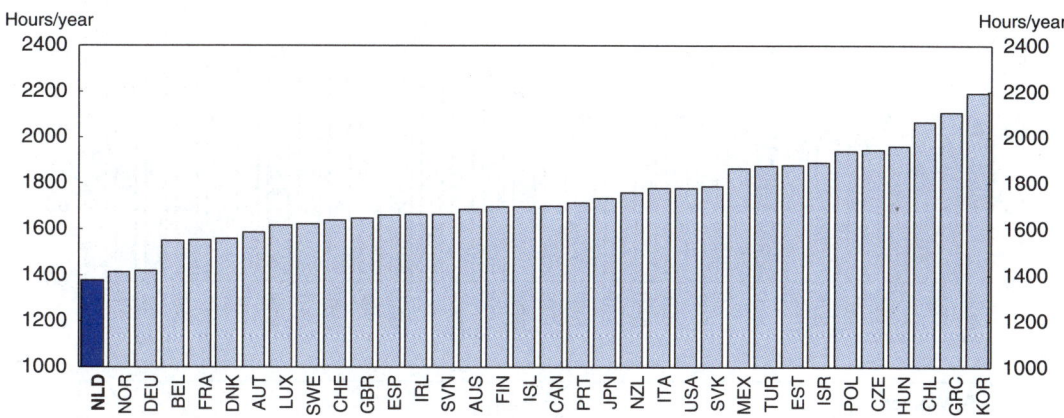

1. 2009 for Denmark, France, and Israel, 2008 for Switzerland.
Source: OECD (2012), *Average Annual Hours Actually Worked per Worker Database.*
StatLink http://dx.doi.org/10.1787/888932614814

recommended in the 2008 *Survey*, the effective marginal tax rates for second earners can be lowered by making child care support provisions more dependent on secondary earners' income rather than family income. In this respect, care should be taken in the design of such a measure to ensure that the effective marginal tax rates for second earners come down. It should be noted that boosting hours worked involve higher fiscal costs – something the government is preventing with the planned reduction in childcare spending of about EUR 1.5 billion by 2015 at a time when population ageing is accelerating. Indeed, given the current bias towards female part-time work, the effects of measures to promote female full-time work may only materialise over the medium-term. In this perspective, cuts in childcare support should be avoided so as not to deter the promotion of female full-time work. Moreover, frequent policy changes in childcare provisions may damage the balance of long-term decisions on how to combine work and care responsibilities. Hence, it is important to secure a long-term commitment to childcare policies to favour work-care decisions towards work.

The effective retirement age of men has increased from 60½ years in 2004 to 63 in 2010, whereas the retirement age for women increased by one year to 61 (Figure 2.15) – a trend that is reflecting past reforms to make early retirement less attractive (Statistics Netherlands, 2012). As the state pension age will be increased from 65 to 66 in 2020 and thereafter be linked to life expectancy, this should together with the "vitality scheme" further boost the effective retirement age.[11] The effectiveness of these measures could be enhanced by securing that older workers do not use a combination of high severance pay and generous unemployment benefits as a route to early retirement.[12] As discussed in the 2010 *Survey*, this would require that the strict EPL for workers with permanent contracts should be eased by, for example imposing an upper ceiling for severance pay and particularly effective if the ceiling declines as workers approach retirement (preferably as a function of the working life remaining before becoming eligible for state pension). In addition, the system of unemployment benefits should be reformed by reducing the

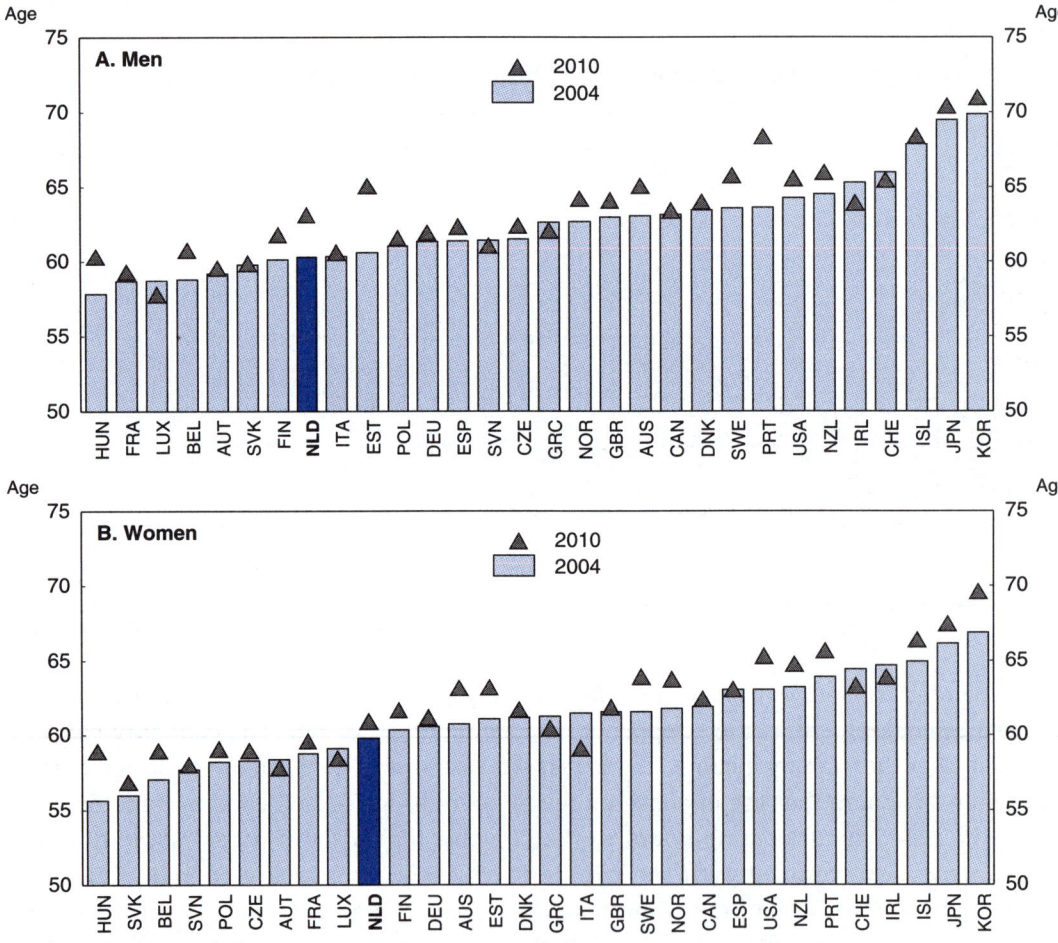

Figure 2.15. **The average retirement age is increasing**[1]

1. The average age of retirement is calculated as the average age of exit from the labour force during a 5-year period. Labour force (net) exits are estimated by taking the difference in the participation rate for each 5-year age group (40 and over) at the beginning of the 5-year period and the rate for the corresponding age group aged 5-years older at the end of the period

Source: OECD (2011), Statistics on average effective age and official age of retirement in OECD countries.

StatLink ⇒ http://dx.doi.org/10.1787/888932614833

maximum duration of 38 months for workers with long tenures. More dynamic search incentives can be given by maintaining the initial generosity of unemployment benefits, but gradually lowering it to the level of social assistance by the end of the benefit period. Moreover, the high upper ceiling for unemployment benefits – of about an annual EUR 35 000 – should be reduced to sharpen search incentives for high-income workers.

Another potentially underutilised labour resource is the high number of disability recipients. Despite a fall in the number of recipients following reforms, the share of the working-age population receiving disability benefits remains high compared to most OECD countries (Figure 2.16). This partly reflects a recent strong inflow in the special system for younger disabled people (Wajong), after decentralising activation responsibilities for social assistance recipients to the municipalities (Box 2.4). To increase employment of these younger workers (as well as older disabled), the government plans to reform and partly merge the schemes for social assistance, younger disabled workers and sheltered work.

Figure 2.16. **The number of disability recipients remains high**[1]
Per cent of population aged 20-64 receiving disability benefits

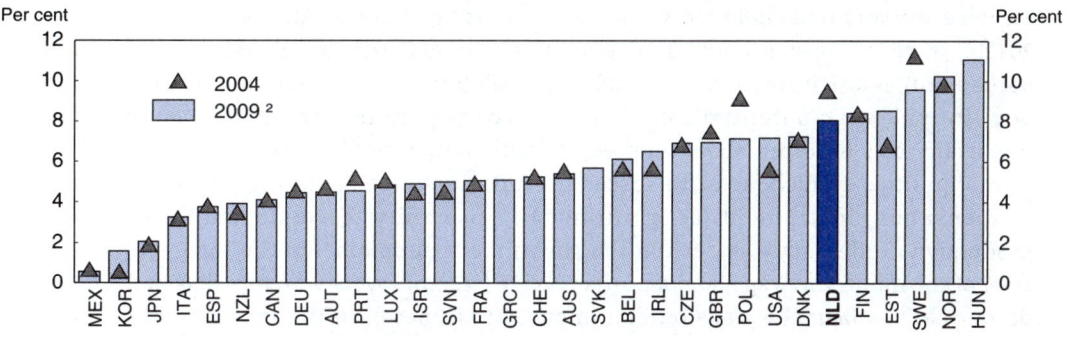

1. Disability benefits include benefits received from schemes to which beneficiaries have paid contributions (contributory), programmes financed by general taxation (non contributory) and work injury schemes.
2. Or latest year available. 2005 for Luxembourg; 2007 for Canada, France, Italy, Spain, and Poland; 2008 for Austria, Belgium, the United Kingdom, Greece, Ireland, Japan, Korea, Slovenia; 2010 for Denmark Estonia, Hungary, Israel and Portugal.

Source: OECD (2012), Going for Growth.

StatLink http://dx.doi.org/10.1787/888932614852

However, integrating (partly) disabled younger workers into the labour market is considerably more challenging compared to other groups, especially in light of globalisation that shifts labour demand towards high-skilled workers. One factor that is likely to hamper the smooth integration of younger workers with low earning potential are the collective minimum youth wages that tend to hover considerably above the statutory minimum wage – depending on the exact age, sector and specific collective agreement (Table 2.2). Hence, for younger workers the social partners should consider bringing the lowest wage of the collective agreements towards the statutory level – an attempt that has already been successfully effectuated for adult wages (for which the average difference between collective and statutory minimum wages is now about 3%).[13] Another concern in this area is the tendency in collective agreements to abolish the salary bands for younger workers (Ministry of Social Affairs and Employment, 2011a), which could worsen employment prospects for (disabled) youth, insofar as this would imply higher entry wages.

> **Box 2.4. Integrating the disabled in the labour market**
>
> The Netherlands experienced a strong inflow in the special system for younger disabled people (Wajong) in recent years, which has been related to the decentralisation of activation responsibilities for social assistance recipients to the municipalities (OECD, 2010b; Van Vuuren et al., 2011). The decentralisation gave municipalities incentives to offload recipients to the central government funded Wajong programme – as the municipalities are allowed to keep social security budget surpluses for other purposes. To reduce the stock of young disabled, the previous Survey recommended that they should be subject to the same controls and activation measures as new applicants to disability benefits. A related problem is the high number of workers in sheltered workplaces (about 1% of the labour force) as well as the diverse conditions to access social assistance, Wajong and sheltered worker places schemes, giving incentives to use the most favourable scheme and too few incentives for searching for regular work (Ministry of Social Affairs and Employment, 2012b).
>
> To increase employment of (partially) disabled workers in the private sector, the government plans to reform and partly merge the schemes for social assistance, younger disabled workers and sheltered workplaces (Ministry of Social Affairs and Employment, 2012b). Under the new scheme (the "Work Capacity Act" that is still being considered by parliament), municipalities will get full responsibility for the integration of workers with any (future) work potential together with corresponding financial accountability. Important tools to foster labour market integration are a single integration budget for the municipalities (which need to foster the efficiency of spending), a wage subsidy (dispensation) instrument (i.e. granting the possibility to employers to pay only a productivity reflecting wage, while the government supplements the income up to the level of the minimum wage) and a no-risk policy (i.e. employers who hire disabled workers do not have to bear the wage burden in case of sickness). In the long run, the reforms should allow budget savings of about EUR 1.8 billion.

Table 2.2. **Lowest collective agreement wage per age category**

% of statutory minimum wage (for corresponding age)

Age	15	16	17	18	19	20	21	22
Agriculture and fisheries	133.4 (4)	140.3 (4)	144.3 (4)	148.8 (4)	149.3 (4)	144.8 (4)	137.1 (4)	121.9 (4)
Construction	100.0 (6)	105.3 (11)	105.9 (12)	108.3 (13)	106.9 (13)	105.4 (13)	104.0 (13)	102.7 (13)
Manufacturing	100.0 (1)	109.0 (4)	108.7 (4)	113.7 (4)	118.9 (4)	120.3 (4)	120.0 (4)	117.4 (4)
Trade and hotel and restaurants	109.4 (16)	111.0 (22)	111.1 (22)	110.6 (22)	110.1 (23)	108.5 (23)	106.9 (23)	111.6 (23)
Transport and telecom	142.6 (5)	141.5 (9)	142.3 (10)	140.1 (10)	137.7 (10)	133.9 (10)	127.9 (10)	119.1 (10)
Business services	100.0 (3)	104.9 (5)	112.0 (8)	114.7 (10)	115.1 (10)	113.5 (10)	111.0 (10)	109.6 (10)
Other services	178.8 (3)	155.5 (3)	129.3 (4)	134.2 (4)	134.4 (4)	131.8 (4)	125.7 (4)	116.7 (4)
Total	**115.4 (38)**	**115.9 (54)**	**116.4 (64)**	**118.0 (67)**	**118.2 (68)**	**116.4 (68)**	**113.7 (68)**	**112.0 (68)**

Note: The brackets indicate the number of collective agreements that have been taken into account for calculations. Figures are weighted for the number of employees.
Source: Voorjaarsrapportage 2011.

> **Box 2.5. Recommendations to support labour reallocation and activation of underutilised labour resources**
>
> **Facilitate the reallocation of increasingly scarce labour resources**
>
> - The social partners should reduce the automatic tenure element in wages to foster the reallocation of older workers as well as support expanding sectors' access to these experienced workers.
> - Renewed efforts to implement an upper ceiling on severance pay should be pursued.
> - The dismissal system should be made simpler, more predictable and less time-consuming.
> - To promote decentralisation of wage formation, the government should limit or abolish ministerial extensions of sector collective agreements.
> - Social partners should facilitate the use of opt-out clauses, including clear procedural guidance for judging opt-out requests. A better alternative would be to let the directly involved parties at the local level decide.
> - The social partners should reorganise the wage formation process to move wage negotiations to the local level to secure an alignment of productivity and wage developments.
>
> **Mobilise underutilised labour resources to counter the ageing related contraction of the labour force**
>
> - The government should make the pilot scheme with short stay work permits permanent to better match labour supply and demand. In addition, the income restrictions in the knowledge worker scheme should be eased substantially.
> - Introduce a scheme to expand the available supply of high-skilled immigrants by granting them job-search visas. The conclusion of a job contract should automatically lead to a work permit. Facilitate job-search by non-EEA graduates from Dutch universities or internationally recognised foreign universities by relaxing or abolishing current income restrictions and time limitations.
> - Reduce the effective marginal tax rate for second earners by making childcare support provisions more dependent on secondary earners' income rather than family income.
> - Avoid cuts in childcare support so as not to deter the promotion of female full-time work.
> - Avoid that older workers use a combination of high severance pay and generous unemployment benefits as an early retirement route by implementing an upper ceiling for severance pay, which would be particularly effective if it declines as workers approach retirement. This should be combined with a reduction in the maximum unemployment benefit duration for workers with long tenures as well as by reducing the high upper ceiling for unemployment benefits.
> - Job prospects for partly disabled younger workers who will be affected by the reforms of the disability system can be strengthened by bringing the lowest wage of the collective agreements towards the statutory level.

Notes

1. Globalisation could have turned out negatively for individual (low skilled) workers, insufficiently mobile to find a new job in another sector, or at a higher skilled level. For instance, the Social and Economic Council considers especially low skilled production workers "the losers" of increased international competition (SER, 2008), although this assumption has not been quantified.

2. On average, people with university education earned twice as much as people with secondary vocational education in the period 2007-09. The income difference is especially pronounced for older workers, while being much more moderate at a younger age (Statistics Netherlands, 2011).

3. Reallocation of labour, has found to be an important driver of productivity growth, insofar as less productive firms tend to destroy more jobs and more productive ones create more jobs. However, the positive relation between job flows and productivity growth does not imply that all labour reallocation is efficiency enhancing (OECD, 2009c, 2010a).

4. The court may determine severance pay roughly according to the following rule: half a month per year of service for workers under 35 years of age; 1 month for workers between 35 and 45; 1.5 months for workers between 45 and 55 and 2 month for workers 55 years and over.

5. By contrast, in industries where firms restructure through internal adjustments, changes in EPL can be expected to have little impact on labour reallocation (Bassanini et al., 2010).

6. Returns to tenure are generally interpreted as the firm-related component of wages, which may act as an impediment to mobility (Deelen, 2011).

7. Studies on inter-industry wage differentials generally find that Dutch workers in financial intermediation and energy sectors are paid relatively well, especially compared to workers with similar characteristics in trade, hotels and restaurants and clothing industries (Du Caju et al., 2010; Advokaat et al., 2005; Van der Wiel, 1999; Hartog et al., 1994).

8. This is reflected by the fact that the number of immigrants that entered the Dutch labour market via a work permit over the last years has substantially exceeded the number of workers who entered the country via knowledge workers scheme. For instance, in 2006 the number work permits mounted to 74 thousand (mainly polish workers), against 2 thousand migrants under the knowledge workers scheme (Ministry of SZW, 2011c). Mainly as workers from most new EU member states do no longer require a permit, the first group declined considerably (to 14 thousand in 2010), but still concerning more than twice as many workers involved in the knowledge migrant schemes.

9. The short-term work permit for high skilled workers does not address the issue of foreign staff (working for foreign companies) that have to be trained in the Netherlands for a short period. There is an income criterion attached to the short-term permit, which is similarly to (the per month ratio of) the knowledge workers scheme.

10. Besides having positive effects on the participation of young mothers, the increase in childcare support replaced some informal care with more formal childcare facilities (Jongen, 2010).

11. A "Vitality" scheme is promoting longer working lives by enhancing training, continuation, mobility, and career incentives for older workers through tax credits and bonuses, although the total impact on employment is estimated to be negligible and only slightly positive on mobility (CPB, 2011).

12. A move that is further facilitated by the generous tax treatment of housing and pension that promotes the accumulation of capital.

13. The youth statutory minimum wage is relatively low, but the collective agreements stipulate higher sector minimum wages, resulting in high entry wages compared to other countries (Van Vuuren et al., 2011).

Bibliography

Advokaat, W., J. van Cruchten, J. Gouweleeuw, E.S. Nordholt and W. Weltens (2005), "Loon Naar Beroep en Opleidingsniveau: Het Loonstructuuronderzoek 2002", *Sociaal-economische Trends*, Statistics Netherlands, The Hague.

Akçomak, I.S., L. Borghans and B. ter Weel (2010), "Measuring and interpreting trends in the division of labour in the Netherlands", *CPB Discussion Paper*, No. 161, Centraal Planbureau, The Hague.

Autor, D.H., L.F. Katz and M.S. Kearney (2006), "The Polarization of The US Labor Market", *American Economic Review*, Vol. 96, No. 2.

Baldwin, R. (2006), "Globalisation, the great unbundling(s)", Secretariat of the Economic Council, Finnish Prime Minister's Office, Helsinki.

Basis en Beleid (2007), "Dispensatiebepalingen in Bedrijfstak-CAO's", July, Utrecht.

Bassanini, A. and R. Duval (2006), "The Determinants of Unemployment Across OECD Countries: Reassessing the Role of Policies and Institutions", *OECD Economic Studies*, No. 42, 2006/1.

Bassanini, A., A. Garnero, P. Marianna and S. Martin (2010), "Institutional Determinants of Worker Flows: A Cross-Country/Cross-Industry Approach", *OECD Social, Employment and Migration Working Papers*, No. 107, OECD Publishing.

Berkhout, E., T. Smid, and M. Volkerink (2010), "Wat Beweegt Kennismigranten?", SEO-rapport nr. 2010-03, April, Amsterdam.

Borghans, L., F. Cörvers, B. Kriechel and R. Montizaan (2007), "Productiviteit, beloning en arbeidsparticipatie van ouderen", ROA-R-2007/5, Researchcentrum voor Onderwijs en Arbeidsmarkt, Maastricht.

Chaloff, J. and G. Lemaître (2009), "Managing Highly-Skilled Labour Migration: A Comparative Analysis of Migration Policies and Challenges in OECD Countries", *OECD Social, Employment and Migration Working Papers*, No. 79, OECD Publishing.

Cörvers, F., R. Euwals and A. de Grip (2011), *Labour Market Flexibility in the Netherlands*, Centraal Planbureau, The Hague.

CPB (2008), *Centraal Economisch Plan*, Centraal Planbureau, The Hague.

CPB (2011), "Houdbaarheidseffect sociaal akkoord AOW, Witteveenkader en Vitaliteitspakket", *CPB Notitie*, December, The Hague.

Deelen, A., E. Jongen and S. Visser (2006), "Employment Protection Legislation: Lessons from Theoretical and Empirical Studies for the Dutch Case", *CPB Document*, No. 135, Centraal Planbureau, The Hague.

Deelen, A. and E. Jongen (2009) "Employment Protection", in *Rethinking Retirement – From participation towards allocation*, CPB Special Publication, No. 80, Centraal Planbureau, The Hague.

Deelen, A. (2011), "Wage-Tenure Profiles and Mobility", *CPB Discussion Paper*, No. 198, Centraal Planbureau, The Hague.

DNB (De Nederlandsche Bank) (2005), "Less Welfare Growth in the Service Economy", *Quarterly Bulletin*, September, Amsterdam.

Du Caju, P., G. Kátay, A. Lamo, D. Nicolitsas and S. Poelhekke (2010), "Inter-industry wage differentials in EU countries: What do cross-country time-varying data add to the picture?", *Working Paper Research*, No 189, National Bank of Belgium.

European Commission (2011), "Industrial Relations in Europe 2010", *Commission Staff Working Paper 2010*, No. SEC(2011)292, March, Brussels.

Euwals, R., R. de Mooij and D. van Vuuren (2009), "Rethinking Retirement – From participation towards allocation", *CPB Special Publication*, No. 80, Centraal Planbureau, The Hague.

Gelauff, G., A. van der Horst and B. ter Weel (2010), "The Netherlands of 2040", *CPB Document*, No. 88, Centraal Planbureau, The Hague.

Gielen, A.C., M.J.M. Kerkhofs and J.C. van Ours (2006), "Prestatieloon en productiviteit", *Economische Statistische Berichten*, No. 91(4491).

Goos, M. and A. Manning (2007), "Lousy and Lovely Jobs: the Rising Polarization of Work in Brittain", *The Review of Economics and Statistics*, No. 89.

Government (2010a), *Werkloosheid. Rapport Brede Heroverwegingen*, The Netherlands, April, The Hague.

Government (2010b), *Het Kind van de Regeling. Rapport Brede Heroverwegingen*, April, The Hague.

Groot, S. and H. de Groot (2011), "Wage inequality in the Netherlands: Evidence, trends and explanations", *CPB Discussion Paper*, No. 186, Centraal Planbureau, The Hague.

Haltiwanger, J., S. Scarpetta and H. Schweiger (2008), "Assessing Job Flows Across Countries: The Role of Industry, Firm Size and Regulations", *Working Paper*, No. 13920, NBER Working Paper Series.

Hartog, J., R. van Opstal en C.N. Teulings (1994), "Loonvorming in Nederland en de Verenigde Staten", *Economische Statistische Berichten*, No. 79(3965).

Heyma, A. and J. Theeuwes (2008), "Offshoring and the Worker", *SEO-Report*, No. 2007-94, Amsterdam.

HSI (2007), "Ontslagkosten van Werkgevers, Rapport Uitgebracht aan de Ministeries van SZW", *EZ en Financiën*, Amsterdam, Hugo Sinzheimer Institute.

IMF (2007), "The Globalization of Labor", *World Economic Outlook*, Chapter 5, October, Washington, DC.

IND Informatie- en Analyse Centrum (INDIAC) (2010), *Trendrapportage Regulier*, May.

Jongen, E.L.W. (2010), "Child Care Subsidies Revised", *CPB Document*, No. 2011, Centraal Planbureau, The Hague.

Jacobs, B. (2004), "The Lost Race Between Schooling and Technology", *De Economist*, Vol. 152, No. 1.

Jacobs, B. and D. Webbink (2006), "Rendement Onderwijs Blijft Stijgen", *Economische Statistische Berichten*, No. 91(4492).

Muysken, J. and T. Ziesemer (2011), "Immigration and Growth in an Ageing Economy", *UNU-MERIT Working Papers Series*, May, Maastricht.

Knegt, R. (2006), "Ontslagvergoedingen in een Duaal Ontslagstelsel", *Sociaal Recht*, 2006-10.

Leering. R. (2007), "Concurrentiepositie Aangetast Door Loonkostenstijging", *Economische Statistische Berichten*, No. 92(4507).

Ministry of Education, Culture and Science (OC&W) (2011), "Internationale mobiliteit", Ref. 352301, December, The Hague.

Ministry of Social Affairs and Employment (SZW) (2008), *Beleidsdoorlichting Arbeidsverhoudingen*, November, The Hague.

Ministry of Social Affairs and Employment (SZW) (2011a), *Voorjaarsrapportage CAO-Afspraken 2011*, June, The Hague.

Ministry of Social Affairs and Employment (SZW) (2011b), *Kinderopvang*, 31 322, No. 138, June, The Hague.

Ministry of Social Affairs and Employment (SZW) (2011c), *Arbeidsmigratie van Buiten de EU*, No. AV/SDA/2011/5618, April, The Hague.

Ministry of Social Affairs and Employment (SZW) (2012a), *Kindregelingen*, Ref. ASEA/CSI/2012/1707, 8 February, The Hague.

Ministry of Social Affairs and Employment (SZW) (2012b), *Memorie van Toelichting, Wet Werken Naar Vermogen*, January.

OECD (2004), *OECD Employment Outlook*, OECD Publishing.

OECD (2007a), "Making the Most of Globalisation", *OECD Economic Outlook*, Chapter 3, Vol. 2007/1, No. 81, June, OECD Publishing.

OECD (2007b), *OECD Employment Outlook*, OECD Publishing.

OECD (2007c), *Staying Competitive in the Global Economy, Moving up the Value Chain*, OECD Publishing, OECD Publishing.

OECD (2008), *Jobs for Youth: the Netherlands*, OECD Publishing.

OECD (2008a), *Growing Unequal? Income Distribution and Poverty in OECD countries*, OECD Publishing.

OECD (2008b), *OECD Economic Surveys: Netherlands 2008*, OECD Publishing.

OECD (2008c), *The Global Competition for Talent: Mobility of the High Skilled*, OECD Publishing.

OECD (2009a), "The Global Competition for Talent", *OECD Policy Brief*, February, OECD Publishing.

OECD (2009b), *International Migration Outlook*, OECD Publishing.

OECD (2009c), *OECD Employment Outlook*, OECD Publishing.

OECD (2010), *Off to a Good Start? Jobs for Youth*, OECD Publishing

OECD (2010a), *OECD Employment Outlook*, OECD Publishing.

OECD (2010b), *OECD Economic Surveys: Netherlands 2010*, OECD, OECD Publishing.

OECD (2011c), *International Migration Outlook, 2011*, OECD, OECD Publishing.

Rae, D. and M. Sollie (2008), "Globalisation and the European Union: Which Countries are Best Placed to Cope?", *OECD Economics Department Working Paper*, No. 586.

Regioplan (2007), "Ervaringen van Werkgevers met de CAO en AVV", No. 1529, June, Amsterdam.

Regioplan (2008), "Aanpassingsvermogen Van Ondernemingen Aan Veranderende Marktomstandigheden: De Rol van Dispensatie en Andere Aanpassingsmogelijkheden", No. 1683, July, Amsterdam.

Roodenburg (2005), "Discussiebijdrage Over Vraag- en Aanbodgestuurde Arbeidsmigratie", *CPB Memorandum*, No. 108, Centraal Planbureau, The Hague.

Sociaal-Economische Raad (SER) (2006), "Welvaartsgroei door en voor iedereen", *Advies Over het Sociaal-economisch Beleid op Middellange Termijn*, Sociaal-Economische Raad, The Hague.

Sociaal-Economische Raad (SER) (2007a), *Industrial Relations and the Adaptability of the Dutch Economy*, No. 06/08IIe, Sociaal-Economische Raad, December, The Hague.

Sociaal-Economische Raad (SER) (2007b), "Summary of Advisory Report on Labour Migration Policy", No. 2007/02e, Sociaal-Economische Raad, The Hague.

Sociaal-Economische Raad (SER) (2008), "On sustainable globalisation: A world to be won", *Advisory Report*, Sociaal-Economische Raad, The Hague.

Sociaal-Economische Raad (SER) (2011), "Werk Maken Van Baan-baanmobiliteit", *Advies 11/05*, April, Sociaal-Economische Raad, The Hague.

Statistics Netherlands (2011), *Inkomens van Afgestudeerden, 2007-09*, The Hague.

Statistics Netherlands (2012), "Pensioenleeftijd werknemers ruim 63 jaar", *Webmagazine*, January, www.cbs.nl.

Theeuwes, J.J.M. (2011), "Gaten vullen met immigranten?", in *Jaarboek Overheidsfinanciën 2011*, Chapter 8, Wim Drees Stichting voor Openbare Financiën, Den Haag, Sdu Press.

Top-team Creative Industries (2011), *Creatieve Industrie In Topvorm: Advies Topteam Creatieve Industrie*, June.

Top-team High Tech (2011), *Holland High Tech: Advies Topteam High Tech Systemen en Materialen*, June, The Hague.

Van Daalen, H., S. Ederveen and K. Henkens (2008), "De productiviteit van de oudere werknemer", *Economische Statistische Berichten*, No. 93(4545).

Van der Wiel (1999), "Loondifferentiatie in Nederland na 1969: Een Sectorale Invalshoek", *Onderzoeksmemorandum*, No. 154, Centraal Planbureau, The Hague.

Van Vuuren, D. and P. de Hek (2009), "Firms, workers, and life-cycle wage profiles", in "Rethinking Retirement – From participation towards allocation", *CPB Special Publication*, No. 80, Centraal Planbureau, The Hague.

Van Vuuren, D., F. van Es, and G. Roelofs (2011), "Van Bijstand naar Wajong", *CPB Policy Brief*, No. 2011/09, Centraal Planbureau, The Hague.

Chapter 3

Health care reform and long-term care in the Netherlands[1]

> The Netherlands, as other OECD countries, faces the challenge of providing high quality health and long-term care services to an ageing population in a cost-efficient manner. In the health care sector, reforms have aimed at introducing more competition. Despite major changes and some positive effects, the reforms run the risk of getting stuck in the middle between a centralised system of state-controlled supply and prices and a decentralised system based on regulated competition, providing insufficient incentives for provision of quality services and expenditure control. The main challenges are to complete the transition to regulated competition in health care provision, to strengthen the role of health insurers as purchasing agents and to secure cost containment in an increasingly demand-driven health care sector. In 2012, reforms expanded the role of the market in the hospital sector and reinforced budget controls. Both measures are not consistent and may jeopardise both objectives. More competitive markets require, at least, provision of good quality information, appropriate financing and better efficiency incentives. In view of population ageing, current policies mean that the cost of long-term care is set to more than double over the coming decades. Insufficient incentives for cost-efficient purchasing of long-term care should be addressed. However, the government's plan to transfer long-term care purchasing to health insurers is unpromising unless additional measures ensure that insurers bear the associated financial risks. In addition, home care should be further encouraged at the expense of institutional care, while screening and targeting should be improved.

Performance of the health care system

The health care sector is effective, as illustrated by relatively low avoidable mortality, but costly. Costs are comparable to other countries with institutionally similar health care systems (market mechanisms in regulating both insurance coverage and health care provision) such as Germany and Switzerland, but relatively high in comparison to most other OECD countries with different systems (Joumard et al., 2010). More specifically, hospital care exhibits mixed efficiency scores, while quality is high in preventive and outpatient care (findings that predate the effects of recent health care reforms). Other studies have emphasised the high equity and access in the Dutch health care system (Davis et al., 2010). This chapter starts with an assessment of health outcomes and resource use. Then the effects of mid-2000s reforms are analysed and the next wave of reforms is discussed. Finally, the chapter assesses reforms of the (distinct) long-term care system.

Health outcomes are relatively good

Health outcome indicators for the Netherlands range from about average to relatively good. Life expectancy at birth is similar to most other western European countries, but remaining years at retirement are only just above the OECD average Figure 3.1). Life expectancy has progressed more slowly than in most other OECD countries over 1995-2005 (Joumard et al., 2010) before rising quite sharply in the second half of the 2000s, largely thanks to a declining mortality among the elderly (Mackenbach et al., 2011). Moreover, the expected number of years of life in good health is fairly high and Dutch citizens seldom succumb to accidental death, implying relatively few potential years of life lost. This average to good performance is also reflected in infant mortality, which is well below the OECD average, but still twice the lowest in the OECD. Similarly, mortality by leading non-communicable causes is generally relatively low except for cancer (Table 3.1). Finally, inequalities in health outcomes are low and lifestyles relatively health despite a high smoking habit (Figure 3.2) (Joumard et al., 2010).

Systematic monitoring of the health care system has been in place since 2006, using 125 indicators to describe quality, accessibility and costs (Westert et al., 2010). Quality indicators show a relatively high uptake of preventive screening and low rates of avoidable hospital admissions, pointing to effective primary and outpatient clinical care. The hospital sector appears less effective, with the death rate within 30 days of hospital admission for an acute condition (heart attack, brain haemorrhage, stroke) being about twice as high as the lowest rates in Europe (Westert et al., 2010). Access to care is facilitated by the comprehensiveness of the basic mandatory health insurance scheme and by the lowest co-payments in Europe (Table 3.2), securing that only few people forgo medical visits for financial reasons (Westert et al., 2010). In addition, essential care services are available at short distance to almost the entire population, while waiting times for almost all treatments are below the agreed acceptable standard (known as "Treek norms") (NZa, 2012). Likewise, health inequalities measured by the dispersion in the age of death are

Figure 3.1. **Life expectancy indicators**

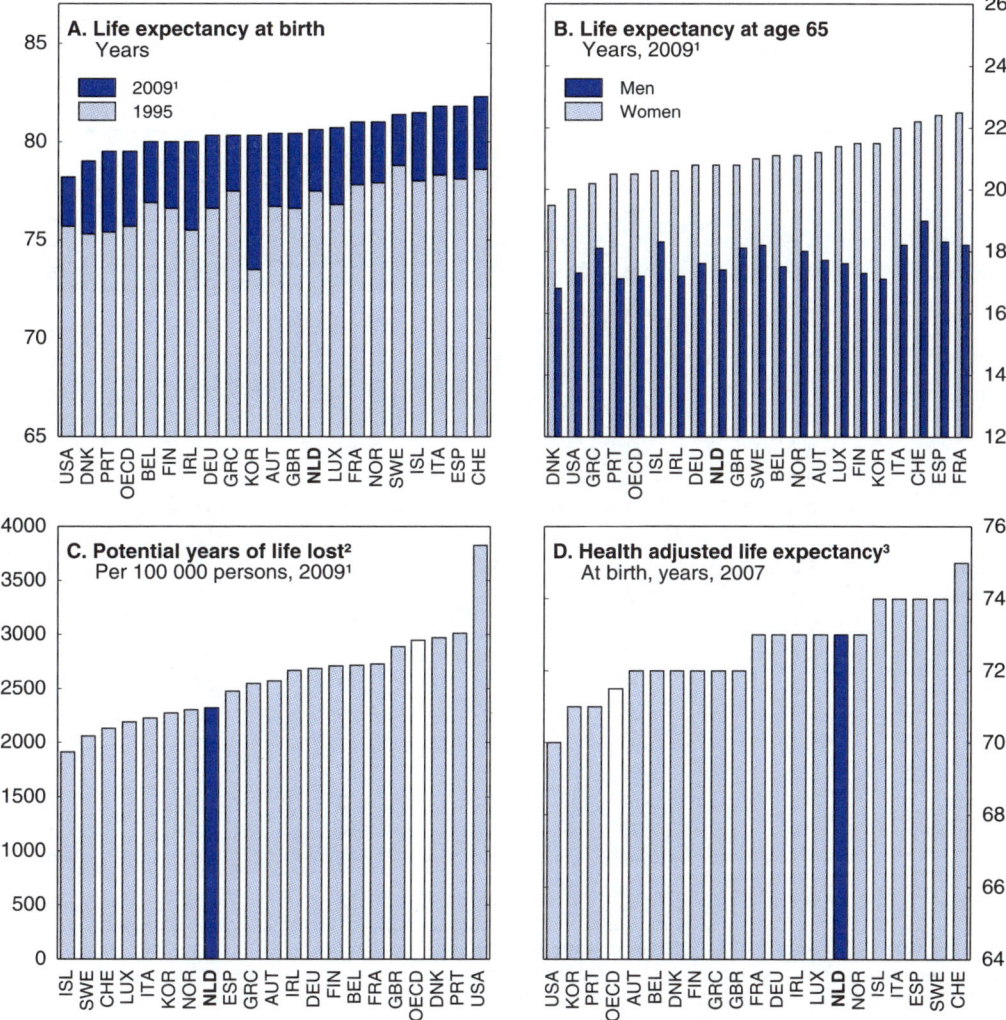

1. Or latest year of data available (2005-09); see source database for detail of country coverage.
2. Adjusted series calculated excluding deaths from land transport accidents, accidental falls, suicides and assaults. Age group 0 to 69.
3. Number of years expected to be lived in what might be termed the equivalent of "full health".

Source: OECD (2011), "OECD Health Data: Health Status", OECD Health Statistics Database, December; and WHO (2011), Global Health Observatory Data Repository, World Health Organisation, May.

StatLink http://dx.doi.org/10.1787/888932614871

among the lowest in the OECD (Joumard et al., 2010). As in many other countries, there is evidence of substantial practice variation (or small-area variation) which cannot be explained by socio-economic factors (Van Beek et al., 2009), pointing to room for efficiency improvements. This is particularly the case for common surgical operations, prescription behavior and a number of diseases, such as otitis media (middle ear infection), pneumonia, and hernia (Vektis and Plexus, 2011).

3. HEALTH CARE REFORM AND LONG-TERM CARE IN THE NETHERLANDS

Table 3.1. **Mortality rates of infants and mortality by leading causes**
2009 or latest year available[1]

	Infant mortality (deaths per 1 000 live births)	Leading causes of mortality (deaths per 100 000 population)				
		Ischemic heart disease	Cerebrovascular disease (stroke)	Lung cancer	Other types of cancer	Liver diseases and cirrhosis
Australia	4.3	74	35	29	116	5
Austria	3.8	92	32	29	121	14
Belgium	3.4	64	41	42	123	9
Canada	5.1	–	–	–	–	–
Czech Republic	2.9	161	75	37	150	15
Denmark	3.1	68	50	50	149	13
Finland	2.6	115	43	24	105	17
France	3.9	32	26	33	125	9
Germany	3.5	93	40	32	125	13
Ireland	3.2	98	39	38	138	7
Italy	3.7	58	44	33	124	9
Japan	2.4	26	40	26	108	6
Korea	3.5	28	57	32	111	11
Mexico	14.7	85	43	10	81	35
Netherlands	**3.8**	**42**	**33**	**44**	**134**	**4**
New Zealand	4.7	98	43	31	136	3
Norway	3.1	62	36	32	118	3
Poland	5.6	97	73	47	146	15
Portugal	3.6	40	71	22	125	12
Slovenia	2.4	61	63	35	154	22
Spain	3.3	45	36	32	115	9
Sweden	2.5	85	40	25	116	5
Switzerland	4.3	62	27	28	111	..
United Kingdom	4.6	77	41	38	127	11
United States	6.5	95	31	45	108	10
OECD average[2]	4.4	85	48	33	126	12

1. The latest year varies from 2007 to 2009 for infant mortality and from 2005 to 2009 for causes of mortality.
2. Unweighted average of latest year of data available. See source database for detail of country coverage.
Source: OECD (2011), "OECD Health Data: Health Status", *OECD Health Statistics Database*, July.

Considerable resources are devoted to the health system

In 2009, the Netherlands was the second largest health spender in the OECD after the United States (Figure 3.3). Other countries with comprehensive social health insurance schemes, such as Belgium, Canada, France, Germany and Switzerland, have almost comparable levels of spending, but spend more on curative care and less on long-term care. Over the decade to 2008, average growth in real health spending per capita was about ½ percentage point lower than in the EU, but spending has increased relatively faster since then, reflecting rather fast growth in the volume of care as inpatient and outpatient admissions grew respectively by 3% and 10% per year. On the other hand, expenditure on outpatient prescription drugs – among the lowest in the OECD – declined in recent years as a policy-induced fall in the prices of generic drugs more than offset an increase in consumption (NZa, 2010b).

Figure 3.2. **Health risks**
2009 or latest year available[1]

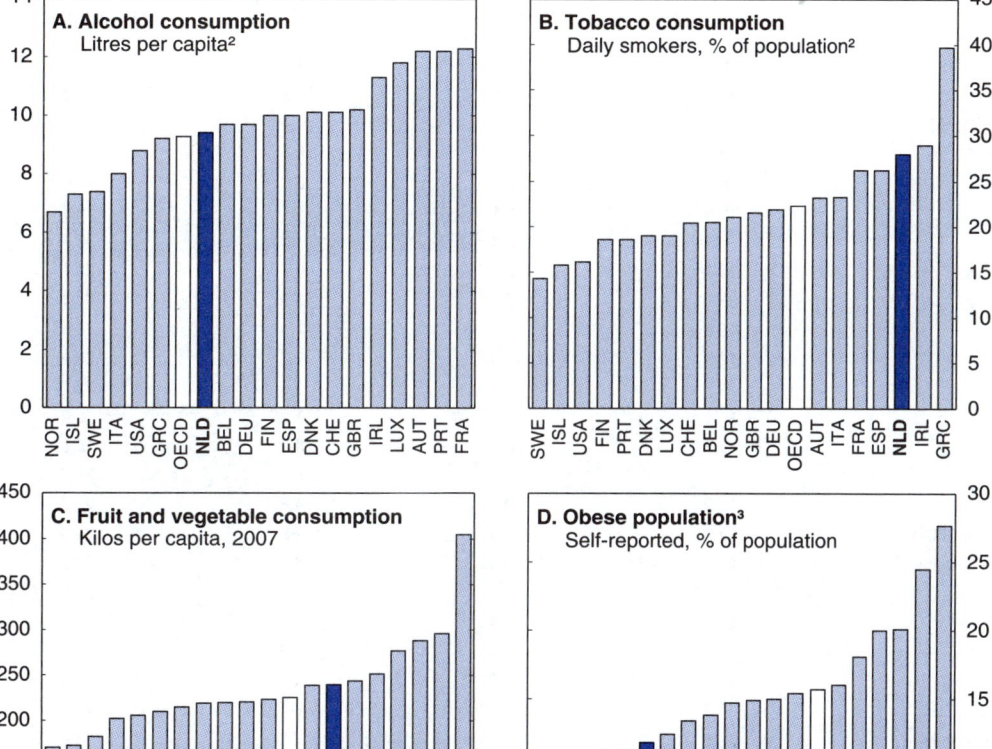

1. The latest year varies from 2005 to 2010; see source database for detail of country coverage. The OECD aggregate is an unweighted average of data available.
2. Population aged 15 and over.
3. Luxembourg, the Slovak Republic and the United Kingdom figures are based on health examination surveys, rather than health interview surveys.

Source: OECD (2011), "OECD Health Data: Non-Medical Determinants of Health", *OECD Health Statistics Database*, December; and OECD (2010), *OECD Health at a Glance: Europe 2010*.

StatLink ⟶ http://dx.doi.org/10.1787/888932614890

In 2010, public expenditure on health care and long-term care accounted for about 10% of GDP (Table 3.3). This share is set to increase as the 2010 Coalition Agreement allows public health expenditure to increase by 3¼ per cent per year in real terms over 2011-15, more than twice the expected expansion of GDP. Nevertheless, overspending appeared in 2011 as the public health care budget (BKZ) was exceeded by about EUR 1.4 billion (2¼ per cent) (Ministry of Health, 2011b), repeating an annual pattern since 2002 of excess spending of 1% to 4% (Algemene Rekenkamer – Court of Audit – 2011). The spending overruns were particularly pronounced in long-term care and mental health care. Excluding long-term care, almost half of public spending on health care goes to hospitals (Table 3.4).

Table 3.2. **Private spending as a share of total health expenditure**
2008

	Out-of-pocket (co-payments)	Voluntary private health insurance	Other private	Total private spending
Austria[1] (2008)	15.5	4.7	1.1	21.4
Belgium[1]	20.0	4.8	0.2	24.9
Czech Republic	14.4	0.2	1.4	16.0
Denmark[1]	13.7	1.8	0.1	15.5
Estonia	20.3	0.2	0.3	20.8
Finland	19.0	2.1	4.1	25.3
France	7.3	13.3	1.5	22.1
Germany	13.1	9.3	0.7	23.1
Hungary	23.7	2.7	3.9	30.3
Iceland	16.6	..	1.4	18.0
Ireland	12.3	11.0	1.7	25.0
Italy	19.7	1.0	1.5	22.1
Luxembourg	11.6	3.1	1.2	16.0
Netherlands[1]	**6.2**	**5.5**	**3.7**	**15.3**
Norway	15.1	..	0.8	15.9
Poland	22.2	0.6	4.8	27.6
Portugal (2008)	27.2	4.9	2.9	34.9
Slovak Republic	25.6	0.0	8.8	34.3
Slovenia	12.9	12.5	1.2	26.6
Spain	20.1	5.4	0.9	26.4
Sweden	16.7	0.2	1.6	18.5
Switzerland	30.5	8.8	1.0	40.3
Turkey[1] (2008)	19.2	..	8.1	27.3
United Kingdom	10.5	1.1	4.3	15.9

1. Current expenditure.
Source: OECD (2011), OECD Health Statistics Database, March.

Figure 3.3. **The Netherlands has high health expenditures**[1]
As a percentage of GDP, 2009[2]

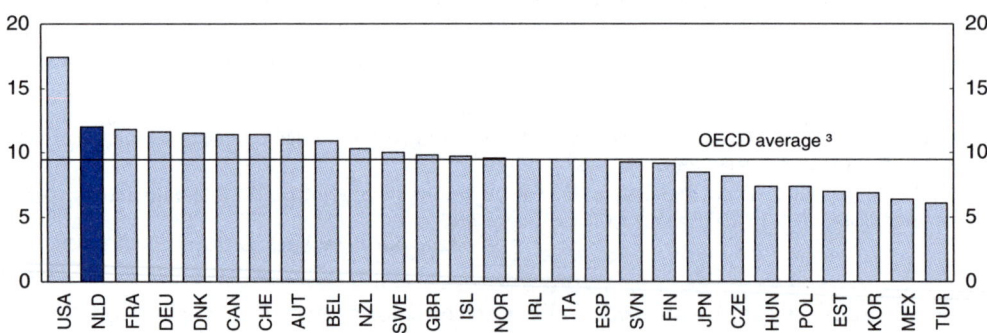

1. For Belgium, excluding investments. For Finland, Japan and Sweden, expenditure on long-term care within the health boundary conforms to a narrower definition for these countries and therefore total spending on health is likely to be underestimated.
2. 2008 for Japan and Turkey.
3. OECD average calculated based on the most recent data available for all countries.
Source: OECD (2011), OECD Health Statistics Database, March.

StatLink http://dx.doi.org/10.1787/888932614909

Table 3.3. **Public expenditures for health care and long-term care**
As a percentage of GDP

	2000	2005	2006[1]	2010[2]	2011[2]	2012[2]
Public health expenditure (% GDP)	**6.0**	**7.1**	**8.5**	**9.9**	**9.9**	**10.1**
Health care (ZFW-ZVW)[1]	2.9	3.3	4.7	5.7	5.7	5.8
Long-term care (AWBZ)	3.1	3.8	3.8	3.7	3.7	3.8
Other	0	0	0	0.5	0.5	0.5

1. In 2006 the former sickness fund scheme (ZFW) (for two thirds of the population) and private health insurance (for one third of the population) were included in a single universal public health insurance scheme (ZVW) carried out by private health insurers. As a result of the expansion of the public health insurance scheme to the entire population, the share of public health care expenditure in GDP substantially increased.
2. Figures for 2010 are preliminary; figures for 2011 and 2012 are projections.

Source: CPB (2011), *Centraal Economisch Plan 2011*, Centraal Planbureau.

Table 3.4. **Public health care expenditure (ZVW) by category**
2011

	EUR bn	% of total
Hospital care[1]	16.5	45.6
Medical specialists (self-employed)	2.1	5.8
General practitioners	2.3	6.4
Mental health care	4.1	11.3
Prescription drugs	5.5	15.2
Other (*e.g.* medical devices, dental care, paramedical care, maternity care)	5.7	15.7
Total public health care expenditure	**36.2**	**100**

1. Including free-standing clinics: ZBCs.
Source: Ministry of Health (2011), "Rijksbegroting 2012. XVI Volksgezondheid, Welzijn en Sport, Tweede Kamer, vergaderjaar 2011-12".

Despite high health care spending, the volume of health care services is low from an international perspective, both in terms of doctor consultations and hospital stays (OECD, 2010a) (Figure 3.4). Regarding hospitals, the number of stays (as measured by the in-patient discharge rate) and their average length in acute care are both below OECD average, but hospital bed occupancy rates are nevertheless very low. The utilisation of coronary angioplasty, which can only be performed by a restricted number of hospitals, is the lowest in the EU. By contrast, hip and knee replacement surgeries occur rather frequently as compared to other OECD countries. Despite high overall spending, the supply side is more constrained than in many other countries with a lower number of hospital beds, doctors, and modern equipment per capita (Figure 3.5).

The health care sector was substantially reformed in the second half of the 2000s

The market failures inherent to health care provision make it very challenging to contain the cost pressures stemming from population ageing. Market failures result from asymmetric information between health insurers and care providers and between care providers and patients, creating scope for supplier-induced demand and up-coding (classifying patients into higher priced diagnostic codes). Empirical analysis suggests that no health care system performs systematically better in addressing these failures and delivering cost-effective health care (Joumard et al., 2010). The Netherlands has opted for a system of regulated competition and private insurance, with wide-ranging reforms

3. HEALTH CARE REFORM AND LONG-TERM CARE IN THE NETHERLANDS

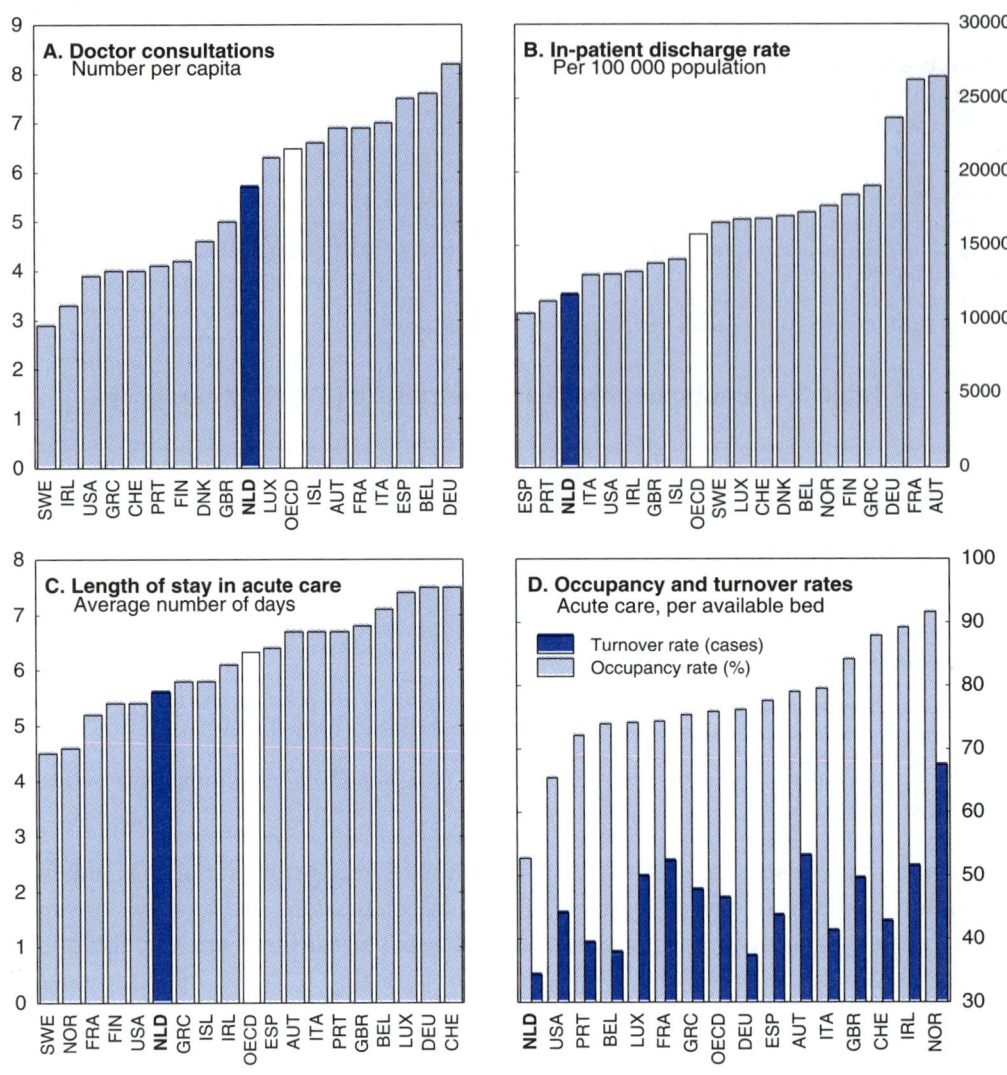

Figure 3.4. **Health care consultations and hospital resource use**
2009 or latest year available[1]

1. The latest year varies from 2005 to 2009; see source database for detail of country coverage. The OECD aggregate is an unweighted average of data available.
Source: OECD (2011), "OECD Health Data: Health Care Utilisation", *OECD Health Statistics Database*, December.
StatLink ⟶ http://dx.doi.org/10.1787/888932614928

implemented since the mid-2000s to reinforce the role of market mechanisms. However, these market failures imply that competition alone is not sufficient to guarantee cost control and that measures are also needed to improve the functioning of the market both on the supply and on the demand side.

In 2006, competition among health insurers was reinforced with the introduction of the Health Insurance Act (*Zorgverzekeringswet, Zvw*), which made private health insurance mandatory for everyone. This replaced a dual system where public insurance was mandatory for about two-thirds of the population while the other third relied on voluntary private insurance. In the new system, all citizens have to pay a flat rate premium (freely set by the insurer) to their chosen health insurer and an income-related contribution to a

Figure 3.5. **Health care resources**
2009 or latest year available[1]

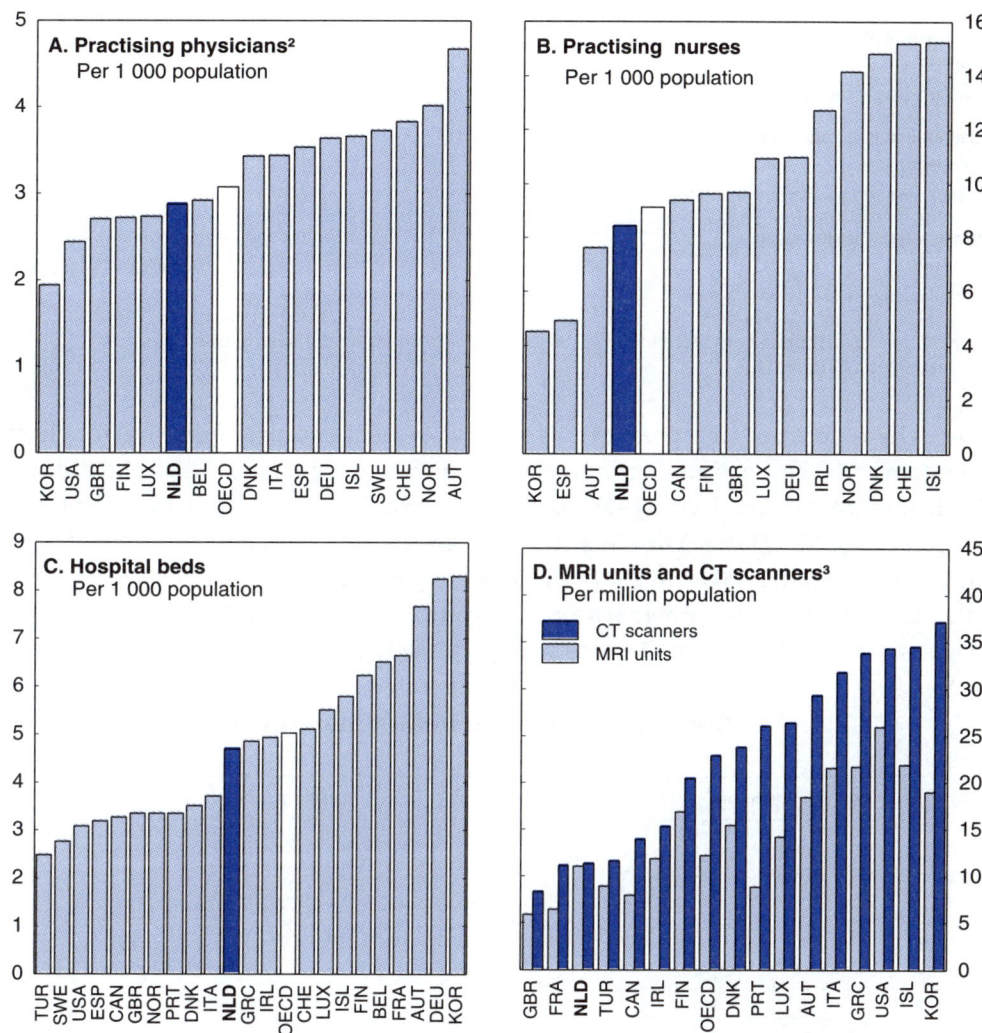

1. The latest year varies from 2006 to 2010. The OECD aggregate is an unweighted average of data available.
2. Professionally active physicians value amongst OECD countries.
3. Magnetic Resonance Imaging (MRI) units and Computed Tomography (CT) scanners.
Source: OECD (2011), *OECD Health Data: Health Care Resources Database.*

StatLink ⟶ http://dx.doi.org/10.1787/888932614947

risk-equalisation fund, which covers 50% of total health expenditure. To ensure affordability, the government provides two thirds of Dutch households with a monthly income-related allowance, accounting for about 6% of health care expenditures (Ministry of Health, 2011b). The basic idea behind the reform was to give health insurers appropriate incentives to act as prudent buyers of health services on behalf of their customers. To that end, the Health Insurance Act allows health insurers to selectively contract with health care providers.

The main result of the reform was the introduction of significant price competition between health insurers, particularly in the early stages as they competed for market share. As a result, health insurers incurred substantial losses on providing basic health insurance coverage during the first three years of the reforms (Table 3.5). The losses in 2007-08 were notably offset by consistently high profits on supplementary health insurance packages, a

Table 3.5. **Profitability of health insurance**[1]

	2006	2007	2008	2009	2010
Financial result basic insurance					
In mln EUR	–422	–125	–262	794	277
% of total revenue basic insurance	–1.5	–0.5	–0.9	2.6	0.8
Financial result supplementary insurance					
In mln EUR	40	149	264	372	376
% of total revenue supplementary insurance	1.2	4.0	6.7	8.9	8.8
Total financial result health insurance					
In mln EUR	–382	24	2	1 166	653
% of total revenue health insurance	–1.2	0.1	0.0	3.3	1.7

1. Financial results comprise both technical results (insurance business) and investment results.
Source: Vektis 2009, 2010, 2011.

market where competitive pressures are weaker because products are much more differentiated. The competition for market share also triggered a rapid consolidation of the health insurance market, leading the four largest health insurers to have a joint market share exceeding 90% (Table 3.6). This has allowed for substantial economies of scale in administration (Vektis, 2009 and 2011) and has increased (regional) buying power vis-à-vis health care providers, as providers now negotiate contracts with only five different purchasers because the five smallest insurers participate in a purchasing co-operative.

Table 3.6. **Concentration of the health insurance market**
2011

Rank	Name insurer[1]	Market share (%)
1	Achmea	32
2	UVIT	26
3	CZ	20
4	Menzis	13
5	DSW	3
6	ONVZ	2
7	Z&Z	2
8	ASR	1
9	Eno	1
Total		**100**

1. The four largest health insurance companies offer health insurance under different labels (risk bearing legal entities). Including these different labels there were 27 health insurers active in the market in 2011.
Source: NZa (2011a).

The consolidation of the health insurance market may reduce competition among health insurers, creating risks of oligopolistic behaviour. Since the beginning of the reform, small insurers have been important to discipline pricing behaviour of the four large insurers. For instance, each year one of the small insurers (DSW) is the first to set a competitive price for the basic insurance package, which serves as a benchmark for other insurers. In 2011, however, the largest of the smaller insurers (DFZ) with a strong regional presence in the province of Friesland merged with the largest health insurer (Achmea) following investigation and approval by the Competition Authority (NMa). Although the Healthcare Authority agreed with the decision, the merger may considerably weaken the collective buyer position of the remaining small insurers, meaning that subsequent takeovers of small insurers may follow, which would reduce competition in the health insurance market (Loozen et al., 2011). Political concern has ensued and the Minister of Health is investigating the possibility of giving the Competition Authority specific directions about the assessment of mergers between health insurers (Ministry of Health, 2011d). Such interference in the work of the Competition authority is not welcome as it risks leading to merger decisions based on political ground instead of competition considerations (which should, naturally, also take into account consumer welfare concerns such as accessibility and quality of services). Moreover, political uncertainty about merger decisions would reduce entry incentives for new (foreign) operators, thus reducing competitive pressures. Thus, clear and transparent competition-based decisions in the area of merger between health insurers should be secured by being based on published merger assessment methodology.

Reforms have had a mixed effect on cost-efficiency in the hospital sector

The reforms of the health care sector have so far had a mixed effect on the supply side. The enhanced competition among health insurers has constrained prices of hospital services and outpatient prescription drugs. Moreover, competition among hospitals has increased due to the entry of a substantial number of freestanding clinics (ZBCs). Nevertheless, health care spending has increased because of a sharp rise in the volume of care, including in mental health care (Box 3.1). This may notably reflect suppliers' efforts to maintain their income despite lower prices, e.g. via supplier-induced demand and up-coding (classifying patients into higher priced diagnostic codes) (Hasaart, 2011; Douven et al., 2012). It is difficult to establish whether health outcomes have improved as a result of the reforms, but public attention for quality of care has increased substantially. On the other hand, providers' administrative costs have increased, along with the increasing number of contractual arrangements, the introduction of a highly complex product classification system (DBC-system) and the increasing information requirements from supervisory bodies and health insurers.

The reforms divided prices for hospital services into a regulated and a freely negotiated segment. The so-called segment A consists of hospital services for which regulated prices are derived from a global hospital budget. The segment B consists of hospital services where prices are freely negotiated with health insurers, and typically comprise less complex services (e.g. knee and hip replacements). The share of segment B has increased from less than 10% in 2005 to more than 30% in 2011 and 70% following the 2012 reform (described below). At the same time, real prices in the segment B have declined, reflecting the increased bargaining power of health insurers (Table 3.8). Nevertheless, substantial price variations across segment B providers remain, with university hospital prices being 7.5% higher and prices in free-standing clinics (ZBCs) 14% lower than average. Because of insufficient information collection, it cannot be established to what extent this can be attributed to differences in efficiency, case-mix or market power.

Despite the decline in real prices in the segment B, total real hospital expenditures have increased by an annual 4%. This may notably reflect supplier-induced volume growth in the segment B – as suggested by the differences between treatments provided by salaried and self-employed specialists – up-coding (classifying patients into higher priced diagnostic codes), and excessive billing (in about five per cent of cases) (Hasaart, 2011; Douven et al., 2012).[2] Since 2003, hospital productivity has increased by 15%, partly thanks to a 35% improvement in labour productivity of nursing personnel (Blank et al., 2011).

> **Box 3.1. Mental health care reform – a step too far?**
>
> Until 2008, mental health care was largely covered by long-term care insurance (AWBZ). To facilitate the co-ordination with somatic (i.e. non-mental) care, mental health care was transferred to the basic health insurance scheme (ZVW), both for primary mental health care (mainly provided by psychologists) and secondary mental health care (provided by mental health care institutions, psychiatric hospitals and self-employed psychiatrists and psychologists). The reform triggered strong increases in expenditure on mental health services (Table 3.7) even though there is no evidence of a higher share of the population having mental health problems over the last decade (De Graaf et al., 2010). The increase in expenditure may notably reflect the fact that health insurers bear only limited financial risks on mental health care because they are largely retrospectively compensated for the cost of mental care. The reason for this is that risk-equalisation for mental health care still is highly imperfect because adequate risk adjusters and data are lacking.
>
> Table 3.7. **Expenditures on curative mental care covered by ZVW**
>
> | | 2008 | 2009 | 2010 | 2011[1] |
> |---|---|---|---|---|
> | Total expenditure (million euro) | 3 313 | 3 575 | 3 897 | 4 095 |
> | % change in expenditure | | 7.9 | 9.0 | 5.1 |
>
> 1. Preliminary figure.
> Source: Ministry of Health 2009, 2010, 2011b.
>
> The government intends to replace the budgeting system of mental health institutions with an output-based payment system by 2013 (Ministry of Health, 2011b). Instead of a collectively negotiated budget with all health insurers, mental health care institutions would be paid an individually negotiated price per service. Since the introduction of an output-based payment system may provide strong incentives for extra production and supplier-induced demand, the government specified a number of preconditions that have to be met: i) a guarantee that total costs can be controlled; ii) sufficiently risk-bearing health insurers; iii) sufficient information about differences in quality and case-mix; iv) sufficient instruments for health insurers to direct patients to efficient providers; v) a good and stable system of product classification; vi) adequate prices per service; vii) unambiguous methods of diagnosis. By 2015, it is planned that health insurers will be fully exposed to the risk for the cost of mental health care. However, none of these preconditions is currently met.
>
> The introduction of an output based financing scheme is particularly risky in mental health care, as this area is more susceptible to market failures, such as risk selection, moral hazard and supplier-induced demand, than other health services (Frank and McGuire, 2000). Moreover, meeting the preconditions is not a trivial task, particularly within such a short time frame. More fundamentally, it is inherently difficult to predict mental care utilisation (and costs) and important explanatory factors cannot be translated into measurable risk adjusters, implying that the full exposure of health insurers to financial risks in this area may result in risk selection and underinvestment in capacity (Frank and McGuire, 2000 and WOR, 2011).

Table 3.8. **Changes in negotiated average prices in the hospital segment B**
Percentage

	2006	2007	2008	2009	2010
Changes in nominal prices[1]	0.0	2.1	1.1	1.5	−1.8
Changes in real prices[2]	−1.2	0.5	−1.3	0.2	−3.3

1. Price changes are weighted by the share in revenues of the clusters of hospitals services by which the free hospital segment B was successively expanded.
2. The consumer price index is used as the deflator.
Source: NZa (2011b), "Marktscan Medisch specialistische zorg. Weergave van de markt 2006-2010".

Further scope for efficiency improvements comes from the fact that general hospitals are often operating on an inefficiently large scale, reflecting a lack of specialisation and a tight network of large hospitals that ensures most people have access to an emergency unit within less than 15 minutes (Blank et al., 2011). Indeed, the hospital sector is consolidating despite limited financial pressure to do so as profitability has remained roughly unchanged and because of the mandatory non-profit status of hospitals (i.e. they are not allowed to pay dividends) (NZa, 2011b).

So far, all hospital mergers have been approved by the Competition Authority. In one particular merger case, a regional monopoly was only allowed in view of efficiency considerations relating to the quality and the accessibility of care. This lenient merger stance reflects a lack of a clear-cut assessment methodology, limited agency capacity, an aversion against potential drawn-out legal procedures and political interference in high-profile cases (Varkevisser and Schut, 2008, 2010). Political concern about mergers has led the Parliament to propose a moratorium on mergers, although associated legal instruments are not in place (Ministry of Health, 2011d). Instead, the Minister of Health wants the Healthcare Authority (NZa) to carry out additional merger assessments in terms of quality and access (Ministry of Health, 2011c, d). However, having several institutions involved in merger assessments would increase unnecessarily regulatory uncertainty without improving the prevention of anticompetitive mergers. To ensure an effective hospital merger assessment, the Competition Authority should develop a clear methodology taking into account all relevant aspects of the problem (including consumer welfare concerns such as accessibility of care). This would boost agency capacity, improve transparency in the decision making and prevent political interference. In addition, given the Dutch hospital market's long-standing tradition of collective bargaining, concerted practice and substantial entry barriers, the Competition Authority should rather risk being too restrictive than too permissive when assessing hospital mergers (Varkevisser and Schut, 2012).

The remuneration of doctors has increased

The health care sector reforms further increased the already high incomes of doctors. Around the time of the reform, the annual remuneration of medical specialists and general practitioners (GP) was high, notably reflecting relatively limited supply (Tables 3.9 and 3.10). Following the reforms, doctors' revenues increased sharply, before moderating. Specialists' total revenues increased by more than an average 20% per year over 2007-08 before slowing to 6½ per cent growth in 2009 (NZa, 2011b), while their number was growing by only 4-5% per year over the period (Capaciteitsorgaan, 2010). GPs' total revenues grew by more than 20% in 2006, but rapidly moderated afterwards (NZa, 2009; Gusdorf et al., 2009).

Table 3.9. **Remuneration, as ratio to average wage in each country**
2009, or latest year available

	GPs		Specialists	
	Salaried	Self-employed	Salaried	Self-employed
Australia (2008)		1.7		4.3
Austria (2007)		2.7		4.4
Canada (2008)		3.1		4.7
Czech Republic (2008)			1.8	3.3
Denmark[1]		2.8		4.0
Estonia	1.7		2.1	
Finland	1.8		2.6	
France(2008)[2]		2.1		3.2
Germany (2007)		3.7		5.0
Greece			2.8	
Hungary[3]	1.4		1.6	
Iceland[4]	3.0		2.8	
Ireland[5]		3.5	4.5	
Italy			2.6	
Mexico	3.5		4.6	
Netherlands (2007)	1.7	3.5	2.9	5.5
New Zealand				
Norway			1.8	
Slovak Republic	1.9			
Slovenia	2.5		2.8	
Spain	1.9			
Turkey	2.0		3.8	
United Kingdom (2008/09)[6]	1.9	3.6	2.6	

1. Data for self-employed specialists is for 2008.
2. Remuneration is net income rather than gross income resulting for an underestimation.
3. Data on salaried doctors relate only to public sector employees who tend to receive lower remuneration than those working in the private sector.
4. Many specialists working in hospitals also earn incomes from private practices which are not included.
5. Data for self-employed GPs include practice expenses resulting in an over-estimation.
6. Remuneration of GPs is for 2008.

Source: OECD (2011), *Health at a Glance 2011*.

Similar factors were behind remuneration developments of specialists and GPs. Nearly half of medical specialists are working within hospitals as self-employed entrepreneurs (mostly as members of a partnership – a "maatschap").[3] In 2008, their remuneration was changed from lump-sum payments per hospital into payments per Diagnosis Treatment Combination (DBC), which essentially is an output-based payment system, giving them much stronger incentives to provide more (or more expensive) services. An additional factor behind higher remunerations was substantially miscalculated prices for certain services by supporting specialists, such as anesthesiologists and radiologists, due to overestimations of the workload associated to these services.

The remuneration system for GPs was reformed in 2006. Previously, it was based on a capitation basis for two thirds of the population and a fee-for-service basis for the other third of the population. The new system is a hybrid system for all patients, with part capitation – an annual "registration fee" per patient – and part fee-for-service. Both registration fee and fee-for-service have regulated maximums, *e.g.* EUR 9 for a standard visit of 10 minutes, which in practice have become fixed prices. This, together with a change in GPs' claims behaviour and an increase in supplier-induced demand (as reflected

Table 3.10. **General practitioners and specialists per 1 000 population**
2010, or latest year available

	GPs	Specialists	Physicians
Australia	1.49	1.5	2.99
Austria	1.57	3.23	4.80
Belgium	1.14	1.79	2.93
Canada	1.12	1.23	2.35
Czech Republic	0.70	2.86	3.56
Denmark	0.67	2.75	3.42
Finland	1.02	2.07	3.09
France	1.60	1.67	3.27
Germany	0.65	2.98	3.63
Greece	0.28	5.84	6.12
Hungary	0.35	2.68	3.03
Iceland	0.57	3.02	3.59
Ireland	0.57	3.65	4.22
Italy	0.78	2.67	3.45
Korea	0.81	1.12	1.93
Luxembourg	0.80	1.93	2.73
Mexico	0.75	..	..
Netherlands	**0.72**	**2.17**	**2.89**
New Zealand	0.75	1.86	2.61
Norway	0.81	3.21	4.02
Poland	0.21	1.96	2.17
Portugal	1.98	2.28	4.26
Slovak Republic	0.41	2.59	3.00
Spain	0.74	..	..
Sweden	0.62	3.10	3.72
Switzerland	0.60	3.23	3.83
Turkey	0.48	0.95	1.43
United Kingdom	0.79	1.94	2.73
United States	0.30	2.14	2.44

Source: OECD (2011), OECD Health Statistics Database, March.

in the more than doubling of the number of long consultations and home visits), explains the rapid increase in GPs' remuneration observed in 2006 (NZa, 2009, CBS, 2011). Since 2010, primary care groups and health insurers are allowed to negotiate bundled payments for providing co-ordinated care to people with specific chronic diseases (diabetes, vascular risk management, chronic obstructive pulmonary disease – COPD). This reform of GP remuneration fostered changes in the organisation of GPs, of which the effects on cost-efficiency are currently evaluated (Box 3.2).

Measures have been taken to rein in the resulting budget overruns. The 30% overrun in the 2008 budget for specialist treatment led the Healthcare Authority (NZa) in September 2010 to impose substantial discounts on regulated prices. Nevertheless, the 2010 budget was exceeded by roughly 10% as the effects on remuneration of the price reductions were more than offset by additional production of medical services, following the introduction of output-based payment. This reflected the lack of countervailing power by health insurers to curb volumes of services, pointing to the benefits of allowing (limited) vertical integration between insurers and hospitals to reduce information asymmetries and thus to strengthen the position of insurers to counter-act supplier-induced demand.

> **Box 3.2. Will the organisation of GPs into primary care groups improve cost-efficiency?**
>
> In recent years, the proportion of GPs participating in primary care groups offering integrated care to patients with chronic diseases rapidly increased to about 80% of GPs in 2010. Since 2010, primary care groups and health insurers are allowed on an experimental basis in the period 2010-13 to negotiate integrated (or bundled) payments for providing co-ordinated care to people with specific chronic diseases (diabetes, vascular risk management, chronic obstructive pulmonary disease – COPD).
>
> It is still too early to assess whether primary care groups are cost-effective (EIB, 2011). On the one hand, primary care groups may improve the co-ordination of care for chronic diseases and reduce unnecessary hospitalisations. Bundled payments could also be a useful first step towards integrated (risk-adjusted) capitation payments for multidisciplinary provider groups offering primary and specialist care for a defined group of patients (De Bakker *et al.*, 2012). On the other hand, there are concerns about potential negative effects, including double payments for the same service (*e.g.* rewarding the treatment of co-morbidities – patients with multiple diseases – both via bundled payments and regular payments), risk selection (providing integrated care primarily to favorable risk groups), abuse of market power (several regional provider groups having a near monopoly position) and high transaction costs.

The number of doctors is still low in comparison to other OECD countries despite a 30% increase in the number of specialists over the past decade (Table 3.10) (Capaciteitsorgaan, 2010). Looking ahead, the Healthcare Authority (NZa) expects shortages to develop as a result of demographic trends and an increasing share of part-time GPs (NZa, 2009). In this context, the government rightly aims at expanding the capacity of medical schools and the number of hospital training positions, as both are identified causes of supply restriction (Capaciteitsorgaan, 2011). Foreign doctors represent another potential source of doctors. In this domain, European candidates (from the European Economic Area) enjoy relatively easy access as their diplomas are recognised, while non-European candidates are subject to a governmental standardised assessment of medical skills and a language test. To facilitate entry for the latter group, it could be considered to exempt holders of diplomas from top universities from the medical-skills components of the assessment.

A concern with increasing the supply of specialists is that it may lead to more supplier-induced demand – a consideration that was a traditional reason for restricting their number. However, restricting the number of specialists is no longer a solution in a more market-oriented system, as it would reinforce their bargaining position and hence their ability to influence prices upwards. Thus, a progressive increase in supply should be encouraged (which, given the lengthy medical training programmes, may take a long time), but it should be preceded by measures to prevent supplier-induced demand, such as changing the payment system (*e.g.* becoming performance based, see below) and strengthening the bargaining position of health insurers. Important steps in this direction are planned in the next wave of reforms (see below). Moreover, the share of self-employed specialists could be further reduced by filling vacancies with salaried specialists when possible.[4]

The reforms have lowered drug costs

Perhaps the strongest effect of the health sector reforms was lower generic drug prices (Boonen et al., 2010). Before 2008, ineffective regulation kept generic drug prices high as pharmacies were allowed to charge health insurers the suppliers' official list price. At the same time, suppliers of off-patent drugs competed for market share by offering discounts to pharmacists, who had no incentive to pass these discounts on to health insurers. Until 2003, health insurers had to reimburse the full cost of all drugs covered by social health insurance, up to a legally determined reimbursement limit. As a result, generic drug prices were all close to the reimbursement limit, allowing pharmacies to make large profits. Attempts from the government to claw back part of the discounts offered to pharmacists were only marginally successful (Boonen et al., 2010).

Encouraged by stronger price competition since the 2006 reform, four of the five biggest health insurers started in 2008 to experiment with "preferred drug" formulas, where patients choosing a non-preferred drug are only reimbursed up to the price of the preferred drug (usually the lowest priced generics within the same therapeutic class). In parallel, health insurers started to issue tenders for contracts to supply several high-volume generic drugs. As a result, list prices of the ten biggest-selling generics fell by between 76% and 93%, leading to estimated savings of EUR 348 million (69%) per year (Boonen et al., 2010). In 2009, the preferred drug formulas were extended to include more generic drugs and adopted by more health insurers. Together with a reduction in the scope of the basic benefits package, this led to a first ever decline (of 5%) in total expenditure on outpatient prescription drugs covered by basic health insurance (NZa, 2010b). Over the period 2007-09, expenditure on multisource drugs (sold under multiple trademarks) decreased by more than 30% despite an increase of about 12% in utilisation (Figure 3.6).

Figure 3.6. **Expenditure on outpatient prescription drugs**
Million euros

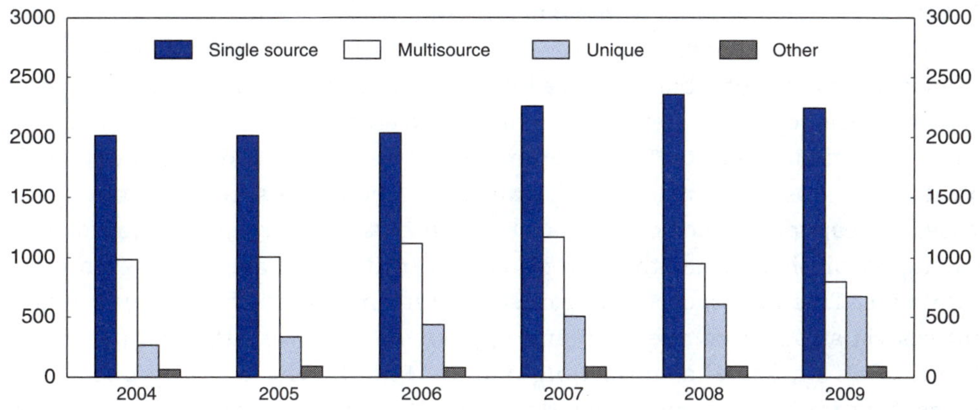

Source: NZa (2010), Monitor Extramurale farmacie 2010, Nederlandse Zorgautoriteit.
StatLink http://dx.doi.org/10.1787/888932614966

The next wave of reform

The reforms in the second half of the 2000s have not (yet) delivered the hoped-for results. In 2010, a government commission concluded that the health care system was "stuck in the middle" between a centrally planned and a market-oriented system, preventing the government from controlling costs and health insurers from being cost-effective purchasers of care (Werkgroep Curatieve zorg, 2010). Health insurers had insufficient incentives because of the still prevailing substantial *ex post* compensations and a lack of adequate instruments because of remaining government regulation of prices, supply and entry in various sectors. These problems were further compounded by a lack of an adequate system of product classification (DBCs) and a lack of reliable and publicly available quality information (performance indicators) due to insufficient patient level data and an inadequate information infrastructure (OECD 2010b, Klazinga et al., 2012).

To address these problems, the government is implementing an extensive set of reforms to strengthen the role of market forces in the provision of health services and to secure cost containment (particularly for hospitals and self-employed medical specialists). The latter is explicitly formulated as keeping public health care expenditure within an annual growth rate of 3¼ per cent. The main policy measures in the hospital sector include both a sizeable extension of the "market-based" segment B (where prices are negotiated) and the introduction of a new powerful legal instrument to enforce overall spending ceilings (Box 3.3). The government also intends to establish a new institute for health care quality to boost the development and dissemination of adequate performance indicators and evidence-based guidelines. Given the prevalence of asymmetric information problems, the production of such (performance) indicators should be given priority.

Despite the stated objective, some of the measures could hamper the emergence of stronger competition in the health sector. For example, the government intends to prohibit vertical integration of health insurers and care providers, with temporary exceptions for starting a new innovative provider and for securing provision of essential services (Ministry of Health, 2011c). The idea is to prevent insurers from foreclosing by directing their customers to their own providers. However, (limited) vertical integration between insurers and providers has the potential to reduce information asymmetry between them and thus to increase efficiency, while mergers resulting in excessive market power can be stopped by the Competition Authority. The government has also concluded agreements with the associations of hospitals, medical specialists and health insurers to limit spending increases on hospital and medical specialist care to 2.5% per year in real terms for 2012-15, by having hospitals and health insurers concentrating and specialising on complex hospital care. This approach goes against the reform thrust of improving efficiency incentives via stronger competition and appears at odds with the competition law's prohibition of market sharing arrangements. Finally, the phasing out of *ex post* compensations for health insurers over the period 2012-15 may not only increase insurers' incentives for efficiency but also for risk selection and underinvestment in the organisation and treatment of chronic diseases that are not sufficiently compensated by the *ex ante* risk equalisation scheme (Van de Ven et al., 2009). Thus, a further improvement of the risk equalisation scheme is necessary to secure unrestricted access to high quality care services.

> **Box 3.3. Main reform measures in the hospital sector 2012-15**
>
> The government's package for reforming the hospital financing system focuses on strengthening incentives for hospital efficiency while trying to contain costs (Ministry of Health, 2011a):
>
> - Expansion of the "market-based" hospital segment (segment B) from 35% to about 70% of hospital revenue.
>
> - Replacing the budgeting system in the regulated hospital segment (segment A) with an output-based payment system with regulated prices, either in the form of maximum or fixed prices. Maximum prices will be set for hospital services for which effective competition is not feasible, such as complex treatments concentrated in a few hospitals (i.e. areas with high entry barriers). Fixed prices will be set for services for which sufficient capacity has to be permanently on standby, but for which demand is irregular and unpredictable (e.g. emergency rooms, trauma centers, burn centers). During the first two years, hospitals will be partly compensated for the reallocation effects as a result of the new payment system (in 2012 for 95% and in 2013 for 70%).
>
> - Ex post compensations for health insurers will be fully phased out by 2015.
>
> - In 2012, a new system of product classification (DOT) has been introduced, reducing the number of hospital products (DBCs) from about 30 000 to about 4 400, which should be more transparent and manageable.
>
> - From 2012 onwards, a new legal "macrobudget instrument" should guarantee that total annual hospital expenditure does not exceed a government-set limit. If the aggregate revenue of all hospitals exceeds this macrobudget, all hospitals have to repay the excess revenue in proportion to their respective market share. The new macrobudget system implies that the budget (or revenues) of each individual hospital not only depends on its own performance but also on the performance of other hospitals.
>
> Starting in 2012, the payment system of self-employed specialists will be reformed, based on a new agreement between the government and the associations of medical specialists (OMS) and hospitals (NVZ) (Tweede Kamer, 2011):
>
> - From 2015, integrated prices for hospital and medical specialist care will be negotiated between health insurers and hospitals (in the segment B) or set by the government (in the segment A).
>
> - During a transition period (2012-14) a macrobudget for medical specialist services (initially set at about EUR 2 billion and increasing by 2½ per cent per year thereafter) is derived from the general macrobudget for health care expenditures covered by public insurance (BKZ). Based on a normative allocation model, the Health Authority (NZa) calculates a budget for medical specialty care for each individual hospital.
>
> - At the individual hospital level, allocation models for the remuneration of medical specialists have to be developed. The largest share of the budget (75% to 85%) will have to be allocated to remuneration of specialists' regular activities, and a smaller variable part (15% to 25%) to the remuneration of practice costs, extra activities and for the hospital management to reward good performance.
>
> - If medical specialists produce more services than allowed by the budget, then the hospital will have to reimburse the additional payments to the Health Insurance Fund.

At the same time, the measures to curb spending growth may not suffice. The threat of a general *ex post* "revenue tax" if total hospital costs exceed the imposed macrobudget gives individual hospitals strong incentives to overspend as they anticipate similar strategic behaviour by other hospitals. The weaker the competitive pressure facing hospitals, the more scope they will have to increase prices (and profit margins) to reduce the impact of a future "revenue tax". This means that, paradoxically, hospitals in the most competitive regional markets may be most hurt, which could, in an extreme case, lead to higher concentration in the market if hospitals in financial distress are taken over. In addition, uncertainty about the revenue tax deters new entry and investments in innovation, further cementing the position of incumbents.

Arguably, health insurers should counteract upward pressures on prices resulting from hospitals' strategic behaviour. However, their ability to do so has been hampered by the introduction of the new product classification system, which has put them at an information disadvantage *vis-à-vis* hospitals. In this respect, the new payment system for medical specialists may be helpful, at least for the period 2012-14, because normative budgets per hospital for medical specialist care may limit incentives for overproduction. In addition, several health insurers have negotiated fixed budgets with hospitals in 2012, which may also reduce incentives to induce demand. However, if these budgets are not sufficiently risk-adjusted, they may induce hospitals to select favourable risks and to refer expensive patients to other hospitals.

The macrobudget instrument may also result in crowding out of complex hospital care with regulated prices (segment A). If prices in the "market-based" segment (segment B) rise faster than regulated prices (segment A) in anticipation of future "revenue taxes", then investing in more complex (regulated) services will become increasingly unattractive due to the relatively lower profit margins. This would induce specialised hospitals to become general, boost waiting lists and reduce consumer welfare. In addition, longer waiting list may lead patients to use their right to go abroad to receive treatment, further reducing the effectiveness of this instrument in controlling costs.

To reinforce macrobudget control, priority should be given to a range of measures to enhance efficiency. These include improving quality information to enable performance-based contracting, creating room for providers and health insurers to develop alternative payment methods based on performance and financial risk-sharing (*e.g.* risk-adjusted capitation payments) and allowing (limited) vertical integration of health insurers and providers. In addition, hospitals' access to capital markets could be expanded by revoking their mandatory non-profit status, a move that should be accompanied with measures to secure the orderly exit of bankrupt hospitals, notably in terms of providing essential services, and to ensure an effective and transparent merger control.

Co-payments, which are among the lowest within the OECD, could be a supplementary tool to control public spending in a more demand-driven system. They could also encourage patients to make choices that take price and quality into consideration. Although low co-payments appear to have contributed to relatively low socio-economic inequalities in health, there is little reason for maintaining them for higher income groups, particularly as high income individuals are substantially less price sensitive than lower income individuals and thus require higher co-payments to achieve the same reduction of moral hazard (Newhouse *et al.*, 1993). Hence, the deductible (*i.e.* the fixed amount of medical expenses that people have to pay out-of-pocket), which in the basic health coverage is set at EUR 220 per year, could be raised for middle and high income groups. In addition, the current exemption of GP consultations from the deductible could be abolished to encourage cost-effective consumer choices. Given that the fee for GP consultations is small (EUR 9), abandoning this exemption would not impede access.

The design of the co-payment system could also be improved for chronically ill people, who currently know in advance that they will inevitably pay the full deductible. In such cases, alternative co-payment structures may generate stronger incentives for cost-effective choices and be more equitable (Van Kleef et al., 2009). For instance, the starting point for the fixed deductible for chronically ill people could be shifted from zero medical expenses (i.e. covering expenses from EUR 0 to EUR 220) to a higher starting level (e.g. expenses from EUR 1 000 to EUR 1 220, depending on a "standard" anticipated average expense for each chronicle disease). For these people, this would make cost-effective choices more rewarding within the threshold of EUR 1 220. It would also entail a more equal distribution of out-of-pocket expenses between the healthy and the chronically ill by giving chronically ill people a chance to spend less than the full deductible.

Population ageing will put pressure on a costly long-term care system

Spending on long-term care, at 3.8% of GDP in 2009, is more than twice the OECD average, reflecting the comprehensiveness and generosity of the system as well as a traditionally high reliance on institutional care (Box 3.4). However, the high spending is not accompanied by obviously better outcomes and is partly the result of a comprehensiveness that include even smaller menial tasks – services that are not provided in many other countries (Eurobarometer, 2007). Over the last decade, spending has been spurred by rising quality standards, higher take-up attracted by the accessibility of the cash benefits scheme and possibly by stricter access to other social safety nets (Mot, 2010).

> **Box 3.4. A comprehensive public long-term care system**
>
> The public long-term care insurance system was created in 1968 – the first in the OECD – and provides universal coverage of a broad range of long-term care benefits. The system mainly serves elderly people (three quarters of patients are over 65) and physically or mentally handicapped persons. Coverage is broad, as it notably includes accommodation costs in nursing homes and home help for domestic activities. Income-dependent co-payments by patients are relatively low by OECD standards, amounting to around 10% of costs (Colombo et al., 2011). They are capped at EUR 12.60 per hour at home (roughly a third of the average cost) and EUR 1 800 per month in institutions, and do not take into account patients' assets but only their revenues. The remaining funding of the system comes from social security contributions (around 60% of costs) and taxes (around 30%).
>
> Care in institutions plays a larger role than in most other OECD countries despite effort to encourage home care over the last decades. Institutional patients account for 40% of the 600 000 long-term care patients (Ministry of Health, 2011e). In 2009, 6.6% of the elderly population (aged over 65) was institutionalised, one of the highest rates in the OECD, even though half of them had only light or moderate care needs (Pommer, 2012).

> **Box 3.4. A comprehensive public long-term care system** *(cont.)*
>
> Long-term care is mostly a central government responsibility, under the framework of the Exceptional Medical Expenses Act (AWBZ), which covers both care at home and in institutions. Only the provision of home help for domestic activities has been delegated to the municipalities in 2007 as part of a broader decentralising pattern. For institutional and home care (with the exception of home help), 32 regional care purchasing agencies (*zorgkantoren*) have been mandated to buy care with public funds. The agencies are generally subsidiaries of the dominant health insurer in each region. These agencies have no budget of their own (except for administrative costs), as care providers are directly paid from a general public fund (AFBZ) on the basis of contracts concluded with purchasing agencies. Hence, purchasing agencies bear no financial risk on purchasing care. Institutional care tariffs are regulated, while home care prices result from bargaining between purchasing agencies and providers. Institutional care providers must be non-for-profit organisations, while the home care market has been opened to for-profit companies.
>
> Patients' eligibility for care is assessed by an independent Care Assessment Centre (CIZ), except for home help where the assessment lies with municipalities. The centre decides if patients are eligible for care in an institution or at home and how much care they are entitled to. Once assessed, patients can opt either to receive in-kind care or a cash benefit ("personal budget") that is equivalent to 75% of the cost of in-kind care. Cash benefits account for 11% of total expenditure, after having grown by an annual 20% since 2002.

Population ageing will boost the number of dependant elderly people by a factor of 2½ to almost 1 million by 2060, which means that, with current policies, long-term care spending would reach 8.1% of GDP by 2060 – more than three times the then EU average (European Commission, 2009). Securing cost-efficient provision of long-term care is key to mitigating spending pressures while maintaining high quality services – a difficult task for which international experience is still limited (Colombo *et al.*, 2011; Schut and Van den Berg, 2010). In this context, the main challenges are to reorganise the system to improve efficiency incentives, to reduce further the dependence on institutional care, and to better target patients as the rapid uptake in the cash benefits system has exposed screening problems.

The main issue with the current organisation of the long-term care system, which is fairly different from the health care system, is the lack of financial incentives of regional care purchasing agencies (*zorgkantoren*). As they face no financial risk on care purchase (Box 3.4), purchasing agencies are not inclined to bargain with care providers on price and quality. In the home care sector, this has led prices to stay very close to the regulated maximum tariff. It has also undermined competition in the home care market, which is highly concentrated and where large providers have been able to charge higher prices (Mosca *et al.*, 2007). The overall cost of these inefficiencies is hard to assess, but may be significant, as suggested by the substantial improvements in cost-efficiency following the decentralisation of home help to municipalities (Box 3.5).

Further decentralisation of home care has the potential to enhance efficiency

The government plans to abolish the regional purchasing agencies by 2013 and to transfer most of their purchasing responsibilities to health insurers and increase municipalities' home care responsibilities. Municipalities will get responsibilities for home assistance (*e.g.* help with administrative tasks) and home care for lightly mentally handicapped young people (Box 3.6).

> **Box 3.5. The decentralisation of home help has improved cost-efficiency**
>
> Home help for domestic activities (*e.g.* house cleaning, cooking) was decentralised to municipalities in 2007 by the new Social Assistance Act (WMO), which provides support services to people in vulnerable situations. Municipalities are given a non-earmarked budget and have a large degree of freedom about how to organise help. They assess patients' needs and purchase help for them.
>
> Because of non-earmarked budgets, municipalities bear financial risks on home help, giving them incentives to bargain intensively with help providers. The resulting spur in competition has helped reducing the average price of an hour of help by more than 20% from 2005 to 2008. Prices subsequently recovered, but they still stand below pre-decentralisation levels (van der Torre *et al.*, 2011).
>
> Overall, municipalities were able to save EUR 150 million in 2007 over a EUR 1.2 billion budget (distributed on the basis of historical spending) and collected EUR 200 million of co-payments, generating EUR 350 million for other spending purposes. The consequences on the quality of home help have been a source of debate, with 40% of clients reporting a quality deterioration following the decentralisation. However, high quality standards have apparently been maintained, as patients still award home help an average score of 8 out of 10 (de Klerk *et al.*, 2010).

Municipalities will receive non-earmarked budgets, giving them strong incentives to contain costs. Better screening and synergies with other decentralised social assistance schemes, such as activation of social security recipients, may also help to improve cost-efficiency. A potential problem is that municipalities will have incentives to redirect patients towards centrally funded and more expensive institutional care to reduce their own costs, leading to higher overall spending. To encourage municipalities to keep patients at home, they should be rewarded financially for reducing institutionalisation rates. To further stimulate home care, this measure could be complemented with making patients bear a larger part of their accommodation costs in institutions.

Health insurers should not be given a bigger role without adequate financial incentives

In the non-decentralised part of the system (*i.e.* institutional care and personal home care), the government intends to give health insurers the responsibility to buy care for their own patients, in the same manner as in the health care system. This would presumably reduce co-ordination costs between health and long-term care. However, there are no plans to make insurers bear the associated financial risks until a risk-equalisation scheme for long-term care is developed, in order to avoid risk-selection issues. An issue is that designing such a scheme is complicated and may not be feasible at all, notably because of the lack of readily available data on potentially good predictors of individuals' future long-term care expenses (Schut and Van de Ven, 2010).[5]

As long as health insurers do not bear financial risk on purchasing care, they will lack incentives to do it efficiently, leading to more costly provision. Moreover, insurers will have incentives to shift patients from insurer-paid health care to publicly funded long-term care, inducing further increases in public spending (Besseling *et al.*, 2011).[6] Thus, transferring care purchasing to health insurers should only be considered if they can bear the financial risks associated, *e.g.* within an appropriate risk-equalisation scheme. If such a scheme can be

> **Box 3.6. The government's reform agenda for long-term care**
>
> **Further decentralising to municipalities and giving a bigger role to health insurers**
>
> - Along the line of the decentralisation of home help to municipalities in 2007, progressive decentralisation of other components of home care by 2013: assistance (budget of around EUR 2 billion) and care for young people with a light mental handicap (around EUR 3 billion).
> - Transfer of the responsibility to purchase the non-decentralised parts of home care (nursing and personal care) and institutional care from regional agencies (*zorgkantoren*) to health insurers by 2013 (Figure 3.7). Insurers would then have to buy long-term care for their own health insured, replacing the current system where regional agencies buy care for all residents of a region regardless of their insurance company.
>
> Figure 3.7. **Main features of the envisaged reorganisation of the long-term care system**
>
>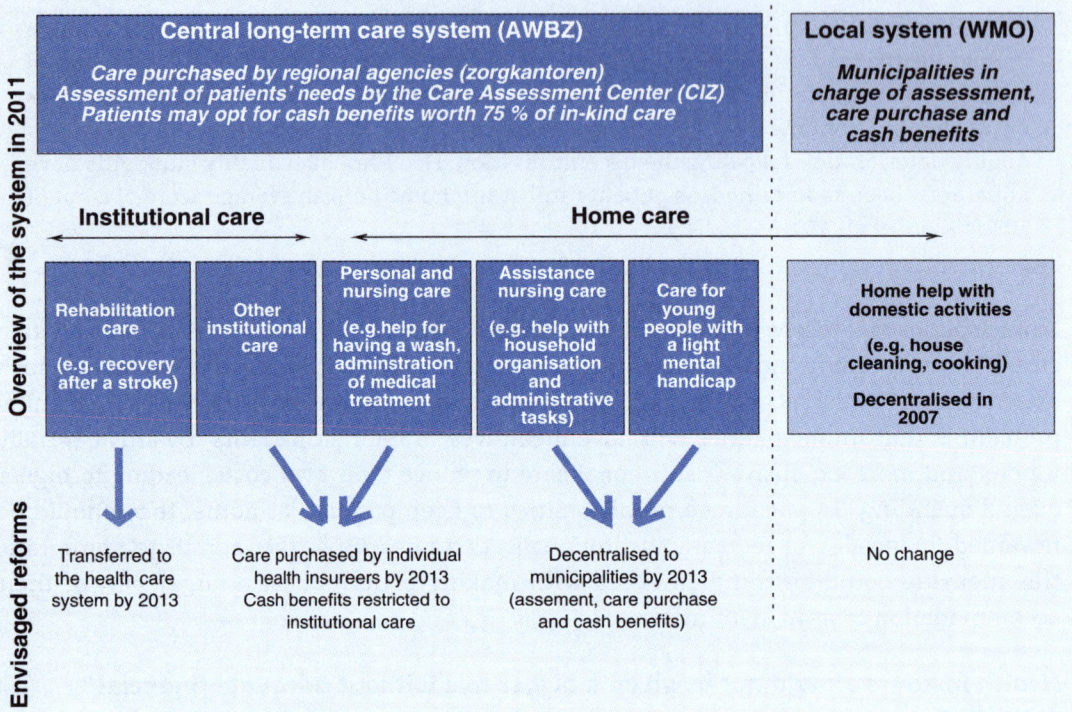
>
> *Source:* Ministry of Health, Welfare and Sport.
>
> **Limiting the target group, notably for cash benefits**
>
> - Reduction of the accessibility of cash benefits to patients eligible for institutional care (10% of the 130 000 cash benefits recipients).
> - Reduction of the accessibility of institutional care for patients with lighter care needs. Lowering of the IQ criteria to assess mental handicap care from 85 to 70 by 2013.
>
> **Improving the quality of care and other measures**
>
> - Measures to strengthen clients' rights *vis-à-vis* care providers. Creation of a Quality Institute to spread good practices. Simplification of assessment procedures.
> - Extra budget of EUR 0.9 billion from 2012 to raise the tariffs of care for self-employed by 5% and encourage hiring and training of care workers.
> - Separation of institutional care costs and accommodation costs in institutions from 2012. Since 2009, care costs are reimbursed on the basis of patients' care needs (ZZP *packages*) and institutions are free to build new capacity but at their own financial risk, with a gradual transition period until 2017.
>
> *Source:* Ministry of Health (2011), *Programmabrief langdurige zorg*, No. DLZ/KZ-U-3067294, and Ministry of Health (2011), *Voortgangsrapportage Hervorming langdurige zorg*, No. Z/M-3089172.

developed, elderly care (both at home and in institutions) could be included in the basic health insurance package. This would also require improving the current health care risk-equalisation scheme to reduce the losses that insurers currently make on long-term care patients' medical expenses (i.e. expenses non related to long-term care), which would make them reluctant to compete for long-term care patients (Schut and Van de Ven, 2010).[7]

Alternatively, there are several other options to improve the system's organisation, which all have in common that they should be combined with better targeting (see below). A first option is to give regional purchasing agencies more incentives for cost-efficiency within the current framework, for example by introducing bonuses for agencies that meet certain performance targets in terms of the quality and efficiency of contracted care. This would require measuring the quality of care with sufficient reliability and broadness, which can be difficult (e.g. in obtaining information from frail patients in declining conditions) as shown by the mixed results of the first international experiments on such pay-for-performance schemes (Colombo et al., 2011). However, the long-term nature of the patient-provider relationship could contribute to addressing such measurement issues. To make purchasing agencies cost-efficient it is also important to ensure that they cannot shift patients to schemes funded under other budget lines. This happened with cash benefits until 2012, allowing the purchasing agencies to respect the regional provider budgets, but at the expense of persistent budget overruns on cash benefits.

A second option is further progressive decentralisation of home care to municipalities, taking advantage of their incentives for cost containment with a non-earmarked budget. Delegating all home care provision (i.e. both personal and domestic care) to municipalities would also present the advantage of reducing co-ordination costs. One exception may be specialised care, for which municipalities could lack economies of scale and scope – which could be addressed via co-operation between municipalities or via centrally provided technical support. As mentioned above, decentralisation should be combined with financial rewards to municipalities to encourage homecare in order to avoid the redirection of patients towards centrally funded institutional care.

A third option could be to give patients a bigger role in the choice of their institutional care provider, which could be combined with larger payment for accommodation costs in institutions. This would give institutions greater incentives to compete for patients. Past and present reforms are paving the way for such a system, as accommodation costs are being progressively separated from care costs (Box 3.6). In such a system, care costs would still be mainly publicly financed, with institutions compensated on the basis of patients' needs, as is the case since 2009 under the so-called "care severity packages" (ZZPs). Institutions would be able to increase capacity to meet new demand, but thanks to new compensation rules for capital expenses, they would be at a financial risk in case of empty beds. Thus, they would have to compete on accommodation costs and quality to attract patients, leading to overall cost-efficiency gains.

The cash benefits boom has exposed targeting problems

The second challenge faced by the Dutch long-term care system is better targeting, as exposed by the recent boom in cash benefits and the fact that almost half of elderly patients receiving in-kind care are not considered frail (SCP, 2011). Both for in-kind care and cash benefits, the government's response has been to restrict eligibility (Box 3.6). This should be combined with improved assessment of patients' needs to improve targeting. For example, assessment procedures could be strengthened by giving regional care purchasing agencies the opportunity to object to inappropriate assessments. This could be particularly effective if combined with giving the agencies stronger incentives for cost-efficiency as mentioned above. Moreover, regional assessment disparities, which have already been reduced over the last decade, could be further addressed (Peeters and Francke, 2007). In addition, it would also be helpful to ensure that the relatively low co-payments for in-kind home care are sufficiently high to encourage patients to make choices that take price and quality into consideration.

The cash benefits option attracted a new and large group of patients, leading to a spending boom (Sadiraj et al., 2011). The higher uptake is not necessarily a problem since it has allowed people to escape waiting lists. However, there has been evidence of unintended use (e.g. grandchildren taking their grandmother to a jazz festival, home help providers who lost the bid for home help in their municipality requesting payments out of their patients' cash benefits) or even in some cases fraud (Mot, 2010; Ministry of Health, 2011e). This led the government to drastically restrict access to cash benefits from 2012 to only people eligible for institutional care – about 10% of the current 130 000 cash benefits recipients – which should save EUR 0.6-0.7 billion by 2015 (CPB, 2011b; Ministry of Health, 2011f). However, this is at the cost of ending the win-win situation where patients choose relatively cheaper cash benefits (worth 75% of the cost of in-kind care) that improve their own welfare thanks to a greater choice of providers and also encourage competition across home care providers.

The root of the problem was not cash benefits themselves, but rather insufficient screening and monitoring. Thus, it would be preferable to keep a cash benefits scheme for home care but to improve screening and monitoring to avoid unintended use. One way of reducing the need for monitoring could be to provide cash benefits in the form of vouchers directly payable to professionals, like in the Nordic countries (Colombo et al., 2011). To be effective, such vouchers should be designed to cover less than the full costs of care, where the implied co-payment on each service purchased would give patients incentives for cost-efficient use of the vouchers.

Conclusion

The focus of the recommendations in this chapter has been on enhancing cost-efficiency. Such a focus could risk impeding the excellent Dutch results in terms of equity and access to health care facilities. However, the increasing role of competition has not had a negative impact on equity so far. The already internationally low waiting times in 2000 have been further reduced since 2006 (Siciliani and Hurst, 2003; Van de Vijsel, 2011; NZa, 2012). In addition, access is assured by some of the lowest out-of-pocket payments in the OECD and the entitlement to a broad basic benefits package at an affordable premium for all citizens. Looking ahead, equity may come under pressure from peoples' unwillingness to subsidise the increasing health care consumption arising from unhealthy lifestyles and the inability of the public sector to continue to finance rapid increases in health expenditures – particularly if such consumption is considered a luxury good (Van der Star et al., 2011; Hall and Jones, 2007). Either way, improved cost-efficiency will be a key factor in securing future high quality health care. A summary of recommendations in this direction is provided in Box 3.7.

> **Box 3.7. Recommendations to promote a more efficient and competitive health sector**
>
> **Establish performance indicators and implement performance-based payment systems**
>
> - Adequate performance indicators should be developed to allow performance-based contracting between health insurers and care providers. In this area, priority should be given to improve data collection at the individual patient level and to develop a better information infrastructure.
> - Health insurers should be allowed to use alternative payment systems based on financial risk-sharing (*e.g.* risk-adjusted capitation payments) and performance as well as to, on a limited scale, vertically integrate with providers to reduce information asymmetries.
> - The risk-equalisation scheme should be further improved to reduce insurers' incentives for risk selection, particularly in view of the government's intention to terminate *ex post* compensations before 2015.
>
> **Facilitate entry to secure contestable provider markets**
>
> - To reduce restricted entry to the medical profession, the current capacity constraints (*numerus fixus*) for medical schools should be lifted. In addition, the recognition of foreign diplomas from outside Europe should be facilitated.
> - For-profit hospitals should be allowed to enter the hospital market. In addition, the orderly exit of bankrupt hospitals should be secured via measures to guarantee access to essential facilities.
> - The Competition Authority should publish a clear methodology for assessing horizontal and vertical mergers between hospital and health insurers, as a way to base merger assessments solely on competition considerations, including consumer welfare concerns.
>
> **Improve incentives for cost-effective choices at the demand side**
>
> - Co-payments for higher income groups could be increased to encourage to make cost-effective choices, alleviate information asymmetries and as an additional budget control tool. Co-payments for chronically ill people should be better designed to give them more incentives for cost-efficiency.
>
> **Long-term care sector**
>
> - Health insurers should not receive more responsibility for purchasing care until they are given proper incentives for cost-efficiency. In the longer term, the decentralisation of home care to municipalities could be completed and institutional patients should directly choose their care provider to push institutions to compete on quality to attract patients.
> - Home care should be encouraged by rewarding financially municipalities for reducing institutionalisation rates, through better screening and by higher co-payments for accommodation costs in institutions.
> - The cash benefits scheme should be kept for home care but combined with better screening and monitoring to avoid unintended use. To this end, a system of vouchers directly payable to professionals and topped up by co-payments should be envisaged.

Notes

1. F.T. (Erik) Schut, Professor of Health Economics at Erasmus University in Rotterdam, was the main author on this chapter.
2. Until 2010, the regulator could not administratively disentangle hospital revenue growth into a price and a volume effect because of the expansion of the segment B and the recalculation of the budgets in the regulated segment A (NZa, 2010a). In 2010, however, the regulator found that the production of services in the segment B increased by 8.6%, a much higher rate than in the segment A (NZa 2011b). An empirical investigation based on more than 2 million inpatient hospital discharge diagnoses also found evidence of a stronger spending growth in the free segment B than in the segment A (Hasaart, 2011).
3. The share of self-employed specialists has declined over the past decade from 56% in 1999 to 44% in 2007 (Capaciteitsorgaan 2010). The mirror image is the increase in the share of salaried specialists, although the practise varies widely across medical specialities with less than one third of cardiologists, radiologists, urologists, orthopaedic and cosmetic surgeons to more than 90% among paediatricians and clinical geriatricians.
4. Often self-employed specialists work in partnerships, implying that if a salaried specialist replaces a (retiring) self-employed specialist. This creates a classic insider-outsider situation where insiders have little incentives to co-operate with the outsider as they want to preserve the goodwill value of the partnership.
5. Having good predictors to assess individual risks is especially important in long-term care because long-term care expenditures are concentrated in a small part of the population and are typically very high. However, there is hardly any research about such predictors so far, and there are no data readily available on potentially good predictors, such as individuals' limitations in activities of daily living (ADL) or the availability of social support networks (an important predictor of the availability of informal care).
6. Another complication of making health insurers financially accountable for covering long term care is that they will have build up financial reserves to meet solvency requirements.
7. Including home care in the basic health package, however, would make the co-ordination with home help and social care more difficult.

Bibliography

Algemene Rekenkamer (2011), *Uitgavenbeheersing in de zorg*, Tweede Kamer, vergaderjaar 2011-2012, No. 33060 (1-2), The Hague.

Besseling, P., W. Elsenburg and C. van Ewijk (2011), "Risicodragende uitvoering AWBZ door zorgverzekeraars verhoogt de kosten", *Me Judice*, www.mejudice.nl/artikel/618/risicodragende-uitvoering-awbz-door-zorgverzekeraars-verhoogt-de-kosten.

Blank, J., A. Dumaij and B. van Hulst(2011), *Ziekenhuismiddelen in verband. Een empirisch onderzoek naar productiviteit en doelmatigheid in de Nederlandse ziekenhuizen 2003-2009*, IPSE Studies, Technische Universiteit, Delft.

Boonen, L.H.H.M., S.A. van der Geest, F.T. Schut and M. Varkevisser (2010), *Pharmaceutical policy in the Netherlands: from price regulation towards managed competition*, in A. Dor (ed.), *Pharmaceutical Markets and Insurance Worldwide*, Advances in Health Economics and Health Services Research, Vol. 22, Bingley: Emerald, pp. 53-76.

Capaciteitsorgaan (2010), *Medisch en klinisch technologische specialisten*, Deelrapport 1, Utrecht.

Capaciteitsorgaan (2011), *Capaciteitsplan 2010 voor de medische, tandheelkundige, klinisch technologische en aanverwante (vervolg)opleidingen, revisie 1.1*, Utrecht.

CBS (2011), *Nieuwe Nederlandse cijfers voor OESO over beloning artsen*, Centraal Bureau voor de Statistiek, published 29 June, on www.cbs.nl/.

CPB (2011a), *Centraal Economisch Plan 2011*, Centraal Planbureau, The Hague.

CPB (2011b), *Effecten van het kabinetsvoorstel voor het pgb*, CPB Notitie, The Hague.

Colombo, F., A. Llena-Nozal, J. Mercier and F. Tjadens (2011), "Help wanted? Providing and paying for long-term care", *OECD Health Policy Studies*, OECD Publishing.

Davis, K., C. Schoen and K. Stremikis (2010), *Mirror, mirror on the wall: How the performance of the US health care system compares internationally, 2010 update*, New York: The Common Wealth Fund.

De Bakker, D.H., J.N. Struijs, C.B. Baan, J. Raams, J.E. de Wildt, H.J.M. Vrijhoef and F.T. Schut (2012), "Early Results from Adoption of Bundled Payment for Diabetes Care in the Netherlands Show Improvement in Care Coordination", *Health Affairs*, No. 31(2), pp. 426-433.

De Graaf, R., M. Ten Have and S. van Dorsselaer (2010), *De psychische gezondheid van de Nederlandse bevolking,Nemesis-2: Opzet en eerste resultaten*, Trimbos-Instituut, Utrecht.

De Klerk, M., R. Gilsing and J. Timmermans (2010), *Op weg met de Wmo. Evaluatie van de Wet maatschappelijke ondersteuning 2007-09*, SCP, The Hague.

Douven, R. and R. Mocking (2012), "The Effect of Physician Fees and Density Differences on Regional Variation in Hospital Treatments", *CPB Discussion Paper*, No. 208, CPB, The Hague.

EIB (2011), *Monitoring integrale bekostiging zorg voor chronisch zieken. Eerste rapportage van de Evaluatiecommissie Integrale Bekostiging*, The Hague.

Eurobarometer (2007), "Health and long-term care in the European Union", *Special Eurobarometer*, No. 283.

European Commission and the European Policy Committee (2009), "2009 Ageing Report: Economic and budgetary projections for the EU-27 Members States (2008-2060)", *European Economy* No. 2/2009.

Frank, R.G. and T.G. McGuire (2000), "Economics and Mental Health", in A.J. Culyer, J.P. Newhouse (eds.), *Handbook of Health Economics*, Elsevier, Amsterdam, pp. 893-954.

Gusdorf, L.M.A., M. Smit and B. Voorbraak (2009), *Huisartsenzorg: een eerste onderzoek*, Zorgthermometer, Vektis, Zeist.

Hall, R.E. and C.I. Jones (2007), "The Value of Life and the Rise in Health Spending", *Quarterly Journal of Economics*, No. 122(1), pp. 39-72.

Hasaart, F. (2011), *Incentives in the Diagnosis Treatment Combination payment system for specialist medical care. A study about behavioral responses of medical specialists and hospitals in the Netherlands*, PhD thesis, University of Maastricht, Maastricht.

Joumard, I., C. André and C. Nicq (2010), "Health Care Systems: Efficiency and Institutions", *OECD Economics Department Working Papers*, No. 769, OECD Publishing.

Klazinga, N., H. Anema and G. ten Asbroek (2012), "De nieuwe kleren van de keizer", *Tijdschrift voor Gezondheidswetenschappen*, No. 90(2), pp. 76-77.

Loozen, E.M.H., F.T. Schut, M. Varkevisser (2011), "Fusie zorgverzekeraars Achmea en De Friesland: hoezo functioneel concentratietoezicht?", *Markt en Mededinging*, No. 14(5).

Mackenbach, J.P., L. Slobbe, C.W.N. Looman, A. van der Heide, J. Polder and J. Garssen (2011), "Sharp upturn of life expectancy in the Netherlands: effect of more health care for the elderly?", *European Journal of Epidemiology*, doi : http://dx.doi.org/10.1007/s10654-011-9633-y.

Ministry of Health (2009), *Rijksbegroting 2010. XVI Volksgezondheid, Welzijn en Sport*, Tweede Kamer, vergaderjaar 2009-2010, No. 32123 XVI (1-2), The Hague.

Ministry of Health (2010), *Rijksbegroting 2011. XVI Volksgezondheid, Welzijn en Sport*, Tweede Kamer, vergaderjaar 2010-2011, No. 32500 XVI (1-2), The Hague.

Ministry of Health (2011a), "Zorg die loont", Tweede Kamer, vergaderjaar 2010-2011, No. 32620 (6), March, The Hague.

Ministry of Health (2011b), *Rijksbegroting 2012. XVI Volksgezondheid, Welzijn en Sport*, Tweede Kamer, vergaderjaar 2011-2012, No; 33000 XVI (1-2), The Hague.

Ministry of Health (2011c), *Fusies in de zorgsector en opsplitsingsbevoegdheid IGZ*, MC-U-3066411, June, The Hague.

Ministry of Health (2011d), *Uitvoering van drie aangenomen moties over fusies in de zorgsector*, Tweede Kamer, vergaderjaar 2011-2012, No. 32620 (31), November, The Hague.

Ministry of Health (2011e), *Programmabrief langdurige zorg*, No. DLZ/KZ-U-3067294, June, The Hague.

Ministry of Health (2011f), *Voortgangsrapportage Hervorming langdurige zorg*, Z/M-3089172, October, The Hague.

Mosca, I., M. Pomp and V. Shestalova (2007), "Market share and price in Dutch home care: market power or quality?", *CPB Discussion Paper*, No. 95, The Hague.

Mot, E. (2010), "The Dutch system of long-term care", *CPB Document*, No. 204, The Hague.

Newhouse, J.P. and the Insurance Experiment Group (1993), *Free for all? Lessons from the RAND Health Insurance Experiment*, Harvard University Press, Cambridge, Massachusetts.

NZa (2009), *Huisartsenzorg 2008. Analyse van het nieuwe bekostigingssysteem en de marktwerking in de huisartsenzorg*, Nederlandse Zorgautoriteit, Utrecht.

NZa (2010a), *Marktimperfecties in de medisch specialistische zorg*, Visiedocument, Nederlandse Zorgautoriteit, Utrecht.

NZa (2010b), *Monitor Extramurale farmacie 2010*, Nederlandse Zorgautoriteit, Utrecht.

NZa (2011a), *Marktscan Zorgverzekeringsmarkt. Weergave van de markt 2007-2011*, Nederlandse Zorgautoriteit, Utrecht.

NZa (2011b), *Marktscan Medisch specialistische zorg. Weergave van de markt 2006-2010*, Nederlandse Zorgautoriteit, Utrecht.

NZa (2011c), *Monitor curatieve GGZ 2010. Een sector in ontwikkeling*, Nederlandse Zorgautoriteit, Utrecht.

NZa, 2012, *Marktscan Medisch specialistische zorg. Weergave van de markt 2006-2011*, Nederlandse Zorgautoriteit, Utrecht.

OECD (2009), *Health at a Glance 2009*, OECD Publishing.

OECD (2010a), *Health at a Glance: Europe 2010*, OECD Publishing.

OECD (2010b), "Improving Value in Health Care: Measuring Quality", *OECD Health Policy Studies*, OECD Publishing.

Peeters, J. and A. Francke (2007): "Indicatiestelling voor AWBZ-zorg, sector Verpleging, Verzorging en Thuiszorg", NIVEL.

Pommer, E. (2012), *Verzorging en verpleging*, SCP, The Hague.

Sadiraj, K., D. Oudijk, H. van Kempen and J. Stevens (2011), *De opmars van het pgb*, SCP-publication 2011-17, The Hague.

Schut, F.T. and B. Van den Berg (2010), Sustainability of Long-Term Care Financing in The Netherlands, *Social Policy and Administration*, No. 44(4), pp. 411-435.

Schut, F.T. and W.P.M.M. van de Ven (2010), "Uitvoering AWBZ door zorgverzekeraars onverstandig", *Economisch Statistische Berichten*, No. 95(4591), pp. 486-489.

SCP (2011), "Frail older persons in the Netherlands", The Netherlands Institute for Social Research (*Sociaal en Cultureel Planbureau*, SCP), The Hague.

Tweede Kamer (2011), *Invoering Diagnose Behandeling Combinaties (DBCs)*, vergaderjaar 2010-11, No. 29248(170).

Van Beek, E., L. Boon and E.J. Vlieger (2009), *Voorstudie naar praktijkvariatie in Nederland*, Plexus, Breukelen.

Van der Star S.M. and B. Van den Berg (2011), "Individual responsibility and health-risk behaviour: A contingent valuation study from the ex ante societal perspective", *Health Policy*, No. 101.

Van der Torre, A., S. Jansen and E. Pommer (2011), "Advies over het Wmo-budget huishoudelijke hulp voor 2012", CP, The Hague.

Van de Vijsel, A.R., P.M. Engelfriet and G.P. Westert (2011), "Rendering hospital budgets volume based and open ended to reduce waiting lists: does it work?", *Health Policy*, No. 100.

Van de Ven, W.P.M.M., F.T. Schut, H.E.G.M. Hermans, J.D. de Jong, M. van der Maat, R. Coppen, P.P. Groenewegen and R.D. Friele (2009), *Evaluatie Zorgverzekeringswet en Wet op de Zorgtoeslag*, Programma evaluatie wetgeving: deel 27, ZonMw, The Hague.

Varkevisser, M., F.T. Schut (2008), NMa moet strenger zijn bij toetsing ziekenhuisfusies, *Economisch Statistische Berichten* 93 (4532).

Varkevisser, M., F.T. Schut (2010), "Fusietoetsing in de zorg", *Economisch Statistische Berichten*, No. 95(4576).

Varkevisser, M. and F.T. Schut (2012), The impact of geographic market definition on the stringency of hospital merger control in Germany and the Netherlands, *Health Economics, Policy and Law*, doi : http://dx.doi.org/10.1017/S1744133112000011.

Vektis (2009), *Zorgverzekeraars en zorgfinanciering. Jaarcijfers 2009*, Vektis, Zeist.

Vektis (2010), *Zorgverzekeraars en zorgfinanciering. Jaarcijfers 2010*, Vektis, Zeist.

Vektis (2011), *Zorgverzekeraars en zorgfinanciering. Jaarcijfers 2011*, Vektis, Zeist.

Vektis and Plexus (2011), *Rapportage indicatoren indicatiestelling (praktijkvariatie)*, Zeist/Breukelen.

Werkgroep Curatieve zorg (2010), *Curatieve zorg. Rapport brede heroverwegingen 11*, Ministry of Finance, The Hague.

Westert, G.P., M.J. Van den Berg, S.L.N. Zwakhals, J.D. de Jong and H. Verkleij (2010), *Dutch Health Care Performance Report 2010*, Bilthoven: RIVM.

WOR (2011), *Advies aan de minister van VWS over de vormgeving van de risicoverevening 2012*, Werkgroep Ontwikkeling Risicoverevening, WOR 580, September, The Hague.

ORGANISATION FOR ECONOMIC CO-OPERATION AND DEVELOPMENT

The OECD is a unique forum where governments work together to address the economic, social and environmental challenges of globalisation. The OECD is also at the forefront of efforts to understand and to help governments respond to new developments and concerns, such as corporate governance, the information economy and the challenges of an ageing population. The Organisation provides a setting where governments can compare policy experiences, seek answers to common problems, identify good practice and work to co-ordinate domestic and international policies.

The OECD member countries are: Australia, Austria, Belgium, Canada, Chile, the Czech Republic, Denmark, Estonia, Finland, France, Germany, Greece, Hungary, Iceland, Ireland, Israel, Italy, Japan, Korea, Luxembourg, Mexico, the Netherlands, New Zealand, Norway, Poland, Portugal, the Slovak Republic, Slovenia, Spain, Sweden, Switzerland, Turkey, the United Kingdom and the United States. The European Union takes part in the work of the OECD.

OECD Publishing disseminates widely the results of the Organisation's statistics gathering and research on economic, social and environmental issues, as well as the conventions, guidelines and standards agreed by its members.